LOOKING AFTER NIETZSCHE

SUNY Series in Intersections: Philosophy and Critical Theory
Rodolphe Gasché and Mark C. Taylor

Nietzsche in 1899

Wood-Engraving
by
Earl Nitschke

Looking After Nietzsche

Edited By

Laurence A. Rickels

STATE UNIVERSITY OF NEW YORK PRESS

All the translations in this book were funded by the University of California, Santa Barbara.

Published by
State University of New York Press, Albany

Printed in the United States of America

For information, address State University of New York Press, State University Plaza, Albany, NY 12246

Library of Congress Cataloging-in Publication Data

Looking after Nietzsche / edited by Laurence A. Rickels.
p. cm.
Bibliography: p.
Includes index.
ISBN 0-7914-0156-1.—ISBN 0-7914-0157-X (pbk.)
1. Nietzsche, Friedrich Wilhelm, 1844–1900. 2. Heidegger, Martin, 1889–1976. I. Rickels, Laurence A. II. Series: Intersections (Albany, N.Y.)
B3317.L59 1990 89-4579
193—dc20 CIP

10 9 8 7 6 5 4 3 2

Contents

Preface

Prefaces, says Nietzsche, would be addressed only to the slow-witted if their readership did not count, instead, only the authors of other prefaces. Within this limited range of reception, the author of a new preface cannot find but can only contrive a rapport with the other. The enemy or appetizer that draws the new preface out into the open must be construed out of precursory prefaces. On this target range *The New Nietzsche*'s star billing of Heidegger as "rediscoverer of Nietzsche" comes into focus.[1] *Looking After Nietzsche* recalls the modality of care or *Sorge*—but only in order to transfer into the Nietzsche account the protection which *The New Nietzsche* paid to Heidegger. The care taken on Heidegger's account would thus be returned to the side of ambivalence where its provenance becomes clear and separable. The return that always follows and exceeds rediscovery now gives Nietzsche his turn to take care of Heidegger.

By naming Nietzsche the last metaphysician, Heidegger anchored the project of transvaluation in a ground which will always slip away from Nietzsche himself.[2] Heidegger reinscribed transvaluation in the history of metaphysics as the unconscious fulfillment[3] of the thought of value, that is, in a larger sense, of nihilism. Or as Heidegger argued with regard to the Myth of the Cave,[4] Nietzsche ought to be considered the greatest Platonist, for he pushed to its last consequences the philosophy of *agathon* above being. Heidegger's reading attains heights which cannot be dismissed—nor reduced to a few motifs. But it nonetheless tends to supplant the abyssal foundation of value (which, according to Nietzsche, governs the history of evaluations) with the abyss of the philosophy of being, from where Nietzsche's enterprise can be envisaged in its entirety, that is, as a restricted one. According to Heidegger, Nietzsche will have repeated the great theses of the philosophical tradition to the point of exhausting their senses. And this reading is produced, in Heidegger's camp, at the price of an interpretive resumption of the notion of *Nichts* and nihilism which, by means of this repetition, acquires a new and vaster significance, and where things or forces now fall together where they tended to separate out.

Heidegger thus determined that the issue of moral imperatives in Nietzsche would remain bound to Plato—or that it could be raised as problematic only by making a move against Heidegger's Nietzsche. Heidegger's diagnosis of Nietzsche's *dependency* on morals or values has indeed attracted a relentless return of rereading which can be characterized as precisely post-Heideggerian. As Nancy demonstrates, the Nietzschean "supermoral" imperative (probity, to give his example) must not be confused with traditionally conceived moral imperatives; these undetermined and extramoral imperatives (which are often of philological pedigree) in turn produce not truth but truth just the same—truth in a nontraditional sense.

The reevaluation of moral imperatives in Nietzsche inevitably takes a detour via Kant, in fact the Heideggerian rereading of Kant, which is borrowed only to be redirected towards another aim. Thus Nancy argues that Nietzsche's renunciation of Kant unknowingly repeats Kant—against Kant's commentators. Although the recasting of imperatives can be found in Heidegger, it is outlawed from Heidegger's Nietzsche. It has proven necessary, in sum, to go beyond Heidegger's rediscovery of Nietzsche by borrowing from another zone of rereading (Heidegger's Kant, for example) and then reapplying the loan towards the reassessment of moral imperatives already under way in Nietzsche.

Hamacher shows that Nietzsche was in fact the first to follow Kant in the examination of precarious connections between ethics and hermeneutics. Nietzsche engaged the Kantian inquiry into the structure of moral consciousness or free will—and hence the historical conditions of history. From the margins and ambivalences surrounding free will, Nietzsche developed the other history of the will's passage from an eccentric position into the center of itself—a passage that does not run on will power, since, as Hamacher makes clear, Nietzsche's genealogy of the will features a will without power over itself. Thus Nietzsche licensed a double reading of the will that aims one barrel at tendencies in his own philosophy which collaborate with interpretations (such as Heidegger's) in which the will is hypostasized as transcendental subject.

The will is also always testament: the metaphors of writing and language that crowd around Nietzsche's characterization of the constitution of acts of will shift the genealogy of nihilism into a grammatological register. Because it never goes without saying, willing is always differentiated with each verbal expression into a will and a separable act of willing. This causative or grammatical split-level construction—language's resentment towards the will—

accordingly observes two laws. The will must, by law, will its own law—its act of not willing. Or as Nietzsche put it in *Genealogy of Morals,* the history of culture can be reduced to the periodic achievement or retention of a few *I will not*s. But this mnemonic intervention always also introduces another law-abiding perspective that faces the other way, towards the dyspeptic nondigestion of the past. Thus resentment or will to nothingness overtakes subservience to the law of the will. With regard to the moral law, then, the will is led to will nothing rather than submit itself to the law of its explication and will not to will. Coming full circle and back to Kant, Hamacher and Nietzsche show free will to be the will of resentment; within the grammatological register, resentment doubles as origin of the stubborn survival of a certain idealism of language.

Between hermeneutics and ethics Derrida too draws the line—along which the name is signed. The original occasion for "Interpreting Signatures" was the debate with Gadamer in which Derrida dismantled received moral imperatives and, on the other side of the Heideggerian reception, the unity of the name "Nietzsche" which only the assumed continuity of Nietzsche's thought could guarantee. The original title of Derrida's response was "Good Wills to Power": the good will that Gadamer offered as precondition of all true dialogue became recognizable on Derrida's side of the exchange as the very proof of dialogue's impossibility.[5] Thus it was only symptomatic that Gadamer's conception of good will, as that context and coherence which understanding invites and requires, was so liberal as to include the consensus of psychoanalysis. But the psychoanalytic perspective, which Gadamer would effortlessly plug into the tradition he advertises, cannot but shortcircuit the hermeneutic currency of understanding's "vital" contextualization. For within this perspective, the relation of understanding that Gadamer would secure as the safety zone of his own polemical positioning is not so much a continuously unfolding disclosure as it is a break—the break the other gets. Good will remains indicative of a metaphysics of will which tends to be asserted with a force (even violence) that does not end up convincing.

Gadamer advanced in exchange a critique of deconstruction's reliance on wordplay and paronomasia as its own ill will toward understanding. But at Derrida's end, wordplay delivers proof that language always has the last word—behind the back of writer or interpreter. In the wake or clearing of the pun one finds that no consciousness, no reason, no logos will have had language at its disposal to the point of rendering it a text that can be assumed or absorbed within the good will to power of a hermeneutic regulatory apparatus. By promoting pun power, Derrida switches on the counter-apparatus and shredding machine that Gadamer overlooks insofar as he invokes psychoanalysis in its place: the Nietzschean machine of transvaluation, advertised for the end of the millennium.

Nietzsche singled out his conception of the project of transvaluation as the gift which had inspired his greatest gratitude—to his life. But *The New Nietzsche* followed Heidegger in banning any reading that turned on Nietzsche's "uninspiring" life. Instead *The New Nietzsche* championed finite but open metaphor in order to eliminate, through this supersemiological challenge, rules of operation basic to "tyranny, capitalism, psychoanalysis."[6] This yawning abyss into which *The New Nietzsche* dropped biography thus resounds with one rediscovery only by scrambling another. The psychoanalytic reception of Nietzsche turns up full blast in Adler, Jung, and Spielrein, and achieves in Freud subliminal heights: are not *Genealogy of Morals* and *Civilization and its Discontents* the "same" book?

The expulsion of biography from Nietzsche attempts to introduce zoning laws into one of philosophy's bad neighborhoods. Here the quarantine imposed on biography could never be enforced. Indeed, as Derrida has established, the politics of the proper name in Nietzsche renders Nietzsche's biography radically nonextraneous and nonaccidental to Nietzsche's philosophizing.[7] Nietzsche went so far as to advise that philosophies could be reduced to dossiers on the philosophers' lives and that the name of a philosopher should be considered the determining force behind the philosophy it signed or countersigned. It may be that in Hegel the truth of the oeuvre makes the name contingent. But Nietzsche signed with his many names, a profusion of naming that could never evaporate with the oeuvre. The many masks of Nietzsche call for further masks, countersignatory gestures of the most varied (even at times contradictory) styles. The post-Heideggerian reading of Nietzsche rides out the splits and frays of the text—following through the anecdote, for example, in which Nietzsche was the first to find cognitive value. *Looking After Nietzsche* remains nonexclusionary in the risks it takes; every thread of "Nietzsche" is pursued throughout its labyrinthine entanglements.

Names and biographies—all the names in history—are irretrievably on the loose in Nietzsche. Although Heidegger canceled all biographical coverage of Nietzsche, he opted to protect the name Nietzsche: " 'Nietzsche'—the name of the thinker stands as title for the subject [*Sache*] of his thought."[8] The proper name, which only comes life-size, is bonded to the return of the biographical. Indeed

Nietzsche's philosophy of metaphor turned on a life-support connection between the biographical and the biological or textual. It is in this sense, as Gasché and Kofman demonstrate, that Nietzsche was the first philosopher to think with his body—to "dance." Gasché describes the scene of writing which Nietzsche's corpus spins out around it in terms of operations of killing time. But the pen that thus fixes the moment at the same time engenders the body—the body conceived, that is, as a happy-faced pile of dead moments. From the footnotes on up, Nietzsche's corpus (his life, his history, his thought) was "posthumously born."

Pautrat builds this body out of the philosophical discourse on truth: what slides to the side—and thus to the inside—are repetition, castration, and desire. The symptomatic interchangeability in this discursivity of Medusa's head and the conception of Eternal Return unveils, according to Pautrat, a fetish doctrine of return (conceived as recycling of identity) which only insures the philosophical coherence it must simulate. For as fetish, this take on return does not take; it cannot but betray the falsity, the vacuity, on which it is erected and instituted. The true version of Eternal Return, it turns out—one that would feature dispersion, selection, and difference—remains a never-to-be-stated statement, a textual hole represented either by the false fetish statement or by no statement at all. This double and dissymetrical censure operates once consciously, on behalf of philosophical clarity and paraphrasability, and once in the unconscious of the text—interrupting the narrative.

In Kofman's reading, Nietzsche installs this interruption or double bind inside his metaphors of metaphor—the building blocks and blockages of his thought. Nietzsche programmed metaphor and concept to drive apart—but on the same pathway of "transference" or "metaphor." Metaphor accelerates beyond concept, which remains but the detritus or exhaust of the "instinct" of metaphor. Art, the multiplication of metaphor, thus reflects a life-serving instinct; idealist philosophy, the vampirology of concepts, articulates only the collected corpse of this vital drive.

Another figure of interruption—the reverberation of detonations set by the double binds Nietzsche deposited in the corners of thought reception or thought control—organizes its after-shock effects along a society-wide, indeed history-wide, trajectory. This is the "Nietzsche-effect" (Nietzsche, remember, *was* dynamite). He was the first to diagnose, in the progress of history which he sought to deter, the auto-destruct program. Thus Nietzsche recognized that the institutional structures of thought already in place when he wrote—or, as with dynamite, issued the warning shout—

would undergo, by the time of the Third Reich (the era he anticipated of great, unknown wars to be fought in his name), radical fast-forwarding. Nietzsche was the premier resistance fighter combating anti-Semites and other "monsters of nihilism" in a paranoid theater of prophesied warfare. Nietzsche: our hero.

On another side of delegation or prophecy—on the side of collaboration of aesthetics and history—Nietzsche and Heidegger advance (in Lacoue-Labarthe's reading) a sublime remedy for Germany's mimetological secondariness or lack of existence: a mimesis without models which, on parallel tracks, would promote the "monumental" reestablishment of history. But Lacoue-Labarthe also shows that this sublime program was at the same time undermined by two side effects: on one side a certain German destiny of psychoticization, embodied close-range by Hölderlin and Nietzsche; on the other a compromise with fixed politics (with the politics of Bismark and Hitler), which was, in theory, never inevitable and yet happened only to recur. Thus Lacoue-Labarthe closes by inserting the sublime conjugations that emerge from his reading of Nietzsche (within Heidegger) into a series of questions left suspended over friable ground.

Summoning Lacanian psychoanalysis to this political front of Nietzsche reception, Canning proves that "how the word became a fable" also always turns around into the fabulational and rumorological production of world events. Thus from the eighteenth century to the millennium, Christianity exercises in its absence that most spectacular self-fulfillment of its prophesies or phantasms. This then was Nietzsche's warning: Christianity has gone unconscious, slipping beneath its secularization to produce on the outside (and by a kind of remote control) the repetition, in place of remembering, of Christian phantasies of pogrom and child abuse.

Nietzsche, as if anticipating the unbounded growth and diversification of the field of nothing, distinguished between bad and good nihilism. He denounced annihilation (*Vernichtung*) as the reactive version of combat (*Kampf*), and likewise anti-Semitism as the reactive, "pitiful" version of the rejection of Judeo-Christian values. Enter Nietzsche's niece (the star of "Friedrich Nichte") obliquely claiming her rights of inheritance. She has poorly digested her past, poorly digested the war—and all the way down to that birth which condemned her to carry like a gibe, like a hump, the name of Nietzsche ironically redoubled in "Nichte." One can discern in terms of this simple spoonerism a significance a good deal more than merely anecdotal. Nietzsche took pains to disclose the forces at work behind such a slippage of the signifier: his niece, by a kind of perversion of delegation, in turn incarnates that which her name designates, that is to say, the nothingness, the *Nichts*, the nihilism at which Nietzsche took aim in his combat against resentment. In a familiar gesture known to post-war German ideologues,[9] the niece has her forebear parade the banner of Naziism in order to distinguish herself from it rather easily. Through her thick and clumsy stammering, however, the niece identifies Nietzsche with Nazi nihilism in order better to identify him secretly with that which she is.

In Kittler's reading the stammer becomes the babble of typographical error, the rhyme of techno-shorthand. The masculinist writing alliance (spectacularly exemplified in the bond of dictation between Goethe and Eckermann) undergoes in Nietzsche its technologization and heterosexualization. This double metamorphosis is introduced by the typewriter, by Nietzsche's typewriter; in the place of his writing machine, Nietzsche found and founded the feminine other, now as taker of dictation and disciple, now as double and god. Thus the philosopher of mysogyny was also, by virtue of being the first philosopher to type, a primal feminist.

Bringing up the rear, Ronell interrogates precursor readers or "writers" of Nietzsche. In the combat zone of master texts, Nietzsche confronts Goethe with the jolting primacy of a debased other. In drawing up his select reading list, Nietzsche stammers over Goethe and names only Eckermann, the otherwise overlooked anchorman of a writing team that yielded at the supplemental closure of Goethe's collected works the memoirs entitled now *The Conversations With Goethe*, now *The Conversations With Eckermann*, but invariably to the credit of the single author "Goethe." Nietzsche's mention of Eckermann in the place of Goethe thus names the scandal of a couplification of writing in which can be observed close up what is otherwise available in Nietzsche only (and in long shot) in analyses of academic decision-making: namely, the psychology of resentment. And it is a lapsus, gap, or stammer which thus discloses the crucial place for Nietzsche of the name Eckermann.

The paradoxical principle[10] to which Nietzsche gave his name, one that was meant to found the most "serious" discipline—the "psychology of resentment"—would appear to destine him, or rather to destine his "thought," which is what Heidegger prefers to address, to a lack of comprehension or to being misunderstood. And such is this principle that, for once, misunderstanding cannot be considered a guilty party.

The stammer, this movement of drifting and contagion (in a word, of association) coincides, beginning with Nietzsche, with the movement itself of truth and of the concept; and it is always this movement that is disclosed at the conclusion of the genealogical inquiry into philosophical theses. Truth (that is to say, judgment) of a strictly moral order, the thesis of the good in itself, has its origin in a clumsy repetition, among slaves, of the term "good" in its aristocratic sense. Philosophical "prejudice" (that is to say, truth), the thesis of free will, has its origin in an absurd scrambling of the useful fiction of cause, become *causa sui* for a demented "philosophical naturalism."

Unflaggingly, the genealogist lifts up the veil of the concept to expose the perverse and at the same time blind manipulation to which it owes its admittance. Such an unveiling of the stammering elaboration peculiar to resentment becomes thus a rule; the basic suspicion that pushes the genealogist towards the subterranean and foul-smelling forges of thought serves as the compass which enables him to retrace the path of its ironical history.

But if there is stammering, and if all that is known as philosophical thought is to be submitted to it ironically, then what could let Nietzsche or his thought escape its hold? What assures him a dominating position to the point, indeed, of sparing him the pitiless treatment of resentment armed with "philosophical interpretations"? What, in short, guarantees the immunity of that which we can call the stammer principle?

According to preference, one can reply that the Nietzschean principle need only be asserted, for it contains within it an announcement of affirmative thought, extricated from the imbroglio of resentment and released from its nihilism, cutting into values instead of remaining entangled in the philosophy of the pre-judged and opposing some sort of conceptual rationality to stammering empirical associations. In short, the question of legitimacy which threatened traditional empiricism would here be out of place. Or else, indeed, one would not produce a response, the absence of a reply being in this case the most authentically aristocritical one: "much is to be passed over in silence here."

But Heidegger marked another, oblique way which can lead to the Nietzschean legacy in order to give assurance of its mastery. And this pathway, which is steep and no longer given to the crudely hacked routes within the heritage, is laid out by Heidegger as an "explication with National Socialism."[11] His reading demonstrates the necessity of a type of thinking beyond all nihilism and thus beyond those ideologies which therein draw their sole substance: the necessity of a thinking of being as such.

But in this encounter, who is stammering: Nietzsche or Heidegger? With a prudence that does them honor, the authors of *Looking After Nietzsche* leave the question suspended.

The philosophical heights to which the Heideggerian reading attains should not induce us to forget the very problematical proximity of the ideology with which Heidegger settles his scores through Nietzsche's intercession. While they are decidedly remote from one another, Heidegger and the niece belong to the same generation. This familiar, all too familiar terrain has barely been explored. Here we traverse an uncanny and barren landscape, one in which everything recalls to us that Nietzsche died without having had children.

NOTES

1. *The New Nietzsche: Contemporary Styles of Interpretation*, ed. David B. Allison (New York: Delta Publishing Co., 1977), p. ix.

2. My thanks to Jason Alès for his assistance in unplugging Heidegger's Nietzsche reception.

3. "Plato's Doctrine on Truth": "Nietzsche entirely ignores the metaphysical origin of 'value.' "

4. "Plato's Doctrine on Truth": "he has sustained the essence of *agathon*, but he has shown less prejudice than others have, who chase after the construction of values valuable in themselves."

5. This debate was first preserved from forgetfulness within Philippe Forget's edition, *Text und Interpretation* (Munich: W. Fink Verlag, 1984).

6. *The New Nietzsche*, p. xvii.

7. See in this regard Derrida's "Otobiographies: The Teaching of Nietzsche and the Politics of the Proper Name," trans. Avital Ronell, in *The Ear of the Other*, ed. Christie V. McDonald (New York: Schocken Books, 1985), pp. 1–38.

8. This is how Heidegger's 1961 preface to *Nietzsche*, vol. 1, opens.

9. Have we not seen a well-known weekly magazine of West Germany have as its front page a sketch representing a character with two heads—one side being Nietzsche and the other Adolf Hitler?

10. The paradox evoked here consists in the principle's capacity to destroy itself.

11. Interview granted to the *Spiegel* magazine.

1

Interpreting Signatures (Nietzsche/Heidegger): Two Questions

Jacques Derrida

The first question concerns the *name* Nietzsche, the second has to do with the concept of totality.

I

Let us begin with chapters 2 and 3 of Heidegger's *Nietzsche*—dealing with "The Eternal Recurrence of the Same" and "The Will to Power as Knowledge," respectively. We will be turning especially to the subsection on chaos ("The Concept of Chaos," I, pp. 562–70) and to "The Alleged Biologism of Nietzsche" (*Nietzsches angeblicher Biologismus*). In view of the fact that the same interpretation is regularly at work throughout, the risks involved in choosing this strategy are, I hope, quite limited. In each instance, a single system of reading is powerfully concentrated and gathered together. It is directed at gathering together the unity and the uniqueness of Nietzsche's thinking, which, as a fulfilled unity, is itself in a fair way to being the culmination of occidental metaphysics. Nietzsche would be precisely at the crest, or ridge, atop the peak of this fulfillment. And thus he would be looking at both sides, down both slopes.

This essay was presented at the Goethe Institute in Paris on April 25, 1981, at a colloquium organized by Philippe Forget which brought together Hans-Georg Gadamer and Jacques Derrida. Papers from the colloquium, including among others the presentation by Gadamer, Derrida's reply, and Derrida's own contribution, appeared in German as *Text und Interpretation*, edited by Philippe Forget (Munich: W. Fink, 1984). The translators wish to thank Philippe Forget for his generous assistance in this project.

What about this unity—this doubled unity? What is its connection to the name—or rather, the signature—of Nietzsche? Does Heidegger take any account of this question—which others might call biographical, autobiographical, or autographical—of the singularity of a signature ostensibly the proper name of Nietzsche? To put the matter another way, if one can glimpse behind Heidegger's reading of Nietzsche the foundations of a general reading of Western metaphysics, then the question arises: To what extent does this interpretation of metaphysics in its totality and as a whole contain an interpretive decision about the unity or singularity of thinking? And to what extent does this interpretive decision also presuppose a decision about the "biographical," about the proper name, the autobiographical, and about signature—about the politics of signature?[1]

Heidegger's position on this subject I will indicate first of all with a summarizing and simplifying statement, which one could, I hope, demonstrate is not wrong: there is a unity in Nietzschean thought even if it is not that of a system in the classical sense. This unity is also its uniqueness, its singularity. A thesis explicitly advanced by Heidegger is that every great thinker has only one thought. This uniqueness was neither constituted nor threatened, neither gathered together nor brought about, through a name or proper name—nor by the life of Nietzsche, either normal or insane. This unique unity is something it draws from the unity of Western metaphysics which is gathered together there at its crest, which one could also compare to the simple unity of a line created by a fold. The result of all this is that biography, autobiography, the scene or the powers of the proper name, of proper names, signatures, and so on, are again accorded minority status, are again given the inessential place they have always occupied in the history of metaphysics. This points to the necessity and place of a questioning which I can only sketch here.

Such would be a simplified version of the question. Now let us read Heidegger a little more closely and seek to confirm the strongest coherence of his interpretation or, beyond its coherence, his deepest thought. As a provisional concession to the classical norms of reading, let us take this book at its beginning, or even before its beginning at the beginning of the preface. Naturally, this preface was, like so many others, written later. As we know, the book goes back to a series of lectures given between 1936 and 1940, and to some treatises written between 1940 and 1946. One should take most careful note of these dates if one is to bring this interpretation, as a whole and in detail, into connection with the historico-political and institutional field of its presentation. The preface, however, dates from 1961. The intention of the two pages in this case, as almost always, is to justify the publication of this collection by reference to the essential unity of its totality: "This publication, re-thought (*nachgedacht*) as a whole (*als Ganzes*) should provide a glimpse of the path of thought which I followed between 1930 and the *Letter on Humanism* (1947)." The unity of this publication and of this teaching is, then, also the unity of the path of thought of Heidegger at a decisive moment and traced through a period of over fifteen years. But at the same time this also means that the unity of his interpretation of Nietzsche, the unity of Western metaphysics to which this interpretation is referred, and the unity of the Heideggerian path of thought are here inseparable. One cannot think the one without the other.

Now what are the first words of this preface? What does one find in that first phrase? To be elliptical, let us say one finds *two things*, and both of them have a literal connection with the *name* of Nietzsche.

First, the name is placed in quotation marks.

Now what happens when a proper name is put between quotation marks? Heidegger never asks himself. Still, his whole undertaking, although entitled "Nietzsche," has perhaps put all its powers together in such a way as to nullify the urgency and necessity of this question.

Second, let me read you the first sentence of the preface in the French translation by Klossowski: " 'Nietzsche'—the name of the thinker here names the *cause* of his thinking" (*intitulé ici la cause de sa pensée*).[2] Heidegger's next paragraph explains and, up to a point, justifies Klossowski's translation of a certain German word (*Sache*) by "cause." For in Heidegger's next paragraph we read: "A case, the legal case, is, in itself, *ex-pli-cation*—or in German, *Auseinander-setzung*—one party taking a position in relation to another. To let our thought be penetrated by this 'cause'—to prepare it for this—that is the content of the present publication."[3]

Now to someone who simply opens up this book without knowing the German text, such an approach could seem both odd and at the same time consonant with the latest modernity, not to say the latest style: the *name* of the thinker would thus be the *cause* of his thought! The thinking, then, would be the *effect* caused by his proper name! And here is a book on the name Nietzsche and on the connections between his name and his thought. Taking into account the fact that in this French edition, through a strange typographical error, the name Nietzsche is cut in two (Niet-zsche), who knows what heights this new reader, in the freshness of his too great or too limited perspective, could attain in his analysis of the schism of the proper name, an analysis which, through a parceling out of the signifier or the semantic elements, could make a connection between the Slavic (Polish) origin of the name, on the one hand, and what Nietzsche himself said about the negativity of his own name and the destructive power of his thought, on the other. And if this analysis were carried to delirious extremes, it would then connect this negative element, *Niet-* (and why not? why stop half-way?) with the only two cities in which he said in 1887 he could think or wanted to think: Venice and Nice (specifically, in a letter to Peter Gast dated September 15, which Heidegger cites near the beginning of the book and chapter on *The Will to Power as Art*).[4] These two cities remain the only cure for Nietzsche, the only possible escape. Ah, says our ingenuous and zealous reader, "I see, I see! *il veut Nice, il Venise, il veut Nietzsche, il veut et il ne veut pas,*[5] there you have the two places, the two said places, the toponyms of his *Will to Power!*" But unfortunately this sequence can only work in French and the delirium must come to a halt the moment one notices that Venice in German is *Venedig* and Nice in German is *Nizza.* As Nietzsche says, cited by Heidegger: *"Somit läuft es auf Venedig und Nizza hinaus. . . ."*—"Therefore it has turned out to be a matter of Venice and Nice . . ." (*N.* I, p. 22; Eng. I, p. 14).

But then, pursuing his reading, our French reader still asks: What does it mean, "Nietzsche, the name of the thinker stands as title for his thinking"? Even within the confines of the French translation the content of the next paragraph is enlightening for it clearly says, Do not take the word *cause* in its opposition to *effect* as material, efficient, formal, or final cause of his thought but understand it as the Latin *causa:* legal debate, litigation, opposition of two parties. Still, this perspective too can exercise a kind of modish temptation for the French reader of today: the name Nietzsche as contentiousness of thinking, as stake in a game, war, or legal battle—that scarcely sounds classical any more. Such, taking this new, fresh start, would be an initial reading. But if he consults the original text, the reader discovers something else, quite different from *cause* either in the derivative sense *or* the usual sense of the word: " 'Nietzsche,' the name of the thinker stands as title for *die Sache seines Denkens,*" the *subject-matter* [*Sache*] of his thought, for *what* he thinks.

The German word that one usually translates into French as *cause* (English "cause") is *Ursache* (the cause or reason for something). Because the two words are alike, Klossowski felt justified in translating *Sache* as "cause." But normally *Sache* designates the "thing"—not the sense object or even the thing at hand but the thing in question, the affair, which eventually can lead to litigation. In this sense, the Latin *causa,* cause in the sense of litigation or a trial, is a good translation. It poses not only the thing in question but the question of the thing (*Die Frage nach dem Ding*), which is dealt with elsewhere, namely in Heidegger's great meditation by that title and above all in reference to the relation to all semantic determinations of cause. Indeed, the translation of *Sache* by the French word *cause* (instead of *chose,* "thing") can find, as we have said, support in the course of the text itself. For Heidegger continues, "Die Sache der Streitfall, ist in sich selbst Auseinandersetzung"—"the matter, the point of dispute, is in itself a placing in opposition, a confrontation."

But when he says that the name of the thinker stands as title "for the *Sache* of his thinking," he certainly does not intend to make the name the cause of an effect that would be the thinking. The genitive "of" here designates the *Sache* ("matter") *as* his thinking. Everything will confirm this once one considers the proper name not as that of an individual or of a signatory; it is the name of a thought, of a thought whose unity gives in return sense and reference to the proper name. "Nietzsche" is nothing other than the name of this thinking. The syntax of the genitive misleads us in the other direction, if one may put it that way, for the name is not before the thought, it is the thing that is thought; it is produced and determined by it. Only in thinking this thought will one think the possessive, the genitive, and the proper name. One will learn *who Nietzsche is* and what his name says only from his thinking—not from card files packed with more or less refined biographical facts.

At this point two paths present themselves. One would consist in taking a new approach to the problematic of the name, at the risk of seeing the name dismembered and multiplied in masks and similitudes. We know what Nietzsche risked in this respect. The name would be constituted on the far side of the "life" of the thinker, from the vantage point of the future of the world, from an affirmation of the "eternal recurrence."[6]

The other path would be to determine the essentiality of the name from the "subject matter of thought," of thought itself defined as the content of theses, and to let fall into inessentiality the particular proper name, which has become the index of the "biography" or a "psychology" of an individual. In legitimately scorning biographism, psychologism, or psychoanalysis, one instead embraces reductionist empiricisms which in turn only cover up what is given as thinking. This is what Heidegger does, for the best reasons in the world. But in doing this does he not thereby fall back on a gesture of classical metaphysics, indeed at the very moment in which he is appealing for something other than metaphysics—i.e., at the moment when he situates Nietzsche on the crest of that metaphysics? This classical gesture also reappears in his dissociating the matter of life or of proper name from the matter of thought. Hence the beginning of Heidegger's lecture course: In a very conventional fashion he dissociates his summary and "official" biography of Nietzsche, on the one hand, from the grand questions which stretch the great philosopher to the limit of his powers, on the other. Such is the form of this first lecture, which conforms to the old pedagogical model: very quickly one runs through the "life of the author" in its most conventional features, then turns to the thought, that which Heidegger calls "the authentic philosophy of Nietzsche." This philosophy, Heidegger notes, "does not arrive at a definitive elaboration nor is it ever published as a work."

Then, criticizing the edition of the complete works, Heidegger notes some of its limitations. They adhered to the principle of integrality (*Vollständigkeit*, "completeness"), that pushed everything and which resurrected nineteenth-century models, to the point of that biologism and psychologism which are like a monstrous perversion of our age. Heidegger criticizes that editorial enthusiasm that "proceeds in the manner of biological and psychological elucidation," which "traces minutely all the data" of the life of the author, including the opinions of contemporaries. It is an "excrescence" (*Ausgeburt*, "monstrosity," "product"), a "monstrous product of the addiction of our time to the psycho-biological [*der psychologisch-biologischen Sucht unserer Zeit*]." Says Heidegger, "Only the proper preparation of an authentic edition of the *Works* (1881–1889), if that task is ever accomplished in the future, will bring access to the 'works of Nietzsche,' properly speaking." Furthermore, Heidegger adds, "This will never be genuinely accomplished if in the questioning we do not grasp Nietzsche as the end of Western metaphysics and press over to the quite different question of the truth of Being" (*N*, I, pp. 18–19; Eng. I, p. 10). To pose the question of the truth of Being, beyond ontology, and to determine the place of Nietzsche as the end of Western metaphysics—these are the prerequisite conditions if one wishes eventually to gain access to the "biography" of Nietzsche, to the name, and above all to the textual corpus of Nietzsche—if one wishes, in other words, to know "who Nietzsche was."

Prior to all other questions, we need to be attentive to the fundamental necessity for such a schema as Heidegger puts forward, and also attentive to everything in a certain historical and political situation which could justify it. The psychological and biological eagerness in the *style* he so often practices circles around and thereby misses the *content* of a thought—its necessity and its internal specificity. A well-known schema. Besides, at the time he was teaching his "Nietzsche," Heidegger had begun to put some distance between himself and Nazism. Without saying anything in his lecture itself that was directed against the government and the use it was making of Nietzsche (on so much prudence and silence one can certainly put an interpretation—but elsewhere), Heidegger is in the process of overtly criticizing the edition that the government is in the process of supporting. Heidegger appears at first to have been associated with it, then he backed out; the issue had to do with instituting, in cooperation with Nietzsche's sister, falsifications in that edition: "For knowledge of Nietzsche's biography," Heidegger continues, "the presentation by his sister, Elisabeth Förster-Nietzsche, *The Life of Friedrich Nietzsche* (published between 1895 and 1904), remains always important. As with all biographical works, however, use of this publication requires great caution. We will refrain from further suggestions and from discussion of the enormous and varied secondary literature surrounding Nietzsche, since none of it can aid the endeavor of this lecture course. Whoever does not have the courage and perseverance of thought required to get involved in reading Nietzsche's own writings has no need to read anything *about* him either" (*N*, I, p. 19; Eng. I, pp. 10–11).

Here and elsewhere one of the targets of Heidegger is what he calls "philosophy of life." The object of Heidegger's attack here was Nazism, but also a classical university tradition as well, which made of Nietzsche a "philosopher-poet," a life-philosopher without conceptual rigor whom one could denounce "from the height of German chairs of philosophy." But in either case one praises or condemns that "philosophy of life" which Heidegger from *Being and Time* onward had combatted as an absurdity.

This critique of psycho-biologism underlies also his critique of Nietzsche's "alleged biologism" ("Nietzsches angeblicher Biologismus," *N*, I, pp. 517–27). It answers the question of the name of Nietzsche, the question "What is that we call Nietzsche?" There, once again, in response to the question, "Who is Nietzsche?", right at the opening of the third chapter, "The Will to Power as Knowledge," in the first subsection (again the first words), which has the title "Nietzsche as Thinker of the Fulfillment of Metaphysics":

> Who Nietzsche *is* and above all who he *will be* we know as soon as we are in a position to think that thought which he stamped into the world-framework of *The Will to Power*. Nietzsche is that thinker who went the way that the train of thought led him—to the will to power. Who Nietzsche is we never find out through a historical account of his life history, and also not through a presentation of the content of his writings. Who Nietzsche is we do not will to know and also are not meant to know if and so long as we have in mind only the personality, the historical figure, the psychological object and its productions. But wait. . . . (*N*, I, p. 473)

At this point, Heidegger brings forward an objection he will soon reject. Before going into this, however, I should like to offer a cautionary remark against oversimplifying the question I am directing to Heidegger's procedure. Doubtless there is an effort by Heidegger to reduce the name of Nietzsche or the "Who is Nietzsche" question to the unity of Western metaphysics, even to the uniqueness of a limit situation on the crest of that metaphysics. Nevertheless, the question "Who is X?" was a rare question when applied to a thinker; it is so still if one does not understand it in a biographically trivial way—as the man and the work, the man behind the work, the life of Descartes or Hegel associated with a kind of doxography. But to ask in another sense "Who is Nietzsche?"—to make his name the title of a book on his thought—that is something not so conventional.

Here is the objection Heidegger raises in a *pro forma* way just after he has rejected psychobiography: "But just a minute! Has not Nietzsche himself as a last act completed a work for publication entitled *Ecce Homo: How One Becomes What One Is?* Does not *Ecce Homo* speak as Nietzsche's last will and testament, to the effect that one must deal with this man, and let it be said of him what the excerpts of that writing suggest: 'Why I am so wise? Why I am so intelligent? Why I write such good books? Why I am a destiny?' Does this not point to an apex in unrestrained self-presentation and measureless self-mirroring?" Heidegger answers: *Ecce Homo* is not an autobiography, and if anything culminates in it, it would be the final moment of the West, in the history of the era of modernity. Without a doubt things get knotted together right in this place. One can admit, easily enough, that *Ecce Homo* is not Nietzsche's autobiographical history. But when Heidegger simply lets stand the conventional concept of autobiography instead of reshaping it, and only opposes to it the destiny of the West whose "carrier" Nietzsche would be, then one has to ask: Does Heidegger himself escape a fairly traditional opposition between biographical factuality—psychobiographical, historical—and an essential thinking on the order of a historical decision? One can also ask what interest is served by this Heideggerian discourse being carried out along these lines.

By means of this strategy, Heidegger intends to rescue Nietzsche from his own singular fate. This fate has remained ambiguous. It has provoked odd uses of his thinking, uses which turned against what Heidegger calls Nietzsche's "innermost will." Thus it is a matter of gaining access to this innermost will and to oppose it to the duplicity of the empirical figure of Nietzsche as well as to the ambiguity of its subsequent effects—its immediate after-effects, for Heidegger believed that the future will work to restore that innermost will. After saying this in order to rescue Nietzsche from ambiguity, Heidegger directs this whole interpretation of Nietzsche's essential and singular thinking to the following argument: this thinking has not really gone beyond the end of metaphysics; it is still itself a great metaphysics and even if it points to such an overcoming, it is just barely, just enough to remain on the sharpest crest of the boundary. Or, in other words, to remain in complete ambiguity.

This, then, is essential ambiguity! Not just Nietzsche's, as Heidegger sees it, but also Heidegger's own ambivalence with regard to Nietzsche. It remains constant. In saving Nietzsche, Heidegger loses him too; he wants at the same time to save him and let go of him. At the very moment of affirming the uniqueness of Nietzsche's thinking, he does everything he can to show that it repeats the mightiest (and therefore the most general) schema of metaphysics. When he is pretending to rescue Nietzsche from this or that distortion—that of the Nazis, for example—he does so with categories which can themselves serve to distort—namely, with that opposition between essential and inessential thinkers, authentic thinkers and inauthentic ones, and with the definition of the essential thinker as someone selected, chosen, marked out or, I would even say, "signed" (*gezeichnet*). Signed—by what? By whom? By nobody—by the history of the truth of Being. Nietzsche was sufficiently chosen for that, and yet he was condemned by this same destiny to bring metaphysics to its completion, and without reaching a decision which he alone had prepared, even without recognizing the scope of that decision: "between the hegemony of *beings* and the lordship of *Being*" (*Zwischen der Vormacht des Seienden und der Herrschaft des Seins*). For all these points I refer you to the first pages of the chapter, "The Will to Power as Knowledge," whose first section carries the heading, "Nietzsche as Thinker of the Fulfillment of Metaphysics" (*N*, I, p. 473ff.).

It was doubtless necessary to set up this interpretation-schema of Nietzsche's *biographein* in order to penetrate to his "alleged biologism." There too it is a matter of rescuing—in a most ambiguous way—the uniqueness of a thinking from the ambiguity of a life and work. The marking out of the boundaries of the biographical and of the proper name opens up the general space in whose interior the interpretation of the biological occurs.

Before the first words I quoted moments ago from the Preface there is an exergue.[7] It is taken from the *Gay Science* and its first word is "life." "Life" stands at the extreme outset of Heidegger's book—even before its beginning, before any decision between biography and biology. Here, strangely enough, Heidegger is not satisfied with breaking off the passage before its end. He also skips over a few words and replaces them with ellipses: "Life . . . more mysterious since the day the great liberator came over me—the thought that life should be an experiment of knowers." Among the words he skips over are the words "true" and "desirable," both of which pertain to life. Here is the fragment from Nietzsche in its—if one may speak this way—integral character.

> *In media vita!* No! [These four words—the title, in short—and above all, these two exclamation points, are omitted by Heidegger—this time without ellipses. JD] Life has not disappointed me! On the contrary, I find it truer, more desirable and mysterious every year—ever since the day when the great liberator came over me: the idea that life might be an experiment of knowers—and not a duty, not a calamity, not trickery! And knowledge itself: let it be something else for others; for example, a bed to rest on, or the way to such a bed, or a diversion, or a form of leisure—for me it is a world of dangers and victories in which heroic feelings, too, find places to dance and play. *"Life as a means to knowledge"*—with this principle in one's heart one can live not only boldly but even gaily, and laugh gaily, too! And who knows how to laugh anyway and live well if he does not first know a good deal about war and victory? (*Gay Science*, § 324)

These are fundamentally secretive assertions, very difficult to interpret, just like the title *In media vita!* That makes life out to be a medium—as much in the sense of a mean between two extremes as in the sense of an elementary milieu in which the experiment of knowledge finds its place. In situating itself within life, this experiment uses life as a means, steers it from the inside, and—with this power to steer the living—comes to be beyond and outside of life, on the side of its end and its death, and so on. One can see why Heidegger took this passage as an exergue. He appears to be making a biological reading of Nietzsche more difficult in advance, whether one understands this reading in the sense of a subordination under the model of biology or as a celebration of life as the ultimate aim—even to the determination of life as the Being of beings, or being as a whole.

This choice of an exergue is sufficient evidence that the question about life and the "alleged biologism" stand at the active center of Heidegger's *Nietzsche.* And yet the paradoxical character of this passage (*In media vita!*) could also thwart Heidegger's hermeneutical strategy. Life does have a beyond, but it does not allow itself to be made into something secondary. As itself and in itself it unfolds the movement of truth or knowledge. It is in itself as its own beyond. Not to mention the stresses and the joys, the laughter and the war, the question marks and exclamation points—those things which Heidegger, considering how he effaces or conceals them, obviously does not want to hear spoken of here. . . .

I would like to point out a second thing about this exergue—or rather, once again, a first thing, something completely first—prefirst. I said "life" was the first word of the citation. Strictly speaking, it is the first word in the quotation from Nietzsche. Before this quotation Heidegger adds a short sentence which—strangely enough—presents the exergue itself: "Nietzsche himself names the experience that determines his thinking: ' . . . ' ". Hence, it is Nietzsche himself who *names* what determines his thinking, the patient experience of his thinking. And, if the name of the thinker designates the matter of his thinking, as Heidegger wants to show immediately afterwards, then the exergue as a whole means: Nietzsche names himself, he names himself from that out of which one must be able to name him. He will give himself a name from out of the experience of his thinking, and from it he receives his name. And so the thinking, so named, must rightly be understood from within this autonomous circle. But is it correct to say, as Heidegger so positively claims, that this thinking is one?—that Nietzsche then has only one name? Does he name himself only once? For Heidegger, his naming takes place only once, even if the place of this event retains the appearance of a borderline, from which one can get a look at both sides at once, at the summit of Western metaphysics, which is gathered together under this name.

But who ever has said that a person bears a single name? Certainly not Nietzsche. And likewise, who has said or decided that there is something like a Western metaphysics, something which would be capable of being gathered up under this name and this name only? What is it—the oneness of a name, the assembled unity of Western metaphysics? Is it anything more or less than the desire (a word effaced in Heidegger's Nietzsche citation) for a proper name, for a single, unique name and a thinkable genealogy? Next to Kierkegaard, was not Nietzsche one of the few great thinkers who multiplied his names and played with signatures, identities, and masks? Who named himself more than once, with several names? And what if that would be the heart of the matter, the *causa*, the *Streitfall* ("point of dispute") of his thinking?

As we have just now seen, Heidegger wants to save Nietzsche at any cost, to save him from ambiguity by a gesture which is itself ambivalent. And what if it would be this rescue, which must be called into question in the name or names of Nietzsche?

When reading Heidegger's lectures on Nietzsche it is possibly less a matter of suspecting the content of an interpretation than of an assumption or axiomatic structure. Perhaps the axiomatic structure of metaphysics, inasmuch as *metaphysics itself* desires, or dreams, or imagines its own unity. A strange circle—an axiomatic structure which consequently demands an interpretation, one, gathered up, around a thinking unifying a unique text and, ultimately, the unique name for Being, for the experience of Being. With the value of the *name* this unity and this oneness mutually guard themselves against the dangers of dissemination. Here, perhaps—to take the words from Heidegger's preface—lies the *Streitfall* or the *Auseinandersetzung* between the Nietzsches and Martin Heidegger, between the Nietzsches and so-called (*ladite*) Western metaphysics. Since Aristotle, and at least up until Bergson, "it" (metaphysics) has constantly repeated and assumed that to think and to say must mean to think and say something that would be a *one*, one *matter*. And that not thinking-saying some one matter or principle is not thinking-saying at all, but a loss of the *logos*. Here is perhaps what the Nietzsches have put in question: the *legein* of this *logos*, the *gathering* of this logic.

This plurality starts to look like the family names of wanderers and tightrope walkers. It leads one away to the feast. Nietzsche and Heidegger speak of this feast with added emphasis. I leave it to you to consider this difference:

> The error will be recognized only when a confrontation with Nietzsche is at the same time conjoined to a confrontation in the realm of the grounding question of philosophy. At the outset, however, we ought to introduce some words of Nietzsche's that stem from the time of his work on "will to power": "for many, abstract thinking is toil; for me, on good days, it is feast and frenzy" (XIV, § 24).
>
> Abstract thinking a feast? The highest form of human existence? Indeed. But at the same time we must observe how Nietzsche views the essence of the feast, in such a way that he can think of it only on the basis of his fundamental conception of all being, will to power. "The feast implies: pride, exuberance, frivolity; mockery of all earnestness and respectability; a divine affirmation of oneself, out of animal plenitude and perfection—all obvious states to which the Christian may not honestly say Yes. *"The feast is paganism par excellence"* (*Will to Power,* § 916). For that reason, we might add, the feast of thinking never takes place in Christianity. That is to say, there is no Christian philosophy. There is no true philosophy that could be determined anywhere else than from within itself. For the same reason there is no pagan philosophy, inasmuch as anything "pagan" is always still something Christian—the counter-Christian. The Greek poets and thinkers can hardly be designated as "pagan." Feasts require long and painstaking preparation. This semester we want to prepare ourselves for the feast, even if we do not make it as far as the celebration, even if we only catch a glimpse of the preliminary festivities at the feast of thinking—experiencing what meditative thought is and what it means to be at home in genuine questioning. (*N,* I, pp. 14–15; Eng. I, pp. 5–6)

What happens in the course of the feast to the *legein* of this *logos,* which demands of the thinking-saying of the essential thinker that it be a thinking-saying of the one and the unique? The Nietzsches' feast risks tearing it into pieces or of dispersing it in its masks. Certainly it would protect it from any kind of biologism, but because the "logism" in it would lose its hold from the start. And another style of autobiography would come into being, bursting open (in every sense of the expression *faire sauter*) the unity of the name and the signature, disturbing both biologism and its critique, so far as it operates, in Heidegger, in the name of "essential thinking."

These are the preliminary remarks that I wanted to suggest for a future reading of Heidegger's *Nietzsche*—for this ambiguous life-saving act, in the course of which one stretches out the net for the tightrope walker, the one who runs the greatest risk overhead on the narrow rope, only insofar as one has made sure that he—unmasked and protected by the unity of his name, which in turn will be sealed by the unity of metaphysics—will not be taking any risks. In other words: he has dead before he landed in the net.

Certainly none of that will have taken place in *Zarathustra*—nor in Basel, Venice, or Nice—but in Freiburg im Breisgau, between 1936 and 1940, during the preparation for a feast, preparation for a "being at home in genuine questioning" (*N*, I, p. 15; Eng. I, p. 6).

II

Since I have been speaking for far too long (and I hope you will excuse me), I will be even more schematic in linking up a second question to the one we have just discussed. All this will be barely even preliminary, and, as I indicated at the beginning, will have to do with the concept of totality. One knows that the reference to the "totality of beings" in Heidegger's interpretation of Nietzsche, as well as in Western metaphysics itself, plays a structuring role. In order to speed things up, I am first of all going to mention two quotations. Heidegger takes the first one from the notes for *The Will to Power:* "Our whole world is the *ashes* of countless *living* creatures: and even if the animate seems so miniscule in comparison to the whole, it is nonetheless the case that *everything* has already been transposed into life and so departs from it." After this quotation Heidegger continues: "Apparently opposed to this is a thought expressed in *The Gay Science,* number 109: 'Let us guard against saying that death is the opposite of life; the living creature is simply a kind of dead creature, and a very rare kind.' "

The first thought points to a paradox in totality as a value. It shows itself disrespectfully in the face of the assurance of all that one generally thinks under the category of totality. But let us not forget that Heidegger defines metaphysics as the thinking of beings as a whole so that the question of the Being of beings is excluded; and on the basis of this definition he often makes Nietzsche out to be the last metaphysician. Without getting tangled up in the complexity of this whole question, one can already surmise just by reading this one passage that Nietzsche by no means trusts any thought of totality. He who says, "Even if the animate seems so miniscule in comparison to the whole, it is nonetheless the case that *everything* has already been transposed into life and so departs from it," expresses a thought about life and death which by no means subordinates itself to an unequivocal meaning of totality, of the relation between a whole and a non-whole. The idea of the eternal recurrence, obviously pervading this statement, is not a thought about totality. But Heidegger presents it *as* a thought about totality. It is one of the most insistent and most decisive themes of his reading. For instance, he writes at the end of the entire interpretation, which began with the two quotations that I recited:

> For one thing, we have circumscribed the field in which the thought of return belongs and which the thought as such concerns: we have surveyed this field of being as a whole and determined it as the interlacing unity of the animate and the lifeless. For another, we have shown how in its foundations being as a whole—as the unity of animate and inanimate—is structured and articulated: it is constituted by the character of force and the finitude of the whole (at one with infinity) that is implied in the character of force—which is to say, the immeasurability of the "phenomenal effects." (*N*, I, p. 355; Eng. II, pp. 96–97)

We must remember that Heidegger takes the will to power to be the principle of the knowledge of the eternal recurrence of the same. It is the *Verfassung* ("composition") of beings (their *quid*, their *quidditas*, their *essentia*); the eternal recurrence is the modality (the *quomodo, die Weise* ["the manner of being"]) of beings as a whole (*N*, I, p. 425). In order to analyze Nietzsche's metaphysical *Grundstellung* ("fundamental position"), Heidegger must examine the accepted answer to the question about beings as a whole. The answer, he finds, is a two-fold one: the totality of beings is will to power and it is eternal recurrence. Whether or not these two answers are compatible, complementary, or combinable is basically less determinable from their content than their mutual relation. In point of fact, they are responses to two questions which throughout metaphysics form a pair (Being as *quidditas* or *essentia;* Being as manner of existing). As Heidegger sees it, because we did not know to identify this "metaphysical" pair of questions, we have erred up to now before the enigma of this twofold answer. But you can very well see that in each of these two questions the question of beings as a totality remains implied. This question about beings as a whole is one that Nietzsche, as the metaphysician he is (according to Heidegger), would stubbornly seek to answer.

And now my question: If in the first of the two statements Heidegger cites (" . . . even if the animate seems so miniscule in comparison to the whole, it is nonetheless the case that *everything* has already been transposed into life and so departs from it") the thought of the eternal recurrence does not coincide either with the thought of totality or any opposition of whole and part, is it perhaps hasty to make Nietzsche out to be a metaphysician, albeit the last one?—At least if a metaphysician is, as Heidegger sees it, a thinker who adheres to the thought of beings as a whole. It just may possibly be that Nietzsche is not at all a thinker of beings, if indeed an essential connection exists between beings as such and totality.

Is it not also worth noting that it is life-death which deprives the value of totality of any privileged status? Is it not to be thought—following a very Nietzschean gesture, for we could well have other indications—that the living (the living–the dead) is not an existent being, does not fall within an ontological determination? Nietzsche had one day proposed to think the word "being" starting from life and not the other way around.

A second preliminary remark: Heidegger has put these two quotations together on the ground of their apparent contradiction. He notes that they appear to "stand opposed" (*entgegenstehen*) to one another. Even if what we have here is an hypothesis or a feigned objection, it seems to me that its very principle is thwarted in Nietzsche's sentence. There, opposition or contradiction no longer constitutes a law dictating prohibitions to thought. And that without dialectic. Life and death (life-death), from which we think everything else—are not the whole. Neither are they opposites: "Let us guard against saying that death is the opposite of life; the living creature is simply a kind of dead creature, and a very rare kind." In one blow Nietzsche thwarts all that governs the thought or even the anticipation of totality, namely the relationship of genus and species. Here we are dealing with a unique inclusion—without any possible totalization—of the "whole" in the "part." With a metonymizing free from limits or positive devices. Let us defend ourselves against all our defenses—Nietzsche seems to be saying, at the beginning of a long aphorism (*Gay Science*, § 109), which, one more time, Heidegger does not quote in its entirety.—Yet another metonymical violence that engages his interpretation, it seems to me. But I do not want to impose upon your time; somewhere else, some other time, perhaps I will come back to these matters. Here I simply wanted to take the risk of sketching out two questions.

Translated by Diane Michelfelder and Richard E. Palmer

NOTES

1. Derrida elsewhere develops this theme further, and in relation to Nietzsche. See his "Nietzsches Otobiographie oder Politik des Eigennamens: Die Lehre Nietzsches," *Fugen: Deutsch-Französisches Jahrbuch für Text-Analytik* (1980). JD. [For the English version of this article, see note 7 below.]

2. Martin Heidegger, *Nietzsche,* trans. Pierre Klossowski (Paris: Gallimard, 1971).

3. Martin Heidegger, *Nietzsche* (Pfüllingen: Neske, 1961), p. 9; English edition, *Nietzsche,* vol. 1: *The Will to Power as Art,* trans. David F. Krell (New York: Harper & Row, 1979), p. xv. Where Derrida provides a French translation, we have worked from the French rather than using Krell's translation. Where the German is presented untranslated, we have sometimes used the Krell translation and sometimes supplied our own.

4. Heidegger, *Nietzsche,* I, 22; Eng. I, 14. Hereafter the abbreviation *N* will refer to the original two-volume German edition. The English translation, when given, will follow a semicolon.

5. The point Derrida is making relies on the French sounds. A translation would be: "He wants Nice, he venices, he wants Nietzsche"—all of which sound close enough to each other in French to invite the play on words.

6. This is the interpretation proposed by Derrida in the essay cited in footnote 1 above. JD.

7. Fr. *exergue.* See the significant reference in Derrida's "Otobiographies: The Teaching of Nietzsche and the Politics of the Proper Name," in *The Ear of the Other: Otobiography, Transference, Translation,* ed. Christie V. McDonald (New York: Schocken Books, 1985), pp. 11–12: "Between the Preface [of *Ecce Homo*] signed F. N., which comes after the title, and the first chapter . . . there is a single page. It is an outwork, an *hors d'oeuvre,* an exergue or a flysheet whose topos . . . strangely dislocates . . . the time of life's *récit.*"

2

The Promise of Interpretation: Reflections on The Hermeneutical Imperative in Kant and Nietzsche

Werner Hamacher

When[1] just about everything became problematic for hermeneutics, from its status within the canon of philosophical sciences to the specific constitution of objects and procedures of understanding, one issue was discussed only fleetingly, as if its clear articulation could shake the entire system of hermeneutics: the fact that understanding *must* take place, the imperative of understanding itself, the obligation presented by every pronouncement—even before any content is expressed—to listen, to understand, to interpret. If the hermeneutical operation begins at that point where understanding itself—as Schleiermacher writes—is no longer a matter of course, then we can wonder if all understanding does not hold its breath in the face of precisely that which escapes understanding, whether it is a linguistic or linguistically mediated fact. If hermeneutics, as Schleiermacher writes again, is "the art" of "understanding correctly the speech of another, especially written speech," and if correct understanding is defined as completely grasping the "speech of the other" in its individuality, then hermeneutics lives in fact off the collapse of its own project "since each [soul] is in its individual existence the non-existence of the other" and therefore "non-understanding refuses to dissolve itself completely."[2] The border separating each individuality from the other is, however, not only a barrier to understanding. Rather, as limit, it entails at the same time the necessity to understand that particular individuality,

First published in *Spiegel und Gleichnis*—Festschrift für Jacob Taubes, ed. N. Bolz-W. Hübener; Würzburg 1983.

as well as every other individuality, because we can gain access to the field of understanding only by understanding that which sets limits on that field.

In Schleiermacher's attempt to offer a methodological grounding for hermeneutic operations the problem of the necessity of understanding will be solved in the form of a paradox: from the very point where understanding cannot exist, comes the demand that understanding must exist. The paradox is unavoidable within the framework of Schleiermacher's fundamental hermeneutical principle which states that all understanding occurs within the dynamic polarity between general language rules and their individual modification in language usage. Only the rule itself can be considered understood, while the individual utterances, from which this rule is abstracted, and which are the actual generative, linguistic productions, can never be totally reduced to the rule. As a result, they must remain inaccessible to the mechanical comprehension gained from linguistic conventions. "The speech of another," if it is to be understood as the speech of this particular other, thus cannot be disclosed to the interpreter through the application of a common norm, a common prior understanding, or even a common interest. Schleiermacher attempted to resolve the conflict between rational knowledge according to generally valid linguistic laws, and the demands of individual, specifically artistic linguistic performances, by appealing to the classical concept of *divinatio.* In divination, interpretation is located neither on the side of a constituted linguistic system nor on the side of its individual application, but rather between the two, at the point where they diverge. As the agent of the "speech of another," divination continues the process of individuation introduced by the other's speech by groping, as it were, in the system of conventions and trying thereby to accommodate by modifying (*anverwandeln*) the singular nature of that speech to speech in general. The mediating movement of divination has no precisely definable techniques at its disposal since it must take over where all techniques fail. Its vanishing point is the messianic moment at the end of history that allows the speech of the other to merge freely with the speech of the one. It is, however, not within the power of the interpreter to induce this moment. Nor is it within the power of the theoretician to conceive of it.

If understanding is not to harden into a mechanism of identifications and projections, it must allow itself to be guided by that which is not eclipsed in identity, but which escapes any assimilation. The "speech of another" can be understood only in an interpretation that makes room in understanding for the otherness of that speech, room for silence, interruption, methodical self-criticism. In all these forms—which the young German romantics developed and applied with an inventive talent hardly attained again since—understanding, by negating itself, points to another understanding; and that other understanding is, for its part, no less relativized, and it points in turn to yet another that would be more appropriate to the other's speech. In this way understanding presents itself as an infinite historical approximation of that one text that it nevertheless must never reach if the text's singular nature is to be upheld. But this approximation is historical only because it is, first of all, semiotic. That is, the interpretation points to its own incapacity to depict the other and thereby evokes *ex negativo* the possibility of a proximity to the other's speech that transcends all exegetical depiction. This act of "pointing" (*Verweisung*), by which understanding refers to another understanding that would be the first understanding of the other, is an instructive "pointer" (*Anweisung*) for all acts of understanding. As the hermeneutical imperative, it demands the infinite unification in understanding of the universal and the individual, the speech of the one and that of the other. But since there is no understanding that could do without suspending one's own speech, and thus without pointing negatively to the speech of the other, and since no language exists that does not respond to an act of understanding, all language must be conceived of as standing implicitly or explicitly under the hermeneutical imperative. All understanding in turn must be understood as striving to fulfill this imperative. The imperative is not uttered positively, either in the speech of the other—since the imperative orders us to hear that speech as speech in the first place—or in the speech of the interpreter (since this speech only arises in the effort to fulfill the imperative). Rather, the hermeneutical imperative can be uttered only negatively in the movement by which every speech relates to another. It is the modification, a priori, of one's own speech, this side of either generality or individuality in the *process* of generalization and individuation.

Understanding is thus, as Schleiermacher says, a "task."[3] It is an "infinite" task that precedes all understanding, one that is incapable of a final solution because it drives finite beings incapable of attaining totality to submit themselves to the form of universality. By using the formula of the "infinite task" of understanding, Schleiermacher allotted a field to hermeneutic reflection which he himself did not cultivate, but which does in fact circumscribe the horizon of his oeuvre. With this concept, he expressed his conviction that the appropriate treatment of hermeneutical problems occurred not in the field and with the methods of epistemology and historical sciences, but rather exclusively under the rubric of ethics.

* * * * *

Kant pointed to the connection between understanding and ethics even more energetically than Schleiermacher, who already assumed the ontology of mediation grounded by speculative Idealism. In his short work of 1791, *On the Failure of all Philosophical Attempts at a Theodicy,* Kant proceeds from the assumption that "the world, as God's work," can be considered an "announcement of the intentions of his will," for which there can be only one "authentic interpretation." This interpretation is that of a practical reason that itself provides all normative laws and postulates, prior to all experience, the concept of God as the origin of that announcement.[4] The interpretation of the divine will by a powerful "authoritative practical reason" can be called "authentic" only because this reason is itself "the unmediated declaration and voice of God," and because as a result God's will interprets itself by means of practical reason's mediation. Since the concept of God arises, however, only where the moral law already functions, the "authentic interpretation" defines itself as self-interpretation not of the divine will but rather of finite reason, and further, as the self-interpretation of the moral law.

Interpretation, insofar as it deserves to be called authentic, does not expound an already given text, but is itself the pronouncement of this text. The law does not exist independently of its interpretation; only because there is no law except in this interpretation, the interpretation that the law's author provides is authentic. Just as the law in its interpretation refers purely to itself, so too does the interpretation in the law refer only to the task of self-realization as both interpretation and as law.

The mode of reality of the moral law differs, however, from every empirical norm, every physical rule, and every behavioral convention that can be the object of descriptive assertions insofar as it can do no more than demand prescriptively the reality to which it refers. Employing equivocation in the concept of law, Kant states that the law as imperative commands a reality of action; and, through this reality of action, reality can appear as a law in the sense of a physical rule. The law demands the law. But only as an imperative demand and not as a law of nature can the law leave man the freedom to choose his own reality. The reality of freedom, which the moral law discloses, is to be dictated, like the law itself, by man himself, and not by any foreign court, either natural or supernatural. It is a "law" of freedom insofar as the will itself "must" dictate such a law to itself in order to be free will. It is a law of "freedom" insofar as the will dictates it to itself. The only law, however, that the will can impose on itself without sacrificing itself is that it itself be law. Independent of every object or purpose of willing (*Wollen*),[5] and independent of every sensual and intellectual motivation, the will itself should possess the form of legality (*Gesetzmäßigkeit*) and be universal in itself. This inner universality of the will, and nothing else, constitutes its autonomy. Only in the form of its universality would the will be itself; only the will that is universal in itself would be, in the strict sense, the subject of its actions. Yet this autonomy of the will, its freedom to determine itself as universal in its absolute individuality, has, of course, no positive reality, but can only be demanded by the law. So the will does not determine itself, but determines only that it should be self-determining. The will is not autonomous, but imposes on itself the demand for autonomy; it is not itself already subject of its actions, but demands of itself to be subject. Unlike the will in Hegel's system of speculative Idealism, it thus does not pass beyond the limits of finite reason. This law is not decreed by the autonomous will, but by the will with a view towards its autonomy. Such is also the case with the "authentic interpretation," the self-interpretation of the law. It is not formulated by an autonomous subject but with a view toward autonomous subjectivity; it entails not an assertion (*Aussage*) as to actual modes of being, but an injunction (*Auflage*) for a mode of knowing. The "authentic interpretation" decrees (for it is law) a mode of acting, knowing and relating to the world as if there were a universal rule of nature according to which all individual actions, including linguistic acts, could communicate with each other in the homogeneous continuum of a universal rule and of a common language.

This common language, which alone could also offer a secure foundation for understanding the speech of the other, is not yet spoken by "authentic interpretation," but rather only ordered by it. Thus within the limits of practical reason Kant's hermeneutic can no more offer a secure basis for concrete acts of understanding than his ethics can guarantee moral actions. On the contrary, his hermeneutics reveals that individual statements can be made subject to universal rule only by a tyrannical linguistic and interpretive regulation and hence solely by means of an individual despotism without foundation in the law. From this insight Kant's hermeneutics draws the conclusion that a theory of hermeneutics cannot be constructed on any one rule of understanding, nor even on a detailed catalogue of rules, but solely on that rule that some rule is, in principle, a precondition of understanding. Since all understanding, regardless of the extent to which it has been distorted on an individual basis, must assume that a universal continuum of understanding should exist, only one option remains for hermeneutics: it must seek its foundation in the vestigial universality of the imperative, which dictates that universality must exist.

At one point Kant reaches back to the metaphor of the book of nature, and grants "authentic interpretation" the capacity "to give meaning [*Sinn*] to the letters of creation." This meaning is by no means that amount of signification (*Bedeutung*) that strenuous exegesis yields.[6] It cannot be deposited, so to speak, as credit into the account of knowledge. Rather, this meaning (*Sinn*) *is* the imperative to act in understanding in accordance with the measure of universalizability inherent in precisely this understanding. Interpretation thus gives meaning to the letter of creation by practical reason—not in the way in which a dictionary attributes to a sign its conventional meaning, but rather meaning (*Sinn*) as a sense of direction (*Richtungssinn*), as a goal, whose obligatory character is all the more binding since only an illusory hope could assume ever to reach it. If, however, the meaning (*Sinn*) of the letter of creation lies in an instructive pointer (*Anweisung*) that shares its source with that letter, then creation itself is also schematized according to the form of this pointer; and its interpretation, like this pointer itself, is not *natura naturata*, but *natura naturans*.

It is of the greatest significance for the correct evaluation of Kant's thought on hermeneutics that the grounding of understanding in reason's command that it be universalizable does *not* mean that it must be grounded in the idea of a limitless community of communication in the future. The finitude of reason, in fact, forbids making the hope for a harmony of languages into *the* explanatory foundation of linguistic action. For in this hope understanding would renouce the possibility of autonomy and would degrade itself to an instrument in the service of an optimistic doctrine of history. The principle of the will can adequately be conceived solely in terms of a structure which is present at all times, and not as a future fact. This structure of the will and its actions—hence the structure of language and understanding as well—is the categorical demand of internal universality. Even if there is no will that fulfills the criterion of this universality at any given time or in any given way, the demand for universality is nevertheless inherent in the very concept of the will. The object of this demand is located outside the will (otherwise it would not be a demand) in a completely good will and its actions. Thus the idea of future fulfillment is associated with an ethics and a hermeneutics of the imperative. Within the will, however, as its constitutive structural impulse, is located the instruction (*Anweisung*) to be immediate universal will—that is, not to be a means for another, but rather an end in itself. This fact is the sole legitimate point of departure for the theory of practical reason.

In the *Foundation of the Metaphysics of Morals*, Kant clarified the specific form of this self-relatedness, in which the will commands its own universality, by analyzing an example that illuminates his entire theory of action, as well as the theory of language latent in it. This example which he offers again and again, and against which he tests the various ways of formulating the categorical imperative, is the promise.[7] It will become clear that this is more than a mere example. The promise is a linguistic act that possesses the character of much more than an empirical speech act. Since, in a promise, I associate myself with a law of my will decreed by myself, the act of promising is a transcendental speech act constitutive of all language. If I wish to make a promise, I must also wish *at the same time* that the rule of this promise could be a universal law. My subjective will must subject itself to a will to the universality of this will, in order even to exist as this subjective individual will. For if my will were not to place itself a priori under the will to universalizability, it would ultimately destroy itself. Under a universal law that allowed lying or deceitful promises, there could be no promising, neither in fact nor in principle. Only that will which fulfills the criterion of inner universality can, under the conditions of time and sociability, assert its identity; it alone is bound at the same time to the idea of existence in any way. The existence of the will is posited (*gesetzt*) only in the law (*Gesetz*).[8] If Kant defines being as "absolute position or positing" (*Position oder Setzung*),[9] then the law (*Gesetz*), as an imperative positing, is to be defined as the a priori demand of a collection of all being under the form of unmediated self-relatedness. Being, because of its being posited in the law, is imperative.

The categorical imperative is thus not primarily one for the "good" will but for the will in general. It is an imperative of identity and existence. Only that which exists in the form of the positing demanded by the imperative can lay claim to the predicate of goodness. And only that which is one with itself within this positing can be called true. Now, Kant treats the promise, of course, as an example of an act—a speech act, in fact—that is subsumed under the categorical imperative insofar as it provides the criterion of the promise's morality. On the basis of this example, it becomes clearer than in all other cases that "the concept of the action in itself already entails a law for me,"[10] for in the promise, a law of action is in fact given. The closest affinity between the imperative and the promise (*Versprechen*) consists in the fact that both are speech acts, and even more, speech acts that premise (*vorsprechen*) that which is to follow.[11] The categorical imperative thus is characterized by its example, the promise, as an unconditional linguistic premise, an absolute promise that does not stand under temporal conditions, but rather out of which the very concept of time originates as a future from which the will can return to itself as its own past. The pre-structure of the imperative determines in every sense not only language but also the will and its self-relatedness. Since the speaking (*Sprechen*) of the imperative absolutely precedes—and must precede in order to determine—every act, every act of speech and of understanding, it cannot be recuperated by any such act. The speaking of the imperative cannot be performed by the will, which can only will insofar as it is spoken to by the imperative. It cannot be attained by the understanding that stands in its every movement under the dictum of the imperative. Language cannot correspond to it (it is *unentsprechbar*), since it asserts its demand even in the slightest linguistic assertion.[12] If the categorical imperative provides the conditions for the possibility of an internally homogeneous will, and thus of the will in general, then it simultaneously provides, as an *absolutely* prior speech act (*Sprachhandlung*), this possibility as one to which no reality can correspond (*entsprechen*), as the possibility of its own impossibility.[13] What is expressed in the categorical imperative is not just a constitutive demand for the rational will—without which it could be neither a will nor rational. At the same time, an absolutely exorbitant demand is expressed under which the will suffers the "infinite disruption"[14] of its natural self-relatedness, the devaluation of its intentions, and even the mortification of its drive for self-preservation.[15] Unavoidably, yet unacceptably, the law's exorbitant demand allows the will to become aware of its finitude. The law is thus the law of the finite and linguistic character of reason.

The absolute precedence of the imperative thus grounds the possibility of the will's self-reference and simultaneously defers it into an irretrievable distance. The practical subjectivity of the will exhausts itself in the infinite reference to its self-posed task. The self-reference (*Selbstbezug*) of the will is grounded in its inevitable deferral (*Entzug*).[16] The will can strive for existence as will only in proleptic reference to the law that is preordained and premised for it. However, insofar as the will, for its own sake, purely wills nothing but the law, it must forsake willing itself. Only when all subjective intention is disrupted can the will step forth in its sublimity—as free will. The ethical consequence of the pre-structure of the imperative as absolute promise is thus characterized by the most extreme self-exercise and self-sacrifice (*Selbstaufgabe*)[17] of the will, namely, that the self-willing will no longer wills itself and no longer wants to will itself. Whoever posits for himself the law of his willing in the promise can no longer see in the law a self-posited (*selbstgesetztes*) goal of his action. Subjective acts of positing are appointed to vanish in the law. The given (*gegebenes*) word is given up (*aufgegeben*) as a task and with it, the very act of giving (*Geben*).

Action can thus only be conceived as rational (*vernünftig*) once the imperative which that action ought to follow is perceived (*vernommen*) as absolute command, as the very law of legality. This perception (*Vernehmen*), which can make one rational (*vernünftig*), is not perceived as a positive gift (*Gabe*) that could enrich or create a feeling of pleasure. Rather it is the perception of the deferral of all images in which empirical persons could confirm their existence, a perception of a sacrificial giving up (*Preisgabe*) of all forms and shapes that should guarantee the stability of sensual experience. It is the perception of an "infinite disruption" of objective reality. The faculty of representation breaks down when confronted with the imperative, since the imperative causes everything in the sphere of representation to tremble.[18] And only as this trembling—as the vibration of finitude—can the imperative impart itself in the "fearful voice" of the conscience.[19] The imperative is the presentation of the unrepresentable, which articulates itself only negatively in the denial of every mimetic, representative, or meaningful shape.[20] All reality that can be the object of language—language itself included—draws its validity solely from that *res* of the law that is itself not subject to the conditions of objectivity and thus not subject to those of representational language. The imperative function of the moral law appears in the form of the command; its function to judge, indeed to condemn (*Urteils- und Verurteilungsfunktion*)[21] appears in the conscience. In both, the representational function of language, exhausted in mere descriptions, yields to linguistic acts that rest on the incommensurability between the assertion and its addressee. Conscience (*Gewissen*) is thus a kind of knowledge or science (*Wissen*) that is defined, not as an aggregate of information concerning factual situations and rules, but rather as an active consciousness of a disparity between the law and the one to whom it applies. In contrast to that intimate self-relatedness of a self-knowledge, whose referents (*Relate*) reflect each other as in a mirror, moral self-consciousness (defined by Kant as conscience) is a consciousness not of the self, but rather of the difference that sunders the self of the moral person from that of the empirical person. This consciousness out of difference—Kant speaks of the "doubled self and the twofold personality as that which man must conceive of himself"[22]—also cannot appear as my "own, proper" consciousness, but only as that consciousness which some irreducibly different other has of me.[23] The voice of conscience appears not as a human one, but rather as the "fearful voice" of God that transcends all human measure. If the law of pure practical reason, and within it the will to existence of this will, expresses (*ausspricht*) itself in a conscience, then this existence *is* confirmed not in an affirmative assertion (*Aussage*) but rather merely demanded in the *claim* (*Anspruch*) that the will makes to itself.[24] The language (*Sprache*) of the law is not one of correspondence (*Entsprechung*), agreement, restitution or representation, but rather one of disparity and pointing (*Anweisung*), dissociation and dissidence, suspension and defiguration. In these *modi,* that are actually not *modi,* but rather the *absolutum* of speaking (*Sprechen*) in every language (*Sprache*), only a claim to be (rather than being itself) is imparted—a claim that disavows whatever cannot correspond (*entsprechen*) to it. The basic postulate (*Grundsatz*) of moral self-consciousness is not "I am," but rather "I am guilty." For this reason self-consciousness is categorical and thus, in the strict sense, accusatory.

While no finite action can ever correspond to the claim raised by the conscience, the position of the corresponding response is occupied by responsibility. "Responsibility, genuineness, integrity"—these are the virtues in which Kant discovers the "authentic interpretation" of the world "expressed allegorically" by the story of Job.[25] This authentic self-interpretation of practical reason is itself imperative. The will interprets in the form of the law. Its interpretation, because it is imperative and categorical, is a guilty verdict for the difference between empirical interpretation and hermeneutical imperative. The genuineness (*Redlichkeit*) of the interpretation, however, consists in rendering in language this knowledge of difference; for this knowledge *is* moral consciousness. In the speech (*Rede*) of interpretation,[26] "the inability of our reason"[27] to satisfy the law of authentic interpretation is expressed. The concern of this speech is not truth, but truthfulness in admitting that it cannot attain truth. Because the object of this speech is the difference between command and performance of understanding, it can be called the allegory of authentic interpretation.

If all ethical action is subject to the categorical imperative, so too, *a fortiori*, are all acts of language. From the perspective of practical reason, an act of language is to be thought of not as the use of linguistic instruments toward ends that lie beyond this use, but rather primarily as an advocation of the very claim to be an end in itself. The structure of action specific to the imperative is inscribed in language as the very condition of its possible existence. Before it can act instrumentally as a prescriptive *pointing* (*Verweisung*), it must have already subjected itself ethically to its own instructive prescription (*Anweisung*) and have appropriated this prescription to the structure of its speaking. Unable to correspond to itself, language becomes the allegorical announcement of its own self-difference. Language as a pure self-correspondence in the law, as an expression corresponding to states of affairs, as communication connecting singular experiences of reality—such language is only promised. However, insofar as language pronounces itself in this promise, it already precedes itself irretrievably. The genuineness (*Redlichkeit*) of an interpretation engenders in language that which in individual speech (*Rede*)—one's own and the other's—does not fulfill the claim of universality of the law. In this way genuineness of interpretation is the agent of the law, because it does not deny the alterity of the other by means of objectification, but *speaks differently*, allegorically, and thereby continues the very process of alteration out of which it arises.

* * * * *

While Kant's concealed statements concerning the relationship between ethics and hermeneutics, or more precisely, concerning the grounding of hermeneutics in a theory of practical reason, were pursued in the *aperçus* of the circle of young romantics—Schleiermacher, Schlegel, Hardenberg—and in the systematic arguments of Hegel and Schelling, the only figure to focus his philosophical attention directly on the precarious connection between ethics and hermeneutics was Nietzsche. He never ceased referring to Kant—either implicitly or explicitly, consciously or without accounting for the filiation. It is uncertain how far Nietzsche's knowledge of Kant extended beyond the distortions of Schopenhauer and Kuno Fischer or beyond his study of the second part of the *Critique of Judgment*, which he subjected to a precise analysis in 1868, in connection with a planned dissertation to be entitled *Teleology since Kant*. But this uncertainty is also relatively insignificant for the attempt to investigate systematically the development of the connection between ethics and the theory of interpretation on the basis of various historical figures. What is certain is that even Nietzsche's earliest studies on the theory of rhetoric and interpretation already stand in irregular but evidently not random proximity to his studies on problems of ethics. This is clear, for example, in the way *On Ethics* (1868) raises the suspicion that ethics has thus far been grounded on aesthetics and proposes to ground it anew on the "ugly and unethical truth."[28] It is clear, furthermore, in *On Truth and Lie in the Extramoral Sense*, which interprets morality as a behavioral convention, and recommends considering it, like truth, as a formation of life-sustaining misinterpretations, whose origin as such has been forgotten. Nietzsche's reflections on morality, all of which are viewed through the lens of their historical origin, are interwoven through all his "major" texts. They tie the threads of his metaphysics of the will, his history of morality, and his theory of interpretation in *Beyond Good and Evil* and *The Genealogy of Morals*—appended to the former "as a supplement and clarification"—all together into a tight knot. In a section of the preface to the *Genealogy* that Nietzsche sketched late and withdrew quickly (probably for stylistic reasons), he refers with considerable emphasis to the universality and determining status of the problem of ethics as "an enormous and as yet completely undiscovered fact." This fact, he continues, "has become clear [to him] slowly, slowly, namely that there have until now been no more fundamental problems than moral ones" and that "it has been their driving force out of which all great conceptions in the realm of existing values have originated." And he then states more precisely just what conceptions are at stake: "Everything, therefore, which is commonly called 'philosophy,' down to its last epistemological premises."[29] The history of moral problems is to be written with a view to "yet more fundamental problems than moral ones," for only the genesis of the problems can illuminate both the foundation upon which they rest and how this foundation has determined and continues to determine conceptions of philosophy and their epistemological premises. Although the problematic nature of the concepts of genesis and foundation—concepts which are themselves only founded in morality—is not alluded to explicitly in this connection, it is nonetheless implied in the comparative formulation: "yet more fundamental problems."

At first, and for long stretches of his argumentation, Nietzsche remains loyal to the moral suggestion—and for him that means conventional suggestion—of the possibility of a history of morals. For Kant ethical consciousness was defined as a consciousness of a self-decreed law by which man distinguishes himself as a rational being. It was not grounded empirically and was therefore in principle independent of all historical experience. In fact, it was that which made experience possible in the first place. Nietzsche, however, inquires into precisely the historical conditions of this moral consciousness, and thus at the same time into the genesis of man as a being capable of autonomy—a genesis which for Kant could only be conceived of aporetically. He does not inquire, as Kant does, into the structure of free will, but rather into its history, and thus into the historical conditions of history. Of course, the history of history cannot be narrated *as* history—Nietzsche leaves no doubt on this point, in spite of his ruthless exploitation of the rhetoric of historical discourse—since it is in the strictest sense pre-history, and, whatever this may mean, nature. It is in fact a "paradoxical" nature to the extent that, as the realm of necessity, it has supposedly produced the sphere which, as the realm of freedom, takes on its form in the sovereign individual, the "master of free will"[30] (*Genealogy of Morals*, II, § 2). A naturally produced freedom could in fact only be a freedom *by* necessity, never a freedom *from* necessity, unless nature were itself already the realm of freedom or an order of necessities whose telos lay in human freedom. But nothing was further from Nietzsche's intention than the assimilation of nature and sovereignty into the concept of teleology. As early as the 1868 essay on teleology, he argues against the necessity, postulated by Kant, to think of organizing causes as acting according to ends or purposes. He points to the "coordinated possibility"[31] of understanding these causes as incalculable accidents. The possibility of teleological organizations, as he argues in later writings, appears for the first time when mechanics and chance no longer determine the world-game; for at that point the autonomous will, which originated in mechanics and chance, develops into the faculty that effects actions according to the idea of self-posited ends. The central concept of ethics, the self-reference of the will, can serve only the interpretation of nature and never knowledge of it. Up until this point Nietzsche agrees with Kant. But he challenges the necessity and the claim to exclusivity of this one scheme of interpretation, since that claim raises this scheme to the status of natural law, and thereby secretly conjures away the differences both between interpretation and knowledge and between knowledge and its objects. If, however, one cannot speak of a *causa finalis* prior to the historical appearance of the autonomy of the will, then sovereign self-determination must for its part be determined by accidents. The history of its emergence thus cannot be teleological, but must rather be a history of the accident. In terms of the structure of the will, this theoretical-historical reflection on its contingent origin yields a paradox which resembles that of the will under the categorical imperative. If the will is to will itself purely, then with respect to its origin, which does not lie within its power, it must will what it did not will, does not will and cannot will, namely itself as an accident and its autonomy as contingency.

Nietzsche presented the collision between history and autonomous subjectivity with great emphasis and in various forms in the *Genealogy of Morals;* it is a collision that leads to the dissolution of both of these traditional concepts. Just as for Kant (and possibly not without his influence), so too for Nietzsche moral consciousness is bound to the ability to make promises: "To breed an animal that can make promises—is that not the paradoxical task that nature has set itself in the case of man? Is that not the real, proper problem of man?" (*GM*, II, § 1). The promise demands from the individual who makes it the ability to develop an affirmative relationship to his own will. He must consistently and repeatedly continue to will what was once willed until it can be realized: "an active will not to rid oneself, a continued willing of that which was once willed, a real, proper memory of the will" (*GM*, II, § 1). The "memory of the will" is the condition for a will that can be a law unto itself. Such a memory of the will conceives of the word given for the future as a word that also refers back to that future's entire past. In this word, the will thus conceives of itself not only as self-identical and uniform in certain temporal conditions; it does not only conceive of itself as subject to a rule to which it corresponds at all times. Rather, the will makes itself into a self-supporting consciousness of freedom against time, into a "conscience." By giving its word, the will gives itself a future for the first time, and thus also temporality and history. The self-reference of the will in its memory produces its own temporality. The teleological time of the will's self-anticipation in its promise is, however, not a phase within a time-continuum that is itself already teleological. For, Nietzsche suggests, "no one ought to have promised it" (*GM*, II, § 3). The promise does not let itself be promised. As a speech act, it posits a new fact whose anticipation would have to have been already a product of this fact. But the promise—and with it temporality, the self-reference of the will, and the conscience,—even though it could not be promised, was "prepared for" by "the monstrous labor, the actual, proper labor of man upon man" (*GM*, II, § 2).[32]

The *Genealogy of Morals* is a genealogy of man and, furthermore, a genealogy of the will. The central problem, with which the genealogy confronts its historiographers, consists in constructing the passage of the will from its eccentric position, where it is not yet will, into the center of itself. This passage, however, must not appear as the passage of a will with power over itself. For this reason, the *petitio principii* inherent in the formula of self-reference—"labor of man upon man"—is placed under the sign of absolute exteriority. This "actual, proper labor," in which man is already one with himself, is at the same time a "monstrous labor" (*ungeheure Arbeit*), a labor that is not just great but one in which man is alienated inhumanely from himself. That which is proper to his productive self-reference is his irrevocable otherness from himself; his self-appropriation is that which is inappropriable—not assimilation, but rather alteration. Philosophical history-writing, no less than nature, is confronted with a "paradoxical task" if it attempts to construct the will. For not only are the prehistorical or historical preconditions of the will differentiated from the will, but so too is the will's self-reference deferred, for it is mediated through them. They are thereby withdrawn from every rational construction of a history that would be the will's "own, proper" one. If one could say of Hegel that he wrote the *Phenomenology of Spirit* as the autobiography of absolute knowledge, one would have to say of Nietzsche that he wrote the history of the will from the standpoint of its decline, that is, not as the history of the will *itself,* but rather as a constitutive movement that constantly eludes the power of the will. Because it can always be struck by chance and is, in fact, at first nothing more than chance, the will's constitution as law is at the same time also its deconstitution. Its genesis is always its degeneration. This structure of the will and its history (if it even makes sense to speak here of structure and history) means that the project of its genealogy cannot positivistically describe a constituted subject in its historical modifications. Instead, genealogy must actively participate in the constitution of this subject and therefore help dissolve certain of the forms that it has adopted. History-writing is subject to the imperative that it make history on its own. But it also cannot avoid acknowledging precisely those aspects that do not subject themselves to the authority of the will. History-writing that understands itself as a performative act that strives to participate in the production of a sovereign, law-giving will, cannot deny the contingency from which the will must extricate itself; rather it must captivate contingency through affirmation. To this end, history-writing is implicated in a process which Nietzsche calls interpretation, but which could be characterized just as well, if not better, as reinterpretation, fabrication, and falsification. Nietzsche legitimates a radically interpretive history-writing by referring to the prehistory of the will itself. For a self-reference of the will does not exist without the will's already being interpreted *as* will. This interpretation makes the promise by means of which the contingent will enters into a secure relationship to itself and thereby to autonomy. The self-reference of the will is produced in the promise. Its—"monstrous"—center is interpretation.

Nietzsche develops this idea of the interpretation of the will in a story of history of virtually mythological proportions. This story deals with the world-historical struggle between two races and deserves a place among the most scandalous passages of great philosophical literature. Nietzsche's description of a struggle among races and prototypes can be read, however, as the allegorical staging of a *gigantomachia peri tēs ousias,* and such a reading mitigates the political and psychological scandal of its composition. It is a struggle over the will and its power to decree itself as law. If it is a precondition of the will that it has become "calculable, regular and necessary" (*GM,* II, § 2) then the noble races, who momentarily enjoyed, it seems, Nietzsche's greatest favor, are the least likely candidates for its representatives. For they are characterized as "insane, absurd, erratic," and their enterprises are called "the incalculable, the improbable itself" (*GM,* I, § 11). On the other hand, the opposite of the "blond beast," namely the man of *ressentiment,* stands in the closest relationship to the memory of the will: "he understands how to keep silent, how not to forget, how to wait, how to be provisionally self-deprecating and self-humiliating" (*GM,* I, § 10). The nobles are "overloaded with energy and are thus necessarily active men" (*GM,* I, § 10), whose spontaneity either expresses itself directly in actions or, where this is prevented, is dissipated and forgotten. They are thus "forgetfulness incarnate," the very concept of necessity, of atemporal momentariness and of non-difference between will and deed. (Nietzsche, who posits this identity for the good, the Goths, the gods and Goethe—*GM,* I, § 6—is thus not far from Kant, who reserves it solely for a god-like being.) On the other hand, the man of *ressentiment* is a prototype of deferral and detour; he needs a "freely choosing 'subject,' " and this differentiates him from his deeds. The idea of freedom, and as a consequence freedom itself, thus has its origin in the sphere of those who, because they lack energy, are not "forced" to identify will and deed, subject and action. The ability of the will to determine itself, and hence sovereignty, develops out of the inability to allow the will to be converted with lightning speed into action. The possibility of speaking the truth is grounded in the compulsion to lie. The ability to give one's word exists thanks to those who can withhold it, falsify it and silence its original meaning which it possessed only in union with its sign.

On the basis of the clearly stunning example of a sentence about lightning—of the sort "The lightning bolt flashes"—Nietzsche demonstrates the ability of *ressentiment* to reinterpret a fact whose power it cannot withstand and to transfer something meaningless into the language of differential references. He writes:

> For just as the popular mind separates the lightning from its flash and takes the latter for a deed, for the effect produced by a subject, called lightning, so the popular morality separates strength from the expressions of strength, as if there existed behind the strong man an indifferent substratum that was free to express strength or not. But there is no such substratum; there is no "being" behind the deed, the effect, the becoming; the "doer" is merely a fiction added to the deed—the deed is everything. The popular mind basically doubles the deed when it allows the lightning to do the flashing, making it the deed of a deed. It posits the same event first as the cause and then as the effect of this cause. (*GM*, I, § 13)

Language separates the event from itself, even if by no other means than by simple doubling. It dissolves an occurrence into imaginary constituent parts; it disintegrates the occurrence into a grammatical relation between a subject and predicate, into a complementary causal relation between cause and effect. In this way it abstracts inductively from the factual event and its traumatic experience; "seduction of language" is a topos of Nietzsche's epistemological reflections. By articulating the occurrence, language masks it. The sentence "The lightning bolt flashes" can make no claim to correspondence with its object; for lightning is the non-referential and meaningless identity of its appearance and its being, while the sentence is a referential structure, an appearance that refers to a being outside of itself. By splitting the event, separating it out into subject and predicate, language suggests behind one world a second world of ideal, unmoved, self-enclosed, constant essences and first principles. Language immobilizes becoming into being, and reduces the former's action to the latter's appearance. In short: language extricates (*legt auseinander*) what belongs together and explicates (*legt aus*) by fabricating what does not exist[33] (*BGE*, II, § 34; III, § 52; *TI*,

"Reason in Philosophy," § 5). Freedom itself has no substantial being. It attains this only after the fact by its linguistic explication *as* freedom, i.e., only when and where it is already past, by means of "that sublime self-deception . . . that interprets and explicates weakness itself as freedom and its mere being-so-and-so as merit" (*GM*, I, § 13).

The spirit of *ressentiment* is not the origin of this idealism of language, but it is the origin of its stubborn survival. For with the aid of this language's grammar and the "fundamental errors of reason ossified in it," *ressentiment* can articulate its "No," its "No to what is 'outside,' to what is 'other,' to what is 'not itself' " (*GM*, I, § 10). Nietzsche's "lightning bolt" is an example of "driving, willing, acting [and] becoming" (*GM*, I, § 13), of the immediate self-affirming Yes. It also serves as an example of his agents in the pseudo-historical history of it that Nietzsche writes, that is, of "any pack of blond beasts of prey, who come like fate without cause, reason, consideration, or pretext, who are simply there like lightning, too terrible, too sudden, too persuasive, too 'other' even to be hated" (*GM*, II, § 17). Against this lightning bolt of the Yes and the sheer alterity of becoming and disappearing, a "No" must be raised which inhibits, delays, defers, and differentiates the bolt so that the lightning itself is at least "something" and so that everything does not disappear under its flash. The speculative grammar of *ressentiment* is the apotropaic interpretation and explication of the lightning bolt; its sentence is the articulated and articulating *No* to the essentially unarticulated, undivided *Yes* of the will. The "self-affirming Yes-saying" (*GM*, I, § 10) is incapable of sense or meaning since it refers without mediation to itself and never to an object external to itself. It is the speech act *par excellence* that glows and fades in the punctual intensity of the lightning bolt, since in it there is no difference between doer and doing, deed and effect, outer and inner, no restraint and no precondition, no reserve and no precedent. The *No* that interprets and explicates this *Yes*, however, doubles, splits it into a deed of a deed, and imposes its deed like an exchangeable mask upon it, rendering it a fixed subject-substratum. In this way the *Yes* is dissolved into a linguistic relation even though it cannot *strictu sensu* belong to language as a conventional system of meaning, since it means the very sphere of pure speaking. The individual members of this relation are equipped with a sturdy function and meaning, but because of their constitution they fall short of whatever it is they are speaking about. As a result of its disjunction into a will and (an act of) willing, willing which in itself is actually already an act, becomes reduced to the mere possibility of willing. By being expressed in language, willing is differentiated into a will and (an act of) willing of which the will is capable, yet to which it should not be compelled.

But the will does not will. It is the simple tautology of willing—without subject, intention, or object. If language makes (the act of) willing into a mere predicate of the will that can be either attributed to or removed from it, then language is the locus not of the will, but of *ressentiment* against the will. It is language which isolates the will from (the act of) willing and, in this way, uses the interpretative and explicative fiction to make the will independent. Itself unfree, the fiction liberates the will. And only where the will is free of its own (act of) willing can it raise itself *as* will to law and subjugate itself freely to this law. The free will is the will of *ressentiment*. By differentiating the will, the inability of *ressentiment* to unite will and deed is interpreted and explicated as the ability not to will this identity. The incapacity to will thereby bestows a will unto itself by means of this interpretation. The hermeneutics of *ressentiment*—the *hermeneuein* of language—is the art of interpreting and explicating the absolute otherness of (the act of) willing as the will of the other. It distances and fixes the movement of (the act of) willing from an outside of itself and reinterprets the will's deficit as will. This interpretation and explication, itself subjectless and unfree, is the invention of the subject, of freedom, and of meaning. To the same extent, however, that the will is betrayed by this interpretation and explication, it is saved by them. The sheer alteration, which announces itself in the speech act of the *Yes*, is also at work in its explication; for the alteration takes no consideration of the explication's "own, proper" structure. Alteration subjects explication, as the act that it is, to a violent change and has no explanation or reason. Explication is the alteration to which alteration must surrender itself if it does not want to stop being absolutely other.

Nietzsche thus divides the world into an active and a reactive will, into the *Yes* and the *No*, into noble beasts of prey and the passive herds. And yet, the *Yes* is as little a self-sufficient quantity as the *No*, the reaction is no less active than the spontaneous act, and *ressentiment* belongs to the structure of *noblesse*. This is obscured for the most part, but becomes sufficiently clear in central passages of his essays and fragments in spite of the rhetorical suggestiveness of his dichotomy in, for example, the eighteenth aphorism of the second section of the *Genealogy of Morals* (the numerical center of the essay).[34] Here he interprets the organizing act of violence, which the "master-race" performs on the as yet unformed "raw material of the masses and half-animals" (described in the seventeenth aphorism), as an act of "self-rape" by the "willingly self-conflicting soul that inflicts suffering upon itself, out of pleasure in inflicting suffering" (*GM*, II, § 18). In this self-relation the individual terms still relate to each other as spontaneity does to receptivity, or as *Yes* does to *No*, although the actors of this drama, as opposed to those in the preceding and following reflections, present themselves as figurations of the one self. This self-relation is exceeded by still another in which the *No*, the contradiction, the *ressentiment*, relates to itself in such a way that out of this self-relation of passivity—a passivity *before* all passivity—it "brings to light an abundance of new, strange beauty and affirmation, perhaps even beauty itself. . . . For what would be 'beautiful' if the contradiction had not first become conscious of itself, if the ugly had not first said to itself: 'I am ugly'? (*GM*, II, § 18). The beauty, which in "the aristocratic equation of values" stands beside power, fortune and the good, arises out of neither a self-sufficient act of positing, nor out of the unmediated positive self-relation of the will to power, nor even out of the influence of this will on opposing objects. Rather it arises out of the self-negation of the No, the division within the ugly, the self-affection of mere receptivity.

The same holds true for being, reality and truth, for beauty serves here merely as an example of the will to power as an organizing aesthetic instinct. Nietzsche writes: "Etymologically, the word ἐσθλός coined (for the noble race) . . . signifies one who is, who possesses reality, who is actual, who is true" (*GM*, I, § 5). Being cannot be attributed to the good, the true, and the beautiful as the result of its simple self-affirmation—as the example of lightning, as unmediated identity of being and appearance, might imply—but rather as the result of the self-affection of that which *is* not. Whatever is called "noble" arises out of the self-negation of *ressentiment;* the *Yes* arises out of the *No* that turns itself against this *No.* And Nietzsche, himself a master of the game of hide-and-seek that he attacks as the genius of *ressentiment,* nonetheless indicates clearly enough that even the will is not to be conceived of as something given, but rather as the result of the self-negation of a deficit of the will. "The active force . . . precisely that instinct for freedom (in my language, the will to power) . . . takes delight . . . in imposing a form upon itself as heavy, recalcitrant, passive matter in branding into itself a will, a critique, a contradiction, a contempt, a *No*" (*GM*, II, § 18). It thus follows from this asyndeton that the will itself is the *No* and the contradiction that the will opposes to itself; it is the very form that delimits it, the critique that splits it off from itself, and the contempt that makes it a pathos of distance. The will, and willing itself (since the will is to be understood in this context entirely in the aforementioned sense of mere willing), is not yet (an act of) willing as long as it has not been separated from itself by the opening of a distance, as long as it has not been torn asunder by its own conflict and in this way limited, formed, stamped, typed—expounded.

Just as there is no will, so too there is no pure alterity of (the act of) willing without the intervention of interpretation and explication. The two sentences: "The will to power brands a will into itself," and, "I am ugly; therefore beauty exists," are both variations of one and the same structure that generates the *Yes* out of the self-negation of the *No*. Only through the immanent repulsion of alteration does the positive image of beauty come forth. Only when unreserved self-sacrifice sacrifices itself does the will become the subject of action in accordance with laws. Not the negation of the self's other—that would be the Hegelian formula—but the *No* to the very self-sameness of mere otherness, the alteration of alteration, produces the self of the will and the very will itself. The conflict within the will is not to be conceived as the relation between two existing wills or modes of will, but rather as a relation that determines the will as will in the first place. The conflict is the difference out of which its two terms result. The will exists only as a "willingly self-conflicting will." It exists only by virtue of its explication, unfolding, and laying asunder.

The conflict within the will, that is the split, crack, break, which allows the will to come into being, is essentially articulation, a linguistic act. Nietzsche reveals this decisive characteristic of the self-relation of the will both by means of the critical linguistic reflections which permeate his text, and by means of the metaphors of writing and language he employs to characterize the constitutive acts of will. For example, when he writes that if the ugly had not first had to *say* to itself: "I am ugly"; or when he speaks of this pleasure of "*branding* a No," a "contra-*diction*," into itself. The conflict opens up in the form of either speech or writing, of carving into, branding into, stamping onto. These are the forms of psychological and physical martyrdom that Nietzsche counts among the "mnemotechnics" of the will, like quartering, breaking on the wheel, flaying and castrating. By means of all these forms, "a few ideas are to be rendered . . . uneradicable, ever-present, unforgettable, 'fixed' " (*GM*, II, § 3). Speech and writing could appear here as interruptions of a physical and psychological continuum. But if it is a question of the genesis of the not yet constituted will, they must possess another status besides that of a foreign body in a homogeneous context or that of the wound in a previously uninjured body. They are, in keeping with the formula of the self-negation of the *No*, the wound that precedes the body and the interruption out of which the continuum results. Since the will articulates itself linguistically and since it is not a will without this articulation, the will is an effect of interpretation and explication. But all that is stamped onto the will by language and writing, by mutilation and castration, by its explication and extrication—all of which belong for Nietzsche to "mnemotechnics"—is the "fivefold, sixfold 'I will not' . . . , in relation to which one has made his promise" (*GM*, II, § 3). The will brands a will into itself by stamping an "I will not" onto itself. The will that is capable of making the law, the will that can make promises by articulating language, this will is one that does not *will*. Rather, it wills its own extrication, its promise, its law and thus its act of not willing. In its law, however, it does not will a particular law or particular moral conventions, but rather the law of legality itself, which, as in Kant, first presents the conditions of the possibility of moral law-giving. It is in this law of the will to will nonwilling, in this law of explication, that Nietzsche formulated one of those "problems even more fundamental than the moral ones." Its danger lies, however, in its implication with the moral law, which leads the will to will nothing rather than to submit itself to the law of its explication and to will not to will. . .

"The will to power interprets"—so reads a now famous note in Nietzsche's unpublished papers (*WP*, III, § 643). This states that interpretation is a necessary, not an arbitrary, predicate of the will to power. Wherever the will is at work, it appears as interpretation. Moreover, the will to power is itself interpretation. Nietzsche's cursory characterizations of the "essence of interpretation" as "raping, adjusting, abreviating, eliding, padding, inventing, falsifying" (*GM*, III, § 24) do not on the surface follow the philological character of interpretation; after all, it is not a question of interpretation, but of its "essence." Rather, his characterizations correspond to those that he applies elsewhere to the will itself. The sentence, "The will to power interprets," states, however, that the act of interpretation, which the will is, first relates to the will itself as an act of self-rape. That is, the act of interpretation is, as interpretation and laying-out, that conflict to which the will itself owes its existence.

The first consequence of the will's structure of interpretation is that the will is not the subject of the explicating. This conclusion runs counter both to what Nietzsche suggests quite often and to any interpretation of his philosophy that, like Heidegger's in particular, hypostasizes the will as transcendental subject. The belief in the will to power as the subject of interpretation is already the result of an interpretation which is imposed upon reason by the restrictions of language and, furthermore, by the process of interpretation itself. Nietzsche sees his task here as one of bringing about a Copernican revolution (*Wende*) according to which not the will but the revolving (*Wendung*) itself, as it were, the alteration and the decentering, stands at the center of the world. In *Twilight of the Idols* he writes:

> It is no different here than with the movements of the sun: in that case, the error is defended by our eyes, and in this case, the error is defended by our language. . . . It sees a doer and a deed everywhere: it believes in the will as the principal cause. . . . Being is projected and insinuated everywhere as a cause. However, from the concept 'ego' follows the concept 'being' as a derivation. . . . In the beginning stands the great and fateful error that the will is something that acts, that will is a faculty. . . . Today we know that it is merely a word. . . . I fear we have not yet rid ourselves of God because we still believe in grammar. (TI, "Reason in Philosophy," § 5)

It is not the will which interprets. Rather, interpretation creates the idea of the will as subject of interpretation in the first place—and with it, the idea of God. A late note confirms this conclusion: "One may not ask: 'So who is it who interprets?' Rather interpretation itself, as a form of the will to power, has existence (but not as 'being,' but as process, becoming) as an affect" (*WP*, III, § 556).

The second decisive consequence of the will's structure of interpretation, which distinguishes Nietzsche's theory of interpretation from all previous hermeneutics, concerns the will's relationship both to the sphere of objects and to the objectivity of that to which it refers. The point of departure for Schleiermacher and the romantic theorists was the principle that every act of interpretation refers to a linguistic or semiotic fact in order to reconstruct the meaning located within it. Nietzsche's concept of interpretation, however, refers to the process by which the perceiving consciousness and its perspectivism, like the will itself, also produce their objects. Interpretation, as laying out, is the process not of its reconstruction, but of its constitution. This idea that the sphere of objectivity is not immediately accessible but must be sketched out time and again in historically varying figurations does not conceal latent subjectivism. On the contrary, one could call it historical-transcendentalist. In fact, Nietzsche insists with the pathos of a phiologist that it must be possible to read a text "*as text* . . . without the intervention of an interpretation." With the ethos of a philosopher, however, he states in the same sentence that the ability to grasp an object or an experience without perspectival distortions is "the latest form of 'inner experience'—one that is perhaps hardly possible" (*WP*, III, § 479). The experience free of interpretation is itself the product of the history of interpretation. It cannot appear until reason reaches the point where it doubts its own ability to grasp reality as it is in itself. In the rape and terror imposed on reason by itself, Nietzsche sees "the ability to have power over one's pro and contra, to use or dispose of them, so that one knows how to put precisely the variety of perspectives and affective interpretations in the service of knowledge" (*GM*, III, § 12). In this way Nietzsche offers a concealed defense of Kant's concept of the intelligible character of things. The "objectivity" of knowledge grows with the degree to which the perspectives of the will and its "interpreting forces" are multiplied. But it can grow only because the perspectives of the will repudiate themselves by this multiplication. Knowledge would thus attain the highest degree of objectivity only once the will itself has been eliminated, the intellect castrated. The entire sphere of objectivity would disappear with the will, however, at that moment when a text can be read *as text*, that is, at that moment without the perspective "through which seeing becomes for the first time seeing-something" (*GM*, III, § 12). Hence, the object, in its pure appearance, is nothing.

A third consequence of the will's structure of explication is that the idea of totality, which is bound up with the concept of knowledge, can no longer be maintained. We can neither take for granted that "all existence is essentially interpreting existence," nor can we be certain that another kind of existence besides interpreting existence exists. "The world has become . . . once again 'infinite' for us insofar as we cannot deny the possibility that it contains within itself infinite interpretations" (*GS*, V, § 374). These "infinite interpretations," however, are not such that they would be *in toto* accessible to mankind or could expand the closed universe of knowledge to an open world of poly-perspectival interpreting. Since the idea of an infinity of possible interpretations cannot be denied by the one humanly possible interpretation, there is no reason for the one interpretation to lay claim to a privileged access to the world, an access that would allow it to unite all interpretive worlds into a single world of worlds. No such human world could produce the totality of knowledge denied to the other interpretive worlds. Because it is merely one of infinitely many possible interpretations, human interpretation is radically finite. Even if its perspectives could multiply, an infinity of other perspectives that it could not incorporate would remain. Human interpretation leaves behind an infinity of interpretations that it cannot exhaust. As long as other possibilities remain open, however, the ones that have been perceived remain incapable of grasping the world and inadequate for providing a total concept of interpretation itself. The possibility of infinite interpretations renders the very concept of interpretation contingent. The world, the perspective of the will, and interpretation could thus always be different or other than the respective one under consideration. This inexhaustible potential of other possibilities introduces into the concept of interpretation itself an uncontrollable alterity and prevents, strictly speaking, the possibility of speaking about interpretation *itself*.

A fourth consequence of Nietzsche's theory of interpretation concerns the traditional concept of truth as *adaequatio*. It is meaningful to speak of measuring an exegetical statement against an object only if the object of the statement is given in advance. An interpretation can correspond to or falsify what is to be interpreted only if what is to be interpreted has a self-supporting reality vis-à-vis every possible interpretation. A theory of interpretation that deals with its objects not as givens but as something to be constituted can offer no correspondence theory of truth, but only a theory of its imperative positing. In a fragment from the period of *Twilight of the Idols*, Nietzsche writes of (the act of) willing (and interpreting is a form of the will): " 'To will' is not the same as 'to desire,' to strive for, to long for: it distinguishes itself from them by the sense of the command."[35] The truth of interpretation is imperative. The will commands, and whatever corresponds to this command of the will possesses, as its correspondence, truth. At first, however, by means of its interpretation, the will commands only itself as not yet corresponding to the will. Since the interpreting will is structurally imperative, its correspondence must remain absent. Only in the law of the will, which is the claim to correspond to itself, can the will be in agreement with itself as in a remainder of correspondence. Its interpretation—and its truth, the will itself—remains, without any substance, a promise.

Translated by Jane O. Newman and John H. Smith

NOTES

1. Translators' note—hereafter TN: As in many philosophical texts, the main word in the title already creates difficulties for translation. The English word "interpretation" has two counterparts in German, *Interpreta-*

tion and *Auslegung*, which have two distinct connotations. Although *Auslegung* is generally translated as "explication," we were often compelled to translate both words simply as "interpretation." What is often lost in both of these translations is a connotation of *Auslegung* which is particularly exploited by Nietzsche and is crucial to Hamacher's argument, namely the aspect of literally "laying out" or "laying asunder" (related to the more concrete *Auseinanderlegung*). The word *Auslegung* echoes the etymological roots of "analysis," and is opposed to the sense of "making clear to the eye" that is implicit in "interpretation."

2. Friedrich Schleiermacher, *Hermeneutik und Kritik* (*Hermeneutics and Critique*), ed. Manfred Frank (Frankfurt, 1977), p. 328.

3. Ibid., p. 94.

4. Immanuel Kant, *Theorie-Werkausgabe* (*Theory: Complete Works*), ed. W. Weischedel, A 211ff.

5. TN: In German, the word for the "will" (*Wille*) is etymologically related to the modal verb "to want" (*wollen*). That verb can be used as a substantive by mere capitalization. When used in a strict sense, the verb *wollen* has been translated as "to will" (though the reader should hear the echo "to want"). As a substantive (*Wollen*), it has been translated either as the gerundive "willing" or with the parenthetical phrase "(act of) willing," since the gerundive is often awkward and confusing.

6. TN: Hamacher distinguishes here between *Sinn* and *Bedeutung* (generally distinguished in English as "sense" and "meaning" or "meaning" and "reference"). Because "sense" was too awkward, we translated *Sinn* as "meaning," *Bedeutung* as "signification." Unfortunately we lost the association with *Richtungssinn* ("sense of direction").

7. Detailed discussions of the promise can be found in the *Grundlegung der Metaphysik der Sitten (Foundation of the Metaphysics of Morals)*, BA 18–19, BA 48–49, BA 67.

8. See Kant's interpretation of the law of nature as the law of being in the *Foundation*, BA 52f. TN: This echo of the word for law (*Gesetz*) in the verb "to posit" or "to set" (*setzen*, as participle *gesetzt*) dates back to the Idealists and has no corresponding echo in English.

9. For example, in his early work from 1763, *Der einzig mögliche Beweisgrund zu einer Demonstration des Daseyns Gottes (The Sole Possible Proof for a Demonstration of the Existence of God)*, A 8. Also *Kritik der reinen Vernunft (Critique of Pure Reason)*, A 598 (B 626). Compare also on the same question, Martin Heidegger, "*Kants These über das Sein*" ("Kant's Thesis on Being"), in *Wegmarken (Signposts)* (Frankfurt, 1967) pp. 276–307.

10. Kant, *Foundation*, BA 18.

11. TN: The verb *versprechen* ("to promise") consists in the prefix *ver-* (generally indicating an exaggeration of the action) and the root *—sprechen* ("to speak"). By changing the prefix, the German writer can therefore create numerous echoes difficult to preserve in English. *Vorsprechen,* e.g., means to "speak before." Such echoes on *sprechen* abound on the following pages (e.g., with *Sprache,* "language").

12. TN: The verb *entsprechen* means "to correspond to," or "to be commensurate to." To capture (at least vaguely) the echo of *sprechen* ("to speak") in this verb, we have opted to write the translation as "correspond" since Hamacher wants to evoke the linguistic aspect of the word. Thus, "to correspond to something" *(entsprechen)* would contain the element of "responding in or with language" *(sprechen).*

13. I choose this formulation well-advisedly, since we can see clearly in it (as well as in some others, such as the structure of the will's self-sacrifice—*Selbstaufgabe*—and in the pre-structure of understanding) the affinity between Heidegger's existential project for an actual being unto death and Kant's notion of the categorical imperative. The distance between the two is so minimal that we are justified in seeing Heidegger's project as an ingenious transformation of Kant's theory of practical reason. In any case, the fact that Heidegger did not write an *Ethics* does not mean that he did not confront the problem of ethics. On the relationship between understanding and being-unto-death in Heidegger, see my essay, *"Peut-être la question"* in *Les fins de l'homme. Ã Partir du travaille de Jacques Derrida,* ed. J.-L. Nancy and Ph. Lacoue-Labarthe (Paris, 1981).

14. *Critique of Practical Reason,* A 131.

15. Compare the series of symptoms of the "pathological feelings" that attest to the effectiveness of the law in *"Von den Triebfedern der reinen praktischen Vernunft"* ("On the Motivations of the Pure Practical Reason"), in the *Critique of Practical Reason.*

16. TN: The echo of the word "to pull or draw" (*ziehen, Zug*) is stronger in the German than in the English (though the Latin root *ferro* is present in "re-fer-ence" and "de-fer").

17. TN: Here, and in the following sentences, Hamacher employs the echo of the root *geben* (literally, "to give") in a number of contexts. The word *Aufgabe* (as verb, *aufgeben*) has two meanings: a "task" or "exercise," and the act of "giving up."

18. Compare the metaphors used in paragraph 27 in the *Critique of Judgment, "Von der Qualität des Wohlgefallens in der Beurteilung des Erhabenen"* ("On the Quality of Pleasing in the Evaluation of the Sublime"), p. 98.

19. *Metaphysik der Sitten (Metaphysics of Morals), "Tugendlehre"* ("On Virtue"), paragraph 13, A 99.

20. On the relationship between the moral law and art in the figure of the sublime, compare Jacques Derrida, *Le Colossal* in *La vérité en peinture* (Paris, 1978) and my study on Kleist, "*Das Beben der Darstellung*" ("The Quaking of Representation") in *Positionen der Literaturwissenschaft ("Positions of Literary Criticism")*, ed. D. Wellbery (Munich, 1984).

21. TN: The echo of *Urteil* ("judgment") in the German *verurteilen* ("to condemn") is lost in English.

22. *Metaphysics of Morals*, A 100.

23. Compare Kant's explanation of the metaphor of the court (loc. cit.) that Schopenhauer criticizes with no understanding in his *Preisschrift über die Grundlage der Moral ("Prize Essay on the Foundations of Morality")*, paragraph 9.

24. TN: Again, in the following passage Hamacher brings out the common root of "speaking" (*sprechen*) in various words: *aussprechen* ("to express," literally, "to speak out"); *Anspruch* ("claim," literally, "spoken to"); *entsprechen* ("correspond"); *Sprache* ("language", literally, "what is spoken").

25. *Über das Misslingen aller philosophischen Versuche in der Theodizee ("On the Failure of All Philosophical Experiments in Theodicy")*, A 218ff.

26. TN: Here Hamacher uses the echo of the word "speech" (*Rede*) in the word for probity: *Redlichkeit*.

27. *Über das Misslingen . . .* , A 218ff.

28. Friedrich Nietzsche, *Gesammelte Werke, Musarion Ausgabe* (Munich, 1922), 1: 405.

29. Friedrich Nietzsche, *Sämtliche Werke. Kritische Studienausgabe*, ed. Colli and Montinari (Berlin: Walter de Gruyter, 1980), 14: 378.

30. TN: Unless otherwise noted, translations of passages from Nietzsche are ours on the basis of Walter Kaufmann's. Citations are included in the body of the text hereafter and by paragraph. *Genealogy of Morals* is abbreviated *GM*.

31. *Musarion Ausgabe*, 1: 412–13.

32. TN: The word for "monstrous" (*ungeheur*) carries with it the connotation of "enormous" and of "uncanny". The word for "actual, proper" (*eigentlich*) means in colloquial speech "actual," but carries the connotation of that which is "proper to" (*eigen*) or even the "property of" (*Eigentum*) something. In rhetoric, literal speech is *eigentlich*, while figural speech is *uneigentlich*.

33. TN: To keep a vague sense of the association at play here, we translated *auseinanderlegen* (literally, "explain, take or lay out into parts") as

"extricate" and *auslegen* (literally, "to lay out") as "explicate." It should be kept in mind, however, that *auslegen*, especially as used by Nietzsche, does not convey the sense of "explication" as "smoothing out (wrinkles)" (OED), but rather the opposite, an act of taking apart. *Beyond Good and Evil* is abbreviated *BGE; Twilight of the Idols* is abbreviated *TI*.

34. The 18th aphorism of the second part of the *Genealogy of Morals* is the 35th out of a total of seventy in the entire essay. *Will to Power* is abbreviated *WP; The Gay Science* is abbreviated *GS*.

35. *Kritische Studienausgabe*, 13: 54. Heidegger energetically emphasized the will's character as command or order in his essay, "Nietzsche's Phrase: 'God is Dead' " in *Holzwege* (Frankfurt, 1950), p. 216f.: "The will is neither a wishing nor a striving for something; rather willing is in itself an order . . . Will means the act of assembling what is given as a task . . . As a command, the will co-ordinates itself with itself, i.e., with the willed object." Just as in his lectures on Nietzsche, especially in the section on *Truth as Justice*, Heidegger identifies the will consistently with its imperative. He *coordinates* the will *with* the imperative, rather than subordinating it *to* it. By speaking of the will's "assembling," he denies the structure of interpretation in the sense of laying out. Hence his interpretation of Nietzsche's philosophy as a metaphysics of subjectivity. For the reading of Nietzsche, one can learn much *in opposition to* Heidegger, as also *in agreement* with Jean-Luc Nancy in his "Our Probity!" (in this volume). Nancy attacks Nietzsche's relationship to Kant's ethics at a point in this text which is, in my estimation, atypical. Namely, for Nietzsche the problem was not so much the enhancement of a particular person in the narcissism of its universalizability, but on the contrary the unreasonable demand placed on the sovereign individual to be universal. To an extent, then, Nancy's objections apply to a limited section of Nietzsche's relationship to Kant.

3

Nietzsche's Thesis on Teleology

Jean-Luc Nancy

To begin with, this title is not meant to be a title. It is simply meant to serve as a kind of pointer, indexing one rubric in the nomenclature of Nietzsche's writings: his 1868 outline for a thesis on teleology.[1]

This essay will do nothing more than set off this piece by Nietzsche (which one would hesitate to call a text), remark momentarily upon its minor, almost insignificant, place in the ensemble of his writings, and observe some of the effects of this move. Our aim here, then, must be a limited one, one which, it must be said, is always susceptible to the nihilist or philological danger of turning into a pious or antiquarian endeavour. Perhaps its only interest lies in this very risk, if it will allow us to show, at least where Nietzsche is concerned, that it is ultimately impossible to be either pious or antiquarian. The draft of 1868, in effect, does not harbor the first fruits of Nietzsche's mature thinking; we will find nothing in it which might allow us to assess, laterally, some simple difference vis-à-vis the later texts. Something else must be at stake.

Placed at the outset of this essay, however, my heading cannot avoid functioning as a title. This places in doubt the provisional and ironic status we would accord it. To some extent, therefore, our task must consist in progressively effacing our title. But it must also consist in showing that it cannot *purely* and *simply* be suppressed; this is what is at least initially at stake here. This is also, incidentally, the sole justification for these preliminary variations on the title, a gesture which would otherwise be a matter of pure convention.

This essay was presented at the Colloque International de Cerisy-la-Salle in 1972, organized around the theme of "Nietzsche aujourd'hui?"

Under this heading then, for the moment, we shall attempt to contribute something to the problematic of Nietzsche's relation to philosophy, or more precisely to philosophic *discourse*.

Nothing new here, then. This question, as you are aware, has been prominent throughout this colloquium. We "know" (though such a "knowing" is precisely what is in question here) that if "Nietzsche Today" means, above all, as this gathering seems to indicate, Nietzsche's place in the domain of philosophy, it is precisely and paradoxically to the extent that *chez* Nietzsche, philosophy is no longer quite at home, is disturbed and displaced, dispossessed of its own estate and properties.

In assessing the extent of this movement in Nietzsche, we are led inevitably to work which has been taken a long way by Heidegger, and more recently by several among us. My essay will add nothing to these works. It can only provide a kind of verification—if this word may be tolerated for a moment. That which is to be verified is not a simple proposition (and this is why there cannot be, properly speaking, any verification). It is rather a matter of the non-simplicity, the complexity, or, to borrow a word from Nietzsche, the *Kombination* ("combination—machination")[2] of Nietzsche's relation to philosophy. To this extent we will be emphasizing the inevitable corrective to (or deformation of) any simple formula that one might try to apply to Nietzsche, concerning for instance his "critique," or his "excess," or his "practice" of philosophy.

And so, then, to a correction, or a deformation, of one of these simple and well known formulae concerning Nietzsche, the one which would have it that Nietzsche *came to* philosophy via some other route or at the end of another road, and that he even came to it more by chance than by design. To this formula we would have to oppose—which is to say we have to compose—the following: Nietzsche also *departed* from philosophy, from a philosophical design or project.

It is this *departure*—to be heard polysemically of course—that will be in question here.

This will oblige us to traverse, however momentarily, the terrain of history, or at least of biography—though not in order to "do" biography, as we shall see. We should point out here that between works of erudition such as Charles Andler's, and works which deal exclusively with Nietzsche's texts, a biography still remains to be *written*, or, a biography still remains to be *read*.[3]

We are dealing with an episode in Nietzsche's university career: the outline that he made for a thesis in 1868.

To date, little or nothing has been made of this episode. This is partly due to a lack of familiarity with Nietzsche's unpublished texts, but more especially due to something which no doubt also accounts for this lack of familiarity, at least as far as the period up to *The Birth of Tragedy* is concerned. The image of Nietzsche as an author of *books,* and as the author of one or several styles, tends to overshadow or obliterate the image of Nietzsche the university man, the studious Nietzsche, author of inventories, of theses, and even of an index.[4] While academic curiosity has turned its attention to those texts of Kant it has dubbed "pre-critical," we have nothing comparable concerning what a mischievous academic mind might well call Nietzsche's "pre-tragic" period. Nietzsche considered *simply* as a philosopher is merely the reverse side of Nietzsche considered *simply* as a writer. It is this double-edged simplicity of approach that needs to be complicated.

We must first of all retrace the history of this thesis. In order to keep within the limits of an intervention at this colloquium, we must excerpt and set in relief a particular sequence of events surrounding the thesis. It should be emphasized that we can present *only* on excerpt from a much more complex ensemble, whose tortuous itinerary would bring into play many other elements and aspects of philology, aesthetics, etc. I can only allude briefly to this ensemble, which might serve as the basis for a second *Der Junge Nietzsche.*[5]

Between 1867 and 1869, Nietzsche was constantly preoccupied with the idea of defending a thesis at the university. This preoccupation was significant in at least two ways, since it corresponds both to his desire to have a university career (especially keen since Ritschl had so dramatically commended the philological excellence of his finest student), and to the concomitant realization that he must renounce a career in music, or what we might perhaps less improperly call an artist's life.

His project, as we know, would end on a paradoxical note, for Nietzsche would not write a thesis, but would nonetheless be granted a doctorate on the basis of his published works. In the end, then, there would be, properly speaking, no thesis by Nietzsche.

But this state of affairs did not come about without a second renunciation,[6] namely, the renunciation of the philosophical thesis: in other words, Nietzsche renounces in the same moment both a *position* in the university as a philosopher, and philosophic *discourse.*

We must disregard the project of 1867, *On the Fundamental Schema of Representation,* which Andler mistakenly attributes to Nietzsche due to a letter Nietzsche wrote recounting the failure of this particular project, which had in fact been submitted by his friend Kleinpaul.[7] The fact remains that Nietzsche's indignation towards the university on this occasion is very revealing, and indeed Andler's mistake seems almost inevitable in light of the text of the letter in which Nietzsche, recounting the misadventures of a "young man," writes as though he were defending his own cause rather than that of Kleinpaul. Throughout this entire period both Nietzsche's strategy and his objective, in the strictest and most academic sense of these words,[8] are philosophical, and he manages to sustain them in a remarkable relational ambiguity with regard to his philological objectives and work.

It is this ambiguity that we shall consider first of all.

The project for a thesis will always in fact be double. In 1867 and 1868 Nietzsche has underway both a project on the authenticity of the works of Democritus, and a project on teleology. We shall see that, in a certain way, we are dealing constantly with the issue of the simultaneity of these two projects, with the interweaving of their motifs. But it would take another essay to sort out this complex network (in which Homer is soon to become involved, vying with Democritus as a subject for the thesis). We will remark upon only a few of the distinctive features of the philological project.

First, the work on Democritus—which, in the sense that it is an inquiry into the authenticity and sources of a body of work, follows the norm of Nietzsche's philological work prior to or contemporaneous with it[9]—is the first that Nietzsche considers to have a "philosophical background," as he expresses it to Rohde.[10]

Second, this "philosophical background" is a reference to materialism, which Nietzsche had encountered through his readings of Lange, whose *Geschichte des Materialismus* Nietzsche held, at the time, to be *the* great philosophical book, coming close at times to surpassing in prestige even Schopenhauer himself. And the materialism of Democritus was, above all, anti-finalism.

Third, Democritus is also an enigmatic figure obscured by an entire tradition of readers. Nietzsche uncovers and denounces the manoeuvers whereby an abundance of writings posterior to Democritus were mistakenly attributed to him. The chief forger was Thrasyllus, an Egyptian astrologer from Tiberia, who used the name of Democritus to "authenticate" an entire science rigorously opposed to the cold positivity (or what Nietzsche would like to see as such) of the Greek thinker.

Thrasyllus himself, moreover, this practically unknown character of whom Nietzsche draws an imaginary portrait curiously resembling a self-portrait[11] (and curiously resembling also, for the first time, a text prepared for publication, an outline for a book rather than a philological article), Thrasyllus, then, must at the same time be regarded as a "Faustian"[12] philologist, which is to say a philologist who deforms and falsifies texts with the power and audacity of Faust translating the prologue to Saint John. This Faustian philology is precisely what Nietzsche will practice from this point onward. His entire denunciation of Thrasyllus, carried out with the aim of reinstating the "real" Democritus, ends up being a eulogy, so that Thrasyllus becomes the first "double" of Nietzsche: Nietzsche himself will be the Thrasyllus, the forger, in his case, of a *Greek* Democritus. Which means of course that Hellenism (in this case philosophic and materialistic Hellenism) cannot be recuperated as a primordial ground, but has to be produced, and produced, if necessary, by a "monstrous," "hair raising"[13] method, such as the one practiced by Thrasyllus.

Democritus thus represents, via Thrasyllus, the first Nietzschean motif of a philology which one would be tempted to call fantastical, but which we should rather call, at this point, and in a very strict sense of the term, romantic, since Nietzsche will define it thus:

> I am coming to believe that in these kinds of works [notably the *Democritea*] what keeps things going is more a certain philological *Witz* [this word cannot be translated], the impulse to make comparisons between unexpected analogies, and the capacity to invent paradoxical questions, rather than strict method (*Methodik*) which is always out of place except when the work of mind (*geistig*) is essentially finished.[14]

Philology as *Witz*[15]—and in this instance, Democritus the materialist philosopher reinstated or instated by means of *Witz*—this then is the project which constantly doubles with the teleological project. We will have time to make only a few points regarding this "dubbing," this "doubling" or "dublet." But it is important to point to its existence as a motif, so that we may consider the thesis on teleology in terms of the bonds which link it to this other.

While the work on Democritus, in 1868, was assuming prolific dimensions, albeit in a rather uncertain way—as if Nietzsche could not quite master the mass of references and hypotheses it had engendered—the work on teleology appears by contrast to be well thought through: its boundaries established, it remained only to write it up. At the beginning of May 68, Nietzsche wrote to Deussen that "the preparatory work is almost finished," and announced that the thesis would be completed by the end of the year and would be entitled *The Concept of the Organism since Kant.*[16] But a few days later, in a later to Rhode,[17] he evokes the importance of the same project only to declare it "too good" for a thesis, as was his *Democritea* and also his *Homerica,* which he was just beginning to think about writing. He will restrict himself, he writes, to the classical philological thesis.

And so things remained for quite some time. Indeed the *Autobiography of 1869* does not say a word about the whole episode. It does contain, however, one allusion, an extremely indirect allusion, and one quite out of keeping with the statements just cited. This occurs in the passage on "renunciation":

> When I look back and consider how I have fallen from art into philosophy, from philosophy into science, and then again into a still more restricted area, it almost looks like a conscious renunciation.[18]

What began, in 1868, as an academically strategic move, and seemed to anticipate, in spite of this strategy, a philosophical work (albeit independent of the thesis) turned in 1869 into the renunciation of philosophy.

What had Nietzsche renounced? We must now consider the thesis itself, or at least the "almost finished preparatory work."

This comprises, in the edition published by Beck, 24 pages of notes, under the title *Zur Teleologie.*[19]

We cannot undertake a detailed analysis of these pages here. Moreover, it will suffice to point out the basic elements of such an analysis, what is most essential. In effect, this essay will rely largely on only one kind of scholarship, that of erudition, aiming therefore to replace around the sentences copied down by Nietzsche a host of quotation marks. (This task has been almost completed by Schlechta in the excellent notes to his edition.) Essentially, then, Nietzsche's notes consist of a series of passages copied down, more or less word for word, from Lange, Schopenhauer and from Kuno Fischer's *Kant,* to mention only the major sources. If we were to comment upon each reference individually, we would first have to make a commentary on each author, which would mean, since Nietzsche draws from their respective discussions of teleology, making a commentary on various commentators of Kant.

By juxtaposing these commentaries in a piecemeal fashion, Nietzsche reconstructs what one might call a composite picture of "midcentury" Kantianism on the motif of teleology.

Very briefly, this Kantianism might be characterized as follows. In part it is the Kantian critique of metaphysical finality, but transposed from the philosophic discourse of the *Third Critique* into a positive scientific or anthropological discourse, strongly marked by Darwinism. Here, the question of teleology comes down to identifying internal finality as the capacity for existence, or with viability, and explaining this viability as a successful "case" in a mechanical series of chance events. This is what Nietzsche, or rather his notes, call(s) "the coordinated possibility" of "mechanism in conjunction with causalism."[20]

But this Kantianism is also in part a thinking of finality as a phenomenon, in contrast to a nature in which there is, as such—Nietzsche copies from Lange—"neither order nor disorder."[21] For Schopenhauer, as we know, finality is the will as it appears to us in its relation to itself, a relation which is not in itself teleological.

One sees, or at least one suspects, that this critique of teleology is fairly muddled, and comes close to resting on a completely uncritical concept of the *telos* itself, which is surreptitiously reintroduced in its most classical and determinative role in philosophic discourse.

In this context, then, what does Nietzsche's thesis represent? One might suggest, to be brief, three things—which at the same time will provide us with three possible reasons for which the thesis will in the end never be written.

First, as we have just pointed out, Nietzsche simply recopies the essential elements of mid-century Kantianism. The outline followed in his notes, and hence the outline of the thesis itself, is significant:

Chapter 1. The Concept of Finality (as the capacity for existence)

Chapter 2. The Organism (the indeterminate concept of life, the indeterminate concept of the individual)

Chapter 3. The supposed impossibility of explaining an organism mechanically (what does mechanically mean?)

Chapter 4. Absence of finality acknowledged in nature, as opposed to finality.[22]

Our first reason, therefore, is very banal: Nietzsche could hardly ignore the fact that this outline contains nothing new, that it is nothing more than a repetition. His self-assured tone in proclaiming the imminent completion of the thesis has changed its tune: Nietzsche hasn't a single philosophical thesis to advance as "his own." Was it not perhaps more a matter of persuading himself that he had mastered the discourse of the thesis?

Second, there is nonetheless one point on which Nietzsche would like to say something new. It is the one proposed for Chapter 3, on mechanism. Nietzsche, who had described his work to Deussen as "half philosophical, half scientific,"[23] wanted to arrive at a definition of a radical mechanism that would be scientific, in other words a position of pure chance that would destroy the concepts of life and individual. (To argue this point he invokes—but here following Goethe—the cellular theory as against the unity of the individual.)

In reality, he lacks the means to effect such a demonstration. For this reason, his notes include a reading prospectus where one finds, for instance, the names of Bichat, Teviranus, Virchow, Helmholtz, etc. But the question cannot simply be re-oriented towards Nietzsche's supposed or actual completion of his reading program (his readings were in any case always quite sporadic and disconnected). It is rather the principle implied by such a program that Nietzsche will not respect: that is to say, the metaphysical temptations of scientific positivism. Although Nietzsche inscribes this principle as a guide, he does not follow the demands it imposes. The naivete of this principle is to be found scattered throughout Nietzsche's writings, though only to be, precisely, dispersed.

The scientific principle, then, could not be expected to produce a *thesis;* this seems to be there for some other purpose.

Finally, and perhaps especially, the objective of this thesis turns out to be something other than a "thesis." In other words, in the final analysis (or even in the first analysis) it is less a matter of establishing a body of knowledge than of achieving a practical "end." Nietzsche remarks very early on, and in one of the very rare notations that actually "belong" to him: "Getting rid of teleology has a practical end. The only important thing is to dismiss the concept of a superior mind: this done, we are satisfied."[24]

It is therefore less a question of constituting a discourse than of affirming a value—which means, of course, rejecting another. Nietzsche realizes that this value is already discursively acquired. In his letter to Deussen he presented his thesis with the following remarks:

> Whoever has before him the physiological research done since Kant can no longer have any doubt about the fact that [the] frontiers [of our knowledge] are established in such a certain and exact way that except for the theologians, some professors of philosophy, and the *vulgus,* no one can still have any illusions on this matter. The kingdom of metaphysics, and with it

the province of "absolute" truth, has been ineluctably brought back to the ranks of poetry [*Poesie*] and religion.

The accumulation of notes that make up *Zur Teleologie* thus assumes another function: it is not a prospectus for a new discourse, but a device for harassing and hammering, a rhapsody that would have, one could even say, almost no consistency, but which would simply be an insistent offensive against "absolute truth."

Nietzsche's thesis does not take place because the grounds for a philosophic discourse are lacking. For Nietzsche something else entirely is at stake, even as he is mapping out the thesis. The letter to Deussen continues: "For some men metaphysics belongs to the domain of the needs of the mind [*Gemüthsbedürfnisse*]; it is in essence piety [*Erbauung*: "edification"]; viewed from another angle it is art, the art of *Begriffsdichtung*." This *Begriffsdichtung* (another untranslatable term) is not *Poesie*—the poetic rendering of the concept—it is the production of the concept by poetry (*Dichtung*), which is to say first of all by composition (and not by edification or architectonics), or, we might say, by writing, and then (at the same time) by fiction. It is the concept as fiction, but also the active *fiction* of the concept, or, to borrow a 'conceit' from Jacques Derrida, its "fictioning."[25]

Nietzsche's thesis or, if you will, his *a-thesis*, this vanishing point in his text (if not in his writing), would be the zero degree of discourse, a philosophy which never takes place, leaving its mark only to bring to prominence the motif it inscribes at once inside itself and outside itself: the *Dichtung* of the concept. Nietzsche's text would be the topographical relief of this operation—and it is here that one might locate the other thesis, now become the other of the *a-thesis:* the *Dichtung* of the concept is none other than the *Witz* of philological authenticity, and it is then a character to be staged, to be *written;* it is Thrasyllus-Nietzsche writing Nietzsche-Democritus.

However, whilst such conclusions are not impertinent, it is obvious that they remain as such too hastily and simply drawn. A commentary on the text of the thesis—or on its non-event—cannot be so simple for at least two reasons.

First, if we suppose that what is at stake is something like a "passage" from the thesis to the text, we should at least signal that this move does not come about all at once.

Indeed, if it came about all at once, if Nietzsche's text could be so easily located and assigned—if one could simply say that the plan for the thesis is not a "text" (but can a "text" be *located, assigned?*) there would no more be a thesis by Nietzsche in the empirical ensemble of his writings than there would be anywhere in the entire theory of philosophemes. The very "fact" of the outline for the thesis defers the birth of the text—and, reciprocally and paradoxically, the text requires the modest imprint of these 24 pages of notes and "recopying" in order to begin its self-inscription.

The "first time" Nietzsche composes (combines) something with a view to producing a book is not a *single* time: it is double. A narrative on Thrasyllus doubles with a project on teleology, and the *Witz* of the former only derives its means from the *Begriffsdichtung* which marks the limit (and failure) of the latter. But if one were to imagine Nietzsche writing *only*, simply, a portrait of Thrasyllus, one would then have, instead of this "doubling," the simply alterity of a fiction behind which the truth would always be holding itself in reserve. Thrasyllus is not only the double of Nietzsche, he is also the double of the philosopher, and not his simple other. Reciprocally, Democritus, reinvented and rewritten by Nietzsche would be the philosophical double of the sage and magus forged by Thrasyllus.

Moreover, this instance is not a *single* instance. If there is only one project for a thesis, there will be *at least* one more project for a philosophical book: *The Book of the Philosopher,* surely intended to be made up of the *Theoretical Studies* and *Philosophy in the Tragic Epoch of the Greeks*.

These drafts are undoubtedly very much woven in the style(s) of *Dichtung* and *Witz*. But they are marked by an entire stratum of discourse, one which recurs insistently, and in which Nietzsche attempts demonstrations, proofs, and theses (often getting himself quite mixed up, as in 1868). Moreover, in these drafts *Dichtung* and *Witz* are *still* objects of inquiry, just as scientific rigor and philosophical probity continue to impose certain requirements: a careful analysis of these texts could thus show that they stem from the desire to construct a philosophy, and that Nietzsche does not yet know (when will he know, when will he *renounce?*) that the project has already miscarried.

And finally, this book will never see the light of day, and the miscarriage will itself be double: certainly, it corresponds to the slow maturation of another project, to be witnessed in the abandoned dramatic sketches (Empedocles, Oedipus, Prometheus)—but in such sketches Nietzsche *also* preserves intact, in that ambiguous reserve of miscarried productions, his scientific program. During these same years he keeps up with his readings (Darwin, Zöllner, Lamarck), and continues to see Rütimeyer in Basel. Does this not seem to announce the coming to be of some other project?

In short must we not say (in lieu of demonstrating it, something time will not permit here) that a double move, brought about by the double thesis, is taking place here, one that will repeat itself even up to what we call, for convenience, *The Will to Power,* the last thesis by Nietzsche not to have taken place?

The second complication is that the failure of the thesis, as we have seen, also marks the "failure" of post-Kantianism. Nietzsche cannot remain unaware (whatever the mode of this "knowledge" might be, its degree of rigor) of the inadequacies of this particular thinking, at least as regards teleology. He was already aware, at the time, that a purely scientific or positivistic approach would not suffice to articulate a philosophical discourse (a systematic study of his texts prior to 1868 would show this). He was also aware that with Schopenhauer's will or Lange's nature, he would come up against a metaphysical principle. The following question from his notes for the thesis, one of Nietzsche's own, bears witness to this: "Is it necessary to set in opposition to teleology an explained world?"[26] The miscarriage of the thesis was not simply due to impotence or a lack of interest in philosophy. It is also due to a philosophical error. Nietzsche remains trapped in the metaphysical or pragmatist reading (they are "the same") of Kant, of a Kant he does not know, since *The Critique of Judgment* is listed only in the last section of his reading list (along with the scientific works).

Thus Nietzsche's "renunciation" is all the more remarkable. It stems from the exigencies of philosophic rigor. But even more remarkable is this: in his very renunciation, it is Kant himself whom Nietzsche is repeating, *against* all the former's commentators.

To establish such a proposition one would have to perform a highly detailed analysis, to which this essay only can serve as an index. For the moment, we can signal two of the cardinal points.

The first is negative: every one of Kant's propositions that Nietzsche criticizes in his notes is in fact a distortion of Kant's text (often Fischer's distortion). These all consist, in one way or another, in attributing to Kant the thinking of a *real finality,* ignoring the paradoxical status of what Kant, it is true, *names* "objective finality," but which he *thinks* explicitly as the impossibility of presenting any such *object*. Kant's genuine propositions dictate much more what is to become established in Nietzsche, little by little, as the thinking of knowledge: for example, the idea of knowledge as recognition, as refuge in the familiar against the "strange" and "uncanny,"[27] repeats the Kantian motif of finality as the "subjective" necessity for escaping—by means of a "symbolism"—a radical heterogeneity of nature, the threat of which can in itself never be eliminated.[28]

The second is positive: in *The Book of the Philosopher* the teleological motif recurs, but this time characterized by a complete scorn for scientific positivities. Here Nietzsche employs, alternately and according to the needs of the particular instance, either finalist arguments or non-finalist arguments when writing about nature (in the same way that he will speak of a "finality without consciousness" in regard to the origin of language).[29] On the other hand, it is the teleology of the philosopher that becomes a motif and a question: "Problem: to know the *teleology* of philosophic genius."[30]

It would be possible to show that the source of this question (beyond any sort of "influence") lies in the discourse of Kant, where the unique function of teleology is to set in play nothing other than the finality and the *end* of philosophic discourse itself.

It would in fact be possible, indeed necessary, to show that the teleology of the third *Critique* does not proceed from an additional examination of the science of nature by the critical system, but that it is in fact a return and a complication (*Kombination?*) of the question of the closing of the system, a question which haunts the discourse of Kant from at least as early as the first *Critique*. If one is willing to accept this reading in its principle—a principle that we cannot fully unfold here—one will also agree that what allows us to return to Kant's discourse (and to his text), and specifically to return to it from Nietzsche, could nonetheless never allow any similar return to neo-Kantian philosophers or to "Kantianism" in general, since the discourse of these latter is on the contrary already full and completed from the very start, albeit in a "relativist" or "finalist" way. The exchange that sets itself up, unbeknownst to Kant, between the Kantian apparatus and the Nietzschean scheme is an exchange set (or upset) according to what one might call, paradoxically (as regards the *doxa* of the "rule"), the functions of the incompletion, the blockage, the rupture or the exasperation of discourse.

One must say therefore that Nietzsche's thesis—or his will to a thesis—is caught up in this strange status: on the one hand, it cannot move beyond the screen of post- or neo-Kantianism, and accordingly Nietzsche renounces philosophy; on the other hand it repeats Kant, but this very repetition brings about an exclusion of the philosophical. For at the close of the analysis begun here, one would have to follow this repetition-exclusion into the moments at which it goes beyond the thesis—or into that by means of which the thesis goes beyond itself; into the *Begriffsdichtung* and the *Witz*, whose connection with the respective positions of art, symbolism and teleology, which after all make up the philosophical economy of the *Critique of Judgment*, would then have to be examined.

In this respect, Nietzsche, instead of extending (one more time) this *Critique* in the romantic mode of a philosophy of life, or in the mode of a science of nature, will be the only one—not to "break" with the prescriptions of philosophy—but to repeat (i.e., "re-inscribe") the Kantian articulation and disarticulation of philosophic discourse.

One therefore has to recognize that the zero degree of discourse is also, in the thesis, the zero degree of the text, and that the text is produced not by a simple difference vis à vis discourse but rather in the stumbling, distressed, and contradictory progression of a projected discourse that will never cease to worry Nietzsche. He notes, in *The Book of the Philosopher,* "Great distress in knowing if philosophy is an art or a science. It is an art in its ends and in its production. But the means, the exposition by concepts (*die Darstellung in Begriffe*) has something in common with science. It is a form of poetry (*Dichtkunst*)."[31]

In a certain sense, nothing will ever overcome this "distress" of Nietzsche's—one that negates the possibility of a thesis, but that also proceeds from it. And Nietzsche's endeavor, inasmuch as it will be that of another *Darstellung*—exposition, presentation, thesis—or of a *Dichtung* in the *place* of a *Darstellung,* will never simply be superior to or more elevated than *Darstellung.* We can only begin to understand what we call Nietzsche's "text"—which after all leaves us, too, in "great distress"—by calling upon, for example, the resources offered in the phrase we used a moment ago: the text is the *relief* of the discourse, which is precisely, once again drawing upon the multiple resources of the word, that which distresses discourse.

From this point on—and this is the only teleology that this essay will propose—we would have to attempt to follow the itinerary of Nietzsche's writings, which would mean, of course, to repeat an itinerary already traveled more than once, by those mentioned earlier on. Such a task would consist in identifying, in a sustained way, the embroiled, implicated, and inter-dependent strands of "text" and "discourse": in following, for example, the persistent motif of a philosophical *Darstellung* on the subject of finality (*The Gay Science,* 360: "We still need a critique of the concept of *purpose*"), in investigating the *Dichtung* that ceaselessly confounds these theses—and here, notably, in confounding discourse with the strategy, so dear to Nietzsche, of announcing a projected task—a task that the thesis of 1868 repeats, in that it never takes place.

To get this underway, one might suggest, *to begin with,* two general movements.[32]

First, there is the movement of the return, the return of the thesis, from 1868 to 1888, from *On Teleology* to *The Re-evaluation of*

All Values, two theses never to be written, "in which" the affirmation of the eternal would not be a thetic affirmation (in the sense of a position on) nor its other, nor its simple outside, but precisely that which always returns, affirming itself: discourse, as relief and distress.

Second, there is the movement of the figure of Zarathustra, finally. For if Zarathustra "completes" the series of figures outlined by Nietzsche, it is precisely the series beginning with Democritus that he completes, the product of *Witz* and the second Thrasyllus, but the *philosophical* product, the philosopher of non-finality (and the non-finality of the thesis). And it is perhaps especially in inscribing the name of Zarathustra that Nietzsche most obscurely and most radically repeats Kant. For in the *Opus Posthumum*—one of the titles foreseen for the exposition of the system (this thesis which the *Critique* will always prevent from taking place)—we read this: "Zoroaster: the ideal of practical reason, physical at the same time as moral, united in a single sensible object."[33]

We said at the outset that we would have to efface, but not *simply* efface, the title of this essay. The "real" title would be:

THE *SECOND* ZARATHUSTRA

Provided that we add right away that the second Zarathustra is not himself (even he) without remainder; he is yet to be succeeded by *the Crucified* and *Dionysos,* the last "signatures."

Translated by Peter Connor

Postscript (1987)[34]: Fourteen years after writing this small essay, of which I see clearly all the insufficiencies, I will not attempt to change or complete it in any way. I would like only to add one remark: Kant's "Zoroaster," as the sensibly presented unity of the whole reason, could not have been (had the figure been actually drawn by Kant) anything other than the presentation of *freedom,* for freedom is the "keystone of the entire system of reason" (2nd *Critique,* Introduction). Freedom is an Idea—it is *the* Idea of reason or of humanity. As an idea, it can never be presented sensibly—but as this particular idea, it has, unlike other ideas, the very special property of being also "given as a matter of fact within experience" (3rd *Critique,* paragraph 91). Understanding this enigmatic assertion by Kant is a task which cannot be outlined here (it will be the topic of an essay to be published about "the experience of liberty").[35] But it should be said here that such a presentation of freedom itself within experience can never be the presentation of a *figure* (Zoroaster or anyone else), and this is not because freedom would be too high and beyond any figure (as is the "sage" himself, according to Kant), but because its essence does not consist in any figure, nor figuration (drawing, model, or "*Dicthung*"), but in the factual *praxis* of existence as such, through the possible figures of human beings as *ex-istants.* Zoroaster as such is therefore a misunderstanding of Kant by Kant himself: a desire to exhibit something like a schema or a symbol of freedom—whereas, to the contrary, it is freedom as such, and as a *fact*, that is the "scheme" of any presentation. The Zarathustra of Nietzsche (of the second Kant) pertains to this same misunderstanding, as perhaps do also "Dionysos" and "the Crucified," for those names are only the last metaphysical attempts by Nietzsche to present the dead God—whereas in truth it is God's *death* itself, and no longer some "dead God" still likely to come back to life, that finally presented itself in Nietzsche's mute and disfiguring paralysis (cf. "Dei paralysis progressiva." *Stanford Italian Review,* 1986).

NOTES

1. References to Nietzsche's texts are from either the *Historisch-kritische Gesamtausgabe,* (Munich: Beck, 1933–1942) (works henceforth cited as W, letters as B), or to Karl Schlechta's edition (Munich: Hanser, 1956), 3 vols.

2. Cf., for example, the letter to Gersdorff (16 February 1868) concerning the Democritic tradition: Beck, B, II: 18, and also the *Autobiography of 1869,* Schlechta, III: 135. We might add that we would thus "verify" what M. Blanchot, in reference to Heidegger, has *written* about this "*Kombination*" in his texts on Nietzsche (collected in *L'Entretien infini,* Paris: Gallimard, 1969).

3. On this question, see Philippe Lacoue-Labarthe, "Le Détour", in *Poétique,* no. 5, p. 55.

4. Nietzsche's own part in this obliteration, indeed, was not inconsiderable.

5. Cf. Elizabeth Förster-Nietzsche, *Der Junge Nietzsche* (Leipzig: Kroner, 1912).

6. On renunciation—*Entsagung,* a key word in Wagner's *Ring*—cf. the *Autobiography of 1869,* Schlechta, III: 150 (quoted below).

7. To Gersdorff, 6 April 1867, Beck, B, II: 133.

8. Nietzsche in fact entertained the idea of founding a philosophical journal: letter to Gersdorff, 16 February 68, ibid., p. 183.

9. For example on Suidas, Diogenes Laertus, Theognis, and Aristotle.

10. 1–3 February 1868, ibid., p. 173.

11. Beck, W, III: 365–367.

12. Ibid.

13. Ibid.

14. To Rohde, 9 December 68, Beck, B, II: 278.

15. Here we would need an analysis of this term and of its origin. Such an analysis would take place in the context of other works concerning German romanticism. Moreover, we should point out at the very least that things are not so simple, and that Nietzsche will see *also* his *Democritea* "crumble before [his] moderately rigorous philological conscience." To Rhode, 3 April 68, ibid., p. 187).

16. Beck, B, II: 194.

17. Ibid., p. 199.

18. Schlechta, III: 150.

19. Beck, W, III: 371–394.

20. Ibid., p. 178.

21. Ibid., p. 375.

22. Ibid., p. 392–393.

23. Letter quoted.

24. Ibid., p. 375.

25. "Positions", in *Promesse,* no. 30–31, p. 53.

26. Ibid., p. 374.

27. *The Gay Science*, paragraph 355.

28. Kant is thus the first philosopher to have "known" the threat of madness. (Translator's note: Cf. *Le Discours de la syncope* (Paris: Aubier Flammarion, 1976.)

29. *Das Philosophenbuch: Le livre du philosophe* (Paris: Aubier, 1969), passim, and "Introduction du cours sur la grammaire latine" (*Poétique*, no. 5, p. 137).

30. Ibid., p. 43; cf. also pp. 159–161.

31. Ibid., p. 69.

32. Clearly—so to speak—such an itinerary, in the end and beyond these figurations, would lead in only one direction, which would not be "one" direction: that of a "rewriting" of "Nietzsche"—and consequently, of course, of Bataille—which is to say that any "program" here would be misguided.

33. *Opus posthumum*, trans. Gibelin (Paris: Vrin, 1950), p. 1.

34. Translator's note: the Postscript (1987) was written in English by the author.

35. Cf. *L'expérience de la liberté* (Paris: Galilée, 1988).

4

"Our Probity!" On Truth in the Moral Sense in Nietzsche

Jean-Luc Nancy

I would like to venture an affirmation on the subject of Nietzsche—an affirmation I advance under the patronage, so to speak, of a remark made by Thomas Mann à propos Nietzsche: "Whoever considers himself an immoralist is in reality the most finely tuned moralist ever to have existed, a being possessed by moral exigency, a brother of Pascal."

It is in fact an affirmation of this order—of the order involving "moral exigency"—that I would like to sketch out here.[1] Or rather, I would like to lend precision to Thomas Mann's comment, perhaps grounding it; for, as it stands, the comment remains at the level of a global and paradoxical intuition, indeed on the level of an accusation, something which calls for a response.

The first clarification I would bring to bear—and urgently so, lest we start out on a misunderstanding—is this: it is not clear what Thomas Mann understands by the word "moralist" here, but the turn of phrase (built as it is on a simple reversal of appearances or of received ideas, indeed on the reversal of Nietzsche's affirmation of his own "immoralism") can only lead us to one of two possibilities: *either* Nietzsche is a moralist in the completely traditional sense of morality, one who upholds Socratic or Christian virtues, or both at the same time; *or* Nietzsche is an immoralist only in the eyes of this tradition, and he is proposing, in opposition to this tradition, another kind of morality.

Now I do not want to scoff at either one of these two interpretations. But we need to be more precise still, for the second hypothesis can itself be understood in two ways. *Either* Nietzsche is the moralist of an anti-morality, let us say, for the sake of brevity, of a morality of "low" ("sensible") values as opposed to the morality of "high" and "ideal" values: this Nietzsche, produced by a simple "reversal" of Platonism, would be the one brought to light by Heidegger *but also* the one whom Heidegger has shown to harbor an entirely other thinking, one that would consist not in reversing the "sensuous/supra-sensuous" schema but rather in "transforming the old schema from top to bottom."[2]

Heidegger's conclusions notwithstanding, it is not some "overturned morality" in Nietzsche that I want to address here.

Or else, Nietzsche is the moralist of an *altogether other morality,* one which, whilst having nothing to do with the sensible/non-sensible couple, would nonetheless still be a morality: that is to say it would have the imperative and normative aim of relating to a value.

In saying this much, I am coming considerably closer to Nietzsche's contention in paragraph 335 of *The Gay Science:* what we have to do, he asserts (to take one quotation from among a thousand possible ones), is "create new and proper tables of values."

It is at this point that the task I have set myself starts to become intricate. The "creation of values" is the true meaning of the "*Umwertung aller Werte.*" But, by the same token, Nietzsche's thought remains subjected to the regime of *value* as such. It is indeed then a morality, but as such it does not transgress in any fundamental way the metaphysical determination of morality, nor the moral determination of metaphysics. Rather, *it brings it to completion.* This *integral* completion is what Heidegger emphasized in Nietzsche.

Let me state briefly what this implies:

1. It implies thinking the *truth* of metaphysics no longer as adequation to a reality, but as an *evaluation* (a "holding-to-be-true," *fürwahrhalten*) of what is necessary to life;
2. It implies thinking *life* precisely as that which *evaluates;* and, in consequence, the supreme value (the one by which we are to evaluate) is evaluation itself;
3. It implies recognizing that life evaluates in two ways: according to "*truth,*" which is to say, according to the lie that holds-to-be-true everything that stabilizes life; and according to "art," or "poetifying transfiguration," as Heidegger calls it, or again life itself as a creation, the incessant creation-evaluation of ever new perspectives (those same perspectives that are themselves stabilized by a holding-to-be-true repeatedly and endlessly shattered by the becoming of creative life);

4. It implies thinking that this double evaluation is only a single one, which is in fact Nietzsche's fundamental evaluation: positing something as true implies always leaving something to be surpassed, and it is through this incessant creative surpassing that the *living* can attain its full *consistency,* or again, according to a fragment quoted by Heidegger at the end of his course of 1939, "becoming [is] stamped with the character of Being."[3] But in this way the evaluation of evaluation (that is to say the will to power as will to will) allows *becoming* to accede to its full presence, or *assimilates chaos* to human life, which then fixes it and transfigures it; thus truth ends up as *homoiōsis*.

Developing Heidegger's argument only a little one can therefore say that Nietzschean *homoiōsis*—truth as assimilation and as self-assimilation—absolutely completes the *moral* essence of truth, as Nietzsche himself brought it to light in metaphysics. It completes it by making clear that the ideal as such—and first of all the ideal of truth—is, in the final analysis, only the evaluation of the evaluator himself, and assigning *Being* within this self-evaluation.

This, then, perhaps rather summarily, is the first meaning that can be given to the formula I have chosen as subtitle to this exposé: "Truth in the moral sense in Nietzsche." Throughout Heidegger's analysis, which doubtless remains incontrovertible, Nietzschean truth appears absolutely moral in its essence—it is not merely a matter of an "overturning" of moral values, but rather, through a strategy which gets to the bottom of every morality, of assigning *the* value in the very subject of evaluation, and of the correlative to this gesture, i.e. assigning this subject in becoming and in chaos (that is to say, once again, in the *will* as that through which becoming and chaos relate to themselves, that is to say are *subjects*).

But I did not choose this subtitle simply to recall Heidegger's reading. I chose it because there is another way to understand it. Not in the sense in which the same words can take on a completely different meaning, but in the sense in which *the same thing*—and so if you like the same meaning—can, while remaining the same, nevertheless be understood in another way. I chose it because it seems to me that in Nietzsche's *moral* completion of metaphysics, in this *same* completion, the *other* of this same is *also* brought into play—an alterity that would be more radical than the sameness of the same, more *abgründlich* (and one which, however, *constitutes,* here as elsewhere—indeed wherever it is a question of "sameness"—the most intimate sameness of the same: constitutes it by dismissing it in some way).

This *other* truth and this *other* morality of the *same* Nietzsche is what the title I have chosen is intended to evoke: "Our probity!"—*Unsere Redlichkeit!* (with an exclamation mark: these two words are to be found at the end of paragraph 335 of *The Gay Science;* we will come to this text presently).

Probity, *Redlichkeit,* this constant motif which Nietzsche so emphasized, perhaps points to this other, this completely other morality. But how?

I am not going to present you with a treatise on Nietzschean probity. This would require more time, and greater competence. I would remind you first of all that it is probity which governs the entire Nietzschean operation I have just been speaking of: in order to be able to begin to recognize Nietzschean truth, one must begin by acknowledging, without dissimulation and without deception, the hidden evaluation and the secret interestedness of truth, of all our truths. The whole enterprise (beginning in particular with *Über Wahrheit und Lüge im aussermoralischen Sinn,* in 1873) rests upon this: one must have the probity to admit the lie of the concept, the lie of language in general. And this is already everything: through this probity we not only designate the lie (that is to say knowledge, truth) but we at the same time liberate this same lie—which is "the instinct that makes metaphors"—by seeing in it the creativity of myth and art.

But of what kind of probity are we talking here? Or what role does probity play in Nietzsche?

In 1873—but also in a number of later texts—everything leads us to believe that this probity consists in the *acknowledgment of reality:* things are not what our concepts make of them, nor what our myths tell us they are. It is precisely the infinite particularities of things that we allow to escape us, and in relation to which we *lie.* Probity, therefore, in one respect, consists in the acknowledgment of truth, of a truth more true than that of our lies.

As you know, it would be easy at this point to try to "corner" Nietzsche, who speaks only in the name of one more truth-adequation, or rather in the name of the always identical truth-adequation. You know as well, and Heidegger has shown this, that anyone who thinks he can denounce Nietzsche by pointing out this truth is in turn claiming the truth of his own discourse about Nietzsche. Thus if one tries to take Nietzsche to task in the name of the proposition that truth is illusion, one in turn falls victim to the accusation, etc. So let us leave this.[4]

What displaces the question in a quite different way is the fact that truth is enunciated *as evaluation.* If probity tells the truth about truth, probity, in its turn, is an evaluation. It is not, of course, the evaluation of Mr. Nietzsche. On the contrary: it is probity that says "But let us leave Mr. Nietzsche!" (Preface to *The Gay Science*). Probity is the absolute and ultimate acknowledgment of evaluation, over and above any evaluator: *it is itself* auto-evaluation. One could say that probity is the most proper character of Nietzschean Being, inasmuch as it includes not only the evaluation but also the evaluation of the evaluation.

Probity is therefore *the* character of ontology, or ontology as moral character. Thus far we have only gained a *word* to name the fundamental auto-evaluation—a *moral* word, and one which would confirm what precedes.

But what is probity without truth, or, to say the same thing another way, probity in the guise of truth? What becomes of probity in the case of someone who happens to have only erroneous information? It would be merely *sincerity,* and the ontological character in question then becomes quite simply a subjective character in the psychological, anthropological sense of the word. We are slipping back into opinion, into Mr. Nietzsche's opinion.

If Nietzsche places great emphasis on this word, and if furthermore we must assent to Heidegger's analysis, this is perhaps because this word, which in fact might be used to baptize Nietzsche's ontology, remains as yet, in spite of everything, unquestioned. Probity exceeds and perhaps unsettles that *homoiōsis* to which it nevertheless corresponds. It brings into play, within the Nietzschean metaphysics of moral identity, an "entirely other" morality.

How and why? This is what I will now attempt to show, first by situating the word "probity" in a number of contexts, and then by examining the precise function that it plays in a text devoted to morality.

There are four points to be made here.

Within the context of this exposé, the first reference will remain of somewhat limited importance. But it would assume much greater importance were we to begin to really "treat" the question of probity in Nietzsche.

It should be pointed out that for Nietzsche probity is undoubtedly not primarily a philosophical nor even a moral issue, but rather a "scientific" one: *Redlichkeit* characterizes the attitude of the *philologist*. The true philologist is *"ein redlicher Philolog,"* as Nietzsche names him in *Homer and Classical Philology.* Or more exactly, perhaps, if philology[5] does not furnish the entire model for *Redlichkeit,* it at least stands for, in opposition to the lie of morality, the *honnêteté* of which Nietzsche speaks in paragraph 84 of *Daybreak*. And it also names, much later on in one of the posthumous fragments (no. 479 of *Die Wille zur Macht*) the most exacting task: "To be able to read a text *as text*, without imposing any interpretation, is the most developed form of 'inner experience'—perhaps a barely possible form." Without elaborating any further, let us make this initial observation: probity is first of all the philological virtue of this face-to-face with the naked word, this guileless confrontation.

The next two references are taken from two passages in which Nietzsche characterizes probity in the most marked way (there are others, of course: for example *Zarathustra*, IV, "On the Higher Man"; *Daybreak*, section 482; *Beyond Good and Evil*, section 227).

First, in paragraph 456 of *Daybreak* Nietzsche states that the assurances given in antique or Christian morality, concerning the links between happiness and virtue, have never been "*honest*" (*probes*), although neither do they stem from a deliberate falsification: he says it is simply that when one feels oneself to be disinterested, one treats truth lightly, and one happily makes do with "this level of truthfulness." On the other hand, he adds:

> Notice, however, that *probity* is among neither the Socratic nor Christian virtues: it is the youngest virtue, still very immature, still often misjudged and taken for something else, still hardly aware of itself—something in process of becoming, which we can advance or obstruct as we think fit.[6]

Probity then is a virtue above and beyond virtues, a virtue yet to come. It cannot therefore be regulated according to any given truth, and its truthfulness—its *Wahrhaftigkeit*—is on a more radical "level" than that of moral truths. Which means most importantly that this truthfulness must elude the liaison between virtue and happiness (beatitude, reward, or satisfaction in general—*Kantian* overtones which I ask you to note and keep in mind). And probity is *in process of becoming* (this is the title of the aphorism: *eine werdende Tugend*): perhaps not only because it still has to complete itself, but also because it is essentially a virtue-in-process-of-becoming, the virtue, precisely, of the tireless reevaluation which is virtue "itself."

This second reference, as you see, is a double one: first, it allows us to identify *Redlichkeit* with becoming itself "as virtue"; second, it also turns this *Redlichkeit* into a strange probity that would in some way precede the truth of which it ought to be the guarantor or the witness, and which would precede or defer indefinitely the *reference* of its truthfulness.

Next—third reference—paragraph 370 of *Daybreak:*

> Never keep back or bury in silence that which can be thought against your thoughts! Give it praise! It is among the foremost requirements of honesty and thought. Every day you must conduct your campaign also against yourself.

In the precise and familiar Nietzschean sense of "thinking against oneself," probity appears perhaps most purely in its essence as becoming. In other words, provided that we do not make this precept into a simple psychological, hygienic recipe, and provided we do not make it into a simple moral maxim (because in this case it would be opposed only to *the* absolute truth of my limited thought), it could well be that this precept signifies the necessity, for Nietzschean thought, of resolutely and incessantly *contradicting* itself, the necessity of not falling back upon itself, of not taking its own truth as ground, *not even its moral truth established as evaluation of evaluation.*

In other words, in this quotation and in the preceding one, *Redlichkeit* names *at the same time* the ultimate moral truth of metaphysics, *and* something which carries this truth outside of itself. If probity consists first in the acknowledgment of being as becoming, the next stage consists in the acknowledgment of becoming and of probity itself. And so it appropriates to itself the essence of becoming in the most fundamental way. But the "fundamental" here opens the ground for its own downfall. Probity towards probity, probity *against* probity, which is to say probity against the *homoiōsis* of becoming in its presence—are we still in a position to create a "truth," and to apply *Redlichkeit* to a *Wahrhaftigkeit?*

Or does this not rather point to a collapsing of the metaphysical ground, not in the sense of a pure and simple ruination for the sake of completion, but in the sense of an unprecedented confrontation with that which truly constitutes its ground? Perhaps *Redlichkeit* has to confront that which at the same time *confers and withdraws its truth on and from truth;* which means confronting also, in every thinking, that which at once bestows and withdraws thought: not an "unthought" which could always be circumscribed and appropriated, but what we might call the "unthinkingness" (*impensement*), let us say thought's aberrations within itself—in brief that *madness* which Nietzsche, in spite of everything, confronts.[7]

Now *Redlichkeit* is also the undissimulating, unrelenting gaze on the universality "of delusion and error": this is how it is described in paragraph 107 of *The Gay Science.* It is the inexorable, cruel insight into the "fundamental" aberration (cf. *Thus Spoke Zarathustra*, IV, "The Leech").

Ecce Homo (which could well be the book of *Redlichkeit par excellence*) meets this madness in playful confrontation, but also plays in confronting it. Because what this book confronts—brutally—is at bottom the impossibility of ascribing to humanity or human thought any act of *Selbstbesinnung*[8] that would not at the same time deny it every basis, all support, all ground and all *selbst* for this *Selbstbesinnung*—thereby leaving only the *selbst* of Nietzsche himself, which is to say (for this argument is in no way subjectivistic; we are not going back to "Mr. Nietzsche") nothing, or a mere puppet, and yet leaving thereby, precisely thereby, the first "*decent* human being," the first *anständig* man, which must surely imply some degree of *Redlichkeit*.

To be even more precise: the probity which leads to *Ecce Homo* is one that involves exposing or exhibiting a subject—and exhibiting the subject as histrionic, even as a ham actor—as the truth of the evaluator at work in every evaluation; but it is a crazed exhibition—in the strongest and *maddest* sense of this word—because what is thereby evaluated is never the subject, nor *this* subject—Mr. Nietzsche—nor *the* Subject, and because the evaluating truth literally shatters to pieces the subjectivity of the subject to which it nonetheless refers. Probity is probity in the face of the *untenable* nature of the thinking of truth. (As such, and also in its proximity to madness, it no doubt stands in the troubling position of the *double* of Descartes's "candor" [*franchise*], the double of the principal evaluation of candor that commands the *Discours de la méthode* and orders it in its entirety as a "fable of candor.")

Probity would then begin to designate less an auto-evaluation than the impossible, unthinkable "self" of evaluation, the irredeemable loss of self and of the Self in evaluation itself. And if evaluation indeed presupposes, in the evaluating subject, an essential *will*, *Redlichkeit* is perhaps *the will to the will which admits to not willing itself*, not being able to will itself, or rather not willing to will itself (cf. "To will is a prejudice," posthumous fragment from *Daybreak;* and *Daybreak*, paragraph 124)—and which would admit therefore the *necessity* of this non-willing, this aberration of self.

But let us not proceed too quickly.

Let us now consider the fourth reference to *Redlichkeit*.

This reference is not in Nietzsche this time, but in language, in the word *Redlichkeit*. (It is therefore a *philological* reference, and so must also be understood in the *witzig* mode Nietzsche himself demanded of philology; cf. my exposé "Nietzsche's Thesis on Teleology," above, pp. 49–65)

What is *Redlichkeit?* It is, first of all, according to one of the very first meanings of *Rede* ("counting," *Rechnung*), commercial honesty, exact or accurate counting and accounting, conformity to calculation, to *arithmos* and to *logos*. It is scrupulous conformity to the law. In terms of discourse, of *Rede* (you will note this word has almost all the properties of *logos,* and that *redlich,* "in this account," is almost *logikos*. Meister Eckhart translated *ratio* [as "human reason"] by *Redlichkeit,* in the sense of "the faculty of speaking, of judging"), it means a statement which conforms perfectly with what it says. A statement that corresponds perfectly to what one is taking into account is *redlich*. It is adequate discourse, a *logos homoios:* the discourse of truth, in a way. This much, but with something more: the quality of *Redlichkeit,* which pertains to a person before it pertains to a discourse, implies that I can be sure of what is being said, that I do not have to be suspicious of it. *Redlichkeit* is that whose truthfulness I do not have to *verify*. It is less an adequation with something that remains elsewhere, behind the discourse, than a discourse which is in itself the restitution—not in the sense of a reproduction, but precisely in the sense of the restitution of a deposit, the canonical example of probity—or the re-presentation (and not the *homoiōsis*) of an account, of a calculation, of a *logos*. It is a truth which is not subjugated to the control of its adequation, or whose adequation—if the concept still has any meaning here—is immediate, evident, given in the statement itself. *Redlichkeit,* which is translated in French by *probité* ("probity") but also by "*loyauté*" ("loyalty"), is a word which cannot be placed in doubt: and this impossibility does not stem from any authority, nor from any kind of verification. It does not belong to the order of knowledge, nor to the order of belief. Here again *Redlichkeit* resembles a *cogito,* without *cogitatio,* and perhaps, as we shall see, without *ego*.

One might try to give a psychological and moral equivalent in the example of what we call "a person of tried and tested probity or loyalty." But this equivalent presupposes precisely that a trial has taken place and a verification of the constant truthfulness of the person, or of his constant respect for the law and the word, or of the law of the word, has been assured through experience. *Redlichkeit,* considered in itself, detached from all moral psychology, would be rather a word which is *in itself legal,* or loyal. And what explains the inadequacy of any psychological equivalent also accounts for the fact that no metaphysical truthfulness can be identical to *Redlichkeit* as such: every truth implies its verification, or implicates itself as auto-verification. Even the truth of Descartes's God implies the testing and the proof that God cannot be deceitful, an assurance which Descartes insists upon very heavily.

In this sense, *Redlichkeit* is not truthfulness. It does not consist in the *homoiōsis* of a statement (or of the intention of the one who makes the statement; I have already dismissed from probity the notion of sincerity) in relation to reality. It is, in a way, the word that is worth only its word, but that is absolutely worthy without verification. In this respect, it is the word at the limit of the word: it is a *virtue*, not a discourse. Or rather, it is a word that not only stands omnipotent, but that is also in need of no defense.

Probity is or does what the word "probity" (*probus*) implies: that which is by itself and for itself its own testing and proof, that which is "of itself" probative; or again, in what the word *loyalty* implies, a presence of the naked law, of the law as such, traversing a subject but finally in spite of himself, or in any case independently of him. *Redlichkeit* at least points towards something before truth, and before the subject. Or rather, it points towards *truth* itself as the absolute law of the word. What *loyalty* implies is that truth is the law of the word—and perhaps we should add that this law is the "essence" of the word. This truth—*the* truth—is not a *homoiōsis:* the law is not that the word must speak the truth *about* something, but that the word alone establishes or opens up the possibility for truth. The lie—and this is a well-known truth—only functions as a lie because it obeys this law.

Equipped with these observations, let us turn to a text which is governed—this is the right word, as we shall see—by *Redlichkeit* in an absolutely essential way, even though it is not a text *about Redlichkeit*.

It is paragraph 335 of *The Gay Science*.

It is entitled "Long live physics!" (*Hoch die Physik!*), but it concludes thus: "*Hoch die Physik! Und höher noch das, was uns zu ihr* zwingt—*unsere Redlichkeit!*" ("Long live physics! But even more so that which *compels* us to turn to physics—our probity!").[9]

How does this conclusion come about, a conclusion that presents itself as the supreme evaluation of probity as supreme value?

The object of the aphorism is a critique of moral judgment: that is to say, not of morality, nor of the content of a given morality, nor yet of its criteria and its values, but of the *act* of moral judgment, taken for itself, or as a critique of such a declaration as "this is fair"/"this is what has to be done" taken for itself. In other words, it is a critique of the act and of the form of moral evaluation.

This critique passes through two major stages: the critique of the "voice of conscience" in general, and the critique of Kant's categorical imperative. After this, Nietzsche appeals to those of "us who want to become . . . those who create themselves and who to that end must become the best . . . inventors of everything that is lawful and necessary in the world," who must therefore "be physicists in order to be able to be creators." Thus "Long live physics!" and, or but, the coda: "But even more so that which *compels* us to turn to physics—our probity!"

The general schema of the aphorism corresponds to something so classical in Nietzsche that it needs no comment: to the moral evaluation which does not suspect for a minute that its judgment of the "good" "could be evidence of personal abjectness, of impersonality . . . or [an] inability to envisage new ideals," Nietzsche opposes the idea of the "creation of new tables" by those who make themselves into "the best disciples" of the "necessity" of life, by "physicists" therefore, who first of all—it is implied—have been able to recognize the physique and the physiognomy of moral judgment and evaluation. ("Your judgment, 'this is right,' has a prehistory in your instincts, likes, dislikes, experiences, and lack of experiences.")

What is less obviously "classical" in this schema is precisely what exceeds it a little, and which has to do with the coda or the point of the aphorism: "Long live physics! But above all, long live our probity!" "Long live physics!" is an evaluation. But what has even more value is what makes us make this evaluation; it is our probity that obliges us, forces us to say: "Long live physics!"

Probity, then, has every appearance of a moral judgment, or rather of what governs it, of a voice of conscience or moral sentiment. What is more, it seems to be flanked by all the attributes of a moral sentiment that has been critiqued: a consciousness of its "solidity," of its "force," the total submission it produces by command etc. There is no need to point out that probity consists here in submitting to physics as opposed to morality: what matters is that this submission *is not physical* but moral. Probity is a necessary part of this submission, *our* probity is necessary to it, and this is doubtless not the probity of one who listens to the voice of his moral conscience (such a one, precisely, lacks probity), but it is surely *the* probity par excellence, and therefore remains—whatever way one goes about it—obedience to a moral conscience, at least in this context and without going into further analysis.

The emergence *in fine* of this probity so much resembles the assurance and the sufficiency of the incriminated moral judgment that one has the right to see some irony in it; it is almost as though Nietzsche were declaring, and in the process annulling, his own theory: "But I myself, before anyone else, I also obey my moral certitude" (and if we have learned from Nietzsche to think against him, we should not exclude this interpretation). But it is also, and in a more easily recognizable way, as though he were saying, "I can, because I have recognized the physiology of moral judgment, rely with absolute certainty on the judgment of my probity, which includes first of all the judgment of judgment, and I have the right to appropriate for myself the 'moral force' which I have denied you." The irony remains: for what the ferocious critique opens a space for is not the positivity of a conformity to nature. It is not a judgment of existence in place of a value judgment, and it is not a truth which would be the adequation to *physis*. Rather it is a value judgment which makes us acknowledge and praise "physics." Indeed, it makes us recognize it as the space or the regime of a "conformity to the law and the necessity of the world," a conformity of which we must be "the best disciples"; but it also makes us acknowledge and choose "physics" as the very space of the creation of new values, for we must also be "the best inventors" of this legality and of this necessity.

To create values, in sum, is to create—to re-create—the necessity of the world; it is to identify oneself with the law as with evaluation itself, as with the true physics and physiology of evaluation. Probity means to submit oneself to the necessity of this evaluating *physis;* or rather, the effect of probity lies in this.

For probity, *as such*, as both the virtue and the virtuous act, is the recognizant evaluation of the evaluating and legislating *physis*. This virtuous act is the very act of moral judgment, an act that displays the powerful affirmation and force of conviction of its inner certitude and discipline. It is an entirely purified act, one might say, an act reduced to its *pure form*, to a *pure gesture*, to what one could call *the schema of probity for every evaluating decision*. This act is rid of all content. It has no other content than "the necessity and the law of the world"; but as such it is still formally (since nothing but form remains) similar to the moral judgment being critiqued, for the critique has not taken into consideration any specific moral content. It is aimed only at the act of judgment.

But "our probity" shows this act to be purified of something else as well as of all moral content. Contrary to what we might think at first, the act of judgment is purified of the *conscience* whence, from the moralist's point of view, it comes.

For Nietzsche asked of this moralist: "For this *belief* of yours (that is to say, once you believe in your judgment, once you have obeyed your moral conscience)—is there no conscience for that? Have you no notion of an intellectual conscience? Of a conscience behind your 'conscience'?" *Our probity* is this conscience behind conscience. It is the "intellectual conscience" of the physiology of moral conscience. In this sense, *Redlichkeit* is purified of "conscience" in that it is the intimate certainty of a subject who relates to an ideal—without knowing the law of this relation. Probity is purified of consciousness as a consciousness of self, as consciousness of the Self inasmuch as this latter would bear moral witness. *Redlichkeit* stems from "intellectual conscience," which is however not a *Selbstbewusstsein,* nor even a *Bewusstsein,* it is rather a knowledge, a *Wissen* (the concept, if not the word, is present in the accusation of the moralists's "ignorance" [*Unerkenntnis*] of the physical.) It is the *Wissen* of necessity, and it is therefore *physical truth* which is to be recognized in *Redlichkeit.* And it makes itself known and is to be recognized elsewhere than in a subject or in self-consciousness.

But *at the same time* this knowledge of necessity, of the truth of necessity, is seen to be a *Gewissen:* this is the word that Nietzsche uses for "intellectual conscience," and it denotes above all a moral conscience. To be clear and accurate, the translation should read: "Have you no notion of a *moral intellectual conscience?" Redlichkeit* is a moral conscience consisting in nothing other than conformity to the law of *physics.* The *moral* character vanishes or is sublimated—or is perhaps itself transvalued—in a knowledge of the law of nature, a knowledge which comes out immediately as evaluation, as a *Gewissen* evaluating this *Wissen* of universal evaluation. Physiology becomes axiology—but in opposition to all axiology. Such is *Redlichkeit.*

As strange as this construction may seem, it can in turn be brought back to a metaphysico-moral model (of the Stoical type, perhaps). Hence we have still not determined what it is that marks the decisive alterity of Nietzschean "morality." In order to approach this morality, we still have to consider the critique of the categorical imperative—which our commentary has been circling around till now.

The categorical imperative is the only instance of a specific morality that Nietzsche takes into consideration in this aphorism.

Why? Because in terms of content *this* morality—let us say Kantian morality—presents nothing other than the imperative itself (in its first, pure, and essential formulation; in fact Nietzsche says nothing here about the subsequent formulations; thus he is not talking in particular about "man as end," but neither does he speak of the second formulation, the one that determines or exemplifies the "universal law" as "the universal law of nature," in other words, as physiology). And the imperative itself offers nothing more or less than the *form* of moral judgment, its "solidity," its "absoluteness" or "unconditionality," and the universality of its compass. Hence Nietzsche attacks the categorical imperative because he wants to expose the very act of judgment as a moral prescription. Nietzsche is attacking an evaluation which is the evaluation of the evaluating judgment itself—and perhaps the evaluation of *judgment* taken absolutely in the universality of its pretension or its compass (which already in Kant is something essential to the judgment of knowledge, as is proved in the *Regulating Use of the Ideas of Reason*), a pretension elevated to the universality of a law, and a law which presents itself immediately in the imperative as an absolute value.

With the categorical imperative, Nietzsche is in fact attacking the exposition of the essence of the evaluating judgment; and the second part of the aphorism, instead of moving on to the examination of a particular instance, radicalizes the attack which the first part had begun. But you will have noticed that the categorical imperative is at the same time in a situation which resembles, in a troubling way, that of probity. In each case the same purification and the same radicalization are at stake; in each case, we are faced with a "morality" whose content is nothing other than the form of the evaluation itself.

Must we then find or read Kant in Nietzsche—at least in the Nietzsche of this aphorism? This is indeed what I consider to be indispensable, and not as a sophisticated (and sophistical) manoeuver, but as the only really adequate way to break through to the interior of *Redlichkeit*.

To introduce Kant into Nietzsche is provocative or paradoxical only at a very superificial level. In fact—and to present a first, historical reason—Nietzsche is taking issue here with a Kant he scarcely knows or knows only through very limited interpretations (and one could show that this is the case for many other passages). The "Kantian morality," or worse still the Kantian moralizing Nietzsche is aiming at, even if they do connect with certain strata and tones of Kant's discourse, are far from constituting a complete account of the true stakes of the latter's thought. Nietzsche, moreover, is not entirely unaware of these stakes, since this passage contains a rare homage to Kant ("he is nonetheless the one who has broken open the cage" of metaphysics, of theology and hence of moralism). Nonetheless, Nietzsche remains captive of a reading which resembles more that of the second or third generation of Kantians than, for example, Hegel's reading. (Unless, another hypothesis not to be rejected, Nietzsche were to be deliberately unhinging the categorical imperative from its strictest Kantian position, so as to be able to make it the foil for his own imperative of probity!)

In fact, the categorical imperative is set forth here under three motifs, none of which is in any way appropriate:

1. The imperative is the "punishment" reserved for "old Kant" for having "spied and obtained by stealth" (*erschlichen*) the "thing in itself." I need hardly remind you that Heidegger, Granel, and others have shown us that Kant neither "captures" nor "swallows up" the "thing in itself." But Nietzsche had not read Heidegger, you might say. He had, however, read Schopenhauer, to say the very least, and he might well have remembered from this reading something else about the "thing in itself" (I refer you to the beginning of the "Critique of Kantian philosophy" at the end of *The World as Will and Representation*). If there is indeed, as Granel proposes, an "ontological equivocation" in Kant, the aspect of this equivocation according to which the thing in itself is the negative index of a pure phenomenality was potentially already accessible to Nietzsche. But, there again, would he not have wanted to reduce Kant to his "other side"—and this precisely because of the too great proximity between his own thought and that of Kant?

2. Kant, writes Nietzsche, "was in his turn spied on and the 'categorical imperative' crept stealthily into his heart and led him *astray—back* to 'God,' 'soul,' 'freedom,' and 'immortality,' like a fox who loses his way and goes astray back into his cage—but it was *his* strength and *his* cleverness that had *broken open* the cage!"

   Here the blindness—or the lack of probity—become even more flagrant. For to pass over the status of the *postulates* of practical reason is really to refuse even the most simple reading of Kant. This status no doubt is not a simple one, but this is not the place to examine it. It is, however, important to point out that *liberty* certainly does not have quite the same status as the other postulates. And in order to assess the extent of Kant's "straying," one need only recall this one statement: "for just as theology can never become *theosophy,* so *rational psychology* can never become *pneumatology*" (3rd *Critique,* paragraph 89). But, more especially, by what error or by what malice can one pretend as though the postulates had something in common with the establishing of the categorical imperative, which is in fact totally apart from it (one only has to read the *Groundwork of the Metaphysic of Morals*)?

3. Finally, Nietzsche characterizes the imperative itself as follows: it would be the "feeling that 'here everyone must judge as I do.' " And Nietzsche goes on to ironize on the "absoluteness" of such a judgment, exclaiming: "Admire rather your *egoism!* And the blindness, the meanness and the lack of rigor of your egoism!" But the articulation of the categorical imperative strictly speaking has nothing to do with these statements, which are in fact those of a totalitarian egoism, which are *imperialist* and not imperative in the sense Kant meant. For the imperative is articulated thus: "Act only on that maxim through which you can at the same time will that it should become a universal law."[10]

The imperative therefore in no way consists, to quote Nietzsche again, in "experiencing one's own judgment as a universal law."

It consists in exactly the *opposite:* in accepting as my judgment (as a maxim) only that which can be presented as universal law. For it is the maxim itself which must be capable of resolving me towards willing it as universal law, and it is not me, especially not me (especially not this pathological "me," as Kant would have said), who can determine it as such. Kant's text is formal: "*nach derjenigen Maxime,* durch die *du zugleich wollen kannst.*" Certainly this is not easy to understand, and this is why certain editors of the *Groundwork* proposed changing it to " . . . *Maxime,* von der *du zugleich wollen kannst*" ("a maxim *of which* you can wish" instead of "*through which*"; indeed, which edition did Nietzsche read, if he read one?). But such a correction misses fundamentally the *thinking,* the difficult thinking of the imperative. It makes the universality heterogeneous with the maxim, and applied to the maxim by an arbitrary will—or at least one could question where such a will might find the criteria for its willing. Nietzsche gets caught in the trap of an error, and an error which is widespread and insistent

> in interpretation (even when Kant's text has not been corrected) only because it consists precisely in bringing the categorical imperative under the communal law of a "moral conscience" of the subject and of the subjective character of its evaluation. And it is this subjectivity of the evaluation which the categorical imperative absolutely eschews.[11]

(I am leaving aside the commentary which would need to be added about another part of the aphorism: Nietzsche makes claims for the *unknowable* nature of moral acts in general. It would be easy to show that this is a Kantian motif.)

In this case, in what kind of a manoeuver is, if not Nietzsche, then at least this aphorism, engaged?

It would be the following: it impugns this pseudo-Kant with creating a morality of the subject, and then in its own way it reinscribes, in *Redlichkeit*, the essence of the categorical imperative.

What does *Redlichkeit* say exactly? That we must—for it constrains us, it *zwingt* us—recognize the law of *physis*, that is to say the only necessity which escapes the arbitrariness and the unconsciousness of "moral conscience." What does the categorical imperative say? That one should acknowledge only that maxim which implies the idea of its universality—and, as you know, in the second articulation of the imperative this idea will be determined according to what the second *Critique* calls the "type" of moral law, as an idea of "the universal law of nature."

Of course, Nietzsche's *physis* and Kant's "nature" are not identical (again, this would have to be looked into). And of course, the conditions of production of the categorical imperative and of *Redlichkeit* are quite different: the former claims to be derived from the testimony of the communal conscience, the latter is violently opposed to any communal conscience of morality. But there again, one would have to look more closely: and one would have to ask if Nietzschean *probity* does not consist precisely in brutally affirming what motivates Kant, something which Kant however conceals up to a point (or conceals from himself), namely the general *devaluation* of every morality founded on the representation of an ideal, a value and an end (which is to say, in Kantian terms, founded on the regime of the hypothetical imperative).

In this regard *Redlichkeit* would allow for a better understanding of the categorical imperative. But it is this imperative that would furnish the true regime of probity.

And it would furnish it essentially as follows: the imperative is not an enunciation by the subject, nor by any subject. The imperative—this verbal mode which Benveniste has shown to be *neither* verbal *nor even* enunciated: no one *pronounces* it—is imposed upon the subject, it *zwingt* the subject, from outside, from an outside so absolutely outside that mixed in it are both Nietzsche's *physis* (for whence comes *Redlichkeit*, whence speaks *Rede*, if not from nature itself in its chaos?) and Kant's "reason" (which in sum receives itself into itself *from the outside* when it receives the imperative).

Hence, something quite different activates the sameness of morality for Kant and for Nietzsche.[12] For Nietzsche accomplishes what emerges in Kant as the resorption of value in evaluation and in the will to evaluation (the measure of the maxim is that it makes me *will* it as law: it is the law of the will of the law). Thus the morality of subjectity, or subjectity *as* morality, is accomplished. But this *same* extreme act—which in fact reduces everything to an act, to the act of judging, of evaluating, to an "evaluating" which is absolute and without subject because *it is the* Subject—this same act is nonetheless carried beyond itself.

No one pronounces the imperative—the *Rede* of *Redlichkeit* is the voice of no one, neither the voice nor the discourse of any consciousness; it is, over and beyond any *verifiable* utterance, that which is imposed as a constraint without having to justifying *itself*, without having to authenticate *itself*. It "befalls" the subject; it happens to him without his being able to master it. The whole aphorism is constructed so as to highlight this "fall." Probity is the admission of this: that the law happens to us, and that we do not have the measure of it. *Ecce Homo* signifies *also* that extreme deprivation which is the lot of each who receives the law. And so Nietzsche writes in the preface to *Daybreak* (paragraph 4): "There is no doubt that a 'thou shalt' still speaks to us too, that we too still obey a stern law set over us."

Nietzsche's probity is to have admitted that he in turn was confronting the truth which Kant had begun to confront—all the while covering it up in "physics," as Kant indeed had covered it up in "morality"—that truth which can be extracted from the *end* of truth, from the end of the "world-truth" (cf. *Twilight of the Idols*), the incommensurable, unpresentable truth (Kant's terms) of that which no longer stems from any *homoiōsis*. The imperative truth of an *ethic* which is not homologous, not adequate, not in keeping with any morality.

This truth—imperative and honest (*probe*)—is no longer a value, no longer stems from an evaluation. For it is no longer what a subject can "hold to be true" according to his needs and interests. It is rather the truth which *holds* the subject. And it does not hold him for true, so to speak; it holds him *under its law.* And if the value as such is always of the order of what Kant calls the *price,* that is to say the value *relative* to an evaluation, then the truth of *Redlichkeit*—of this imperative probity—does not have a relative value, but, still in Kant's terms, an "intrinsic value, that is to say a *dignity (Würde)*" (*Groundwork of the Metaphysic of Morals*). Dignity, or absolute value, escapes all evaluation.

Dignity (or nobility, or excellence) is at bottom what Nietzsche never stopped trying to think. All I have tried to show here is epitomized in the following passage from *The Greek State* (one of the *Five Prefaces to Unwritten Books*):

> Every man has dignity only insomuch as he is, consciously or unconsciously, the instrument of genius: and from this one must immediately draw the ethical consequence that "man in himself," absolute man, has neither dignity, nor rights, nor duties: it is only when entirely resolute, and in the service of unconscious ends, that man can excuse his existence.

The "genius" might well be in the categorical imperative. It would then have, following the third formulation of the imperative, "humanity as end." No doubt. But this *final* humanity is not that of "man in himself." Kant never knew what "man in himself" was. Rather, along with Nietzsche, he prepared for us the awesome task of thinking man beyond essence and beyond value. Probity of thought consists in conceding nothing to this inevaluable dignity.

As for the probity which was *also* Nietzsche's own probity towards Kant, one can measure this from the way in which he one day transcribed in his notes Kant's most famous, or in any case most popular text. I reprint it here without commentary, noting only the few divergencies in its transcription:

> Two things fill the mind with ever new and increasing admiration and awe, the oftener and the more steadily we reflect on them: the starry sky above us and the moral law within us." [Nietzsche writes "us" where Kant has "me."] The former view of a countless multitude of worlds *annihilates, as it were, my importance* [Nietzsche's emphasis] as an *animal creature,* which after it has been for a short time provided with vital power, one knows not how, must again give back the matter of which it was formed to the planet it inhabits (a mere speck in the universe). The second, on the contrary, *infinitely* elevates my worth as an *intelligence.* . . . " [Nietzsche cuts off

the sentence at this point, which Kant continues,] "through my personality, in which the moral law reveals to me a life independent of animality."[13]

Translated by Peter Connor

NOTES

1. This text was first presented as a lecture in Jean-Pierre Schobinger's seminar at the Philosophische Falkultät 1, University of Zurich. The seminar was devoted to Nietzsche, and particularly to "On Truth and Lie in an Extra-Moral Sense." "Notre Probité" was published in *L'impératif catégorique* (Paris: Flammarion, 1983).

2. Cf. Martin Heidegger: *Nietzsche,* trans. David Farrell Krell (New York: Harper and Row, 1981), 1: 200–210.

3. Ibid., 4: 202; cf. *The Will to Power,* § 617.

4. Cf. ibid., 3: 26–27.

5. The historical and theoretical role of philology in Nietzsche's thought need hardly be recalled here: cf. Sarah Kofman, *Nietzsche et la métaphore,* (Paris: Galilée, 1972) and also the texts by Eric Blondel and Heinz Wismann in *Nietzsche aujourd'hui,* vol. 2 (Paris: 10:18, 1973); this last text is in fact entitled and treats *Nietzsche et la philologie.*

6. *Daybreak,* trans. R. J. Hollingdale (Cambridge, 1982), p. 191 (translation slightly modified: all further quotations from *Daybreak* are Hollingdale's).

7. This confrontation is not a simple one, and the way in which Heidegger obliterates it in his reading of Nietzsche is not simple either; on this subject I refer you to "L'oblitération," by Philippe Lacoue-Labarthe, in *Le Sujet de la philosophie* (Paris: Flammarion, 1979).

8. In this respect, it is somewhat similar to the way *Umwertung* is qualified in this book; cf. *Ecce Homo,* "Why I am a Destiny," I.

9. *The Gay Science,* trans. Walter Kaufmann (New York: Vintage, 1974), pp. 263–266.

10. Kant: *Groundwork of the Metaphysic of Morals,* trans. H. J. Paton (New York: Harper and Row, 1964), p. 88.

11. One might note further, though not in regard to Nietzsche's text, another—and parallel—current alteration of the imperative. It is often cited in the following form: "Act *as if* your maxim could become universal law." But the *as if* only appears in the *second* formulation, which refers to the

"type" of a "law of nature." It does not appear in the first, nor in the third (where the law is replaced by the final and law-making nature of humanity in each one of us). Finally, the single formulation from the second *Critique:* "So act that the maxim of your will can always at the same time be valid as a principle making universal law."

12. I note, after having written this text, that an analysis by Henri Birault converges in a most illuminating way with the one outlined here. Cf. *Heidegger et l'expérience de la pensée,* (Paris: Gallimard, 1978, pp. 175–191).

13. In *Oeuvres philosophiques complètes,* vol. 12 (Paris: Gallimard, 1978, p. 265). The comments on Nietzsche's treatment of the quotation are those of the French translator, J. Hervier.

5
Metaphoric Architectures

Sarah Kofman

Genoa—For quite a while now I have been looking at this city, at its villas and pleasure gardens, and the far-flung periphery of its inhabited heights and slopes, and in the end I must say: I see faces *from generations gone by, this region is strewn with images of bold and autocratic human beings. They have lived and wanted to live on: this is what they are telling me with their houses, built and adorned to last for centuries and not for a fleeting hour; they were well disposed toward life, however ill-disposed they may often have been toward themselves. I keep seeing the builder, how his gaze rests on everything built around him, near and far, and on the city too, and the sea, and the contours of the mountains, and how there is violence and conquest in his gaze. All this he wants to fit into* his *plan, to make it ultimately* his property [Eigentume] *by making it a part of his plan. This whole region is overgrown with this magnificent and insatiable selfishness of the lust for possessions and spoils; and even as these people refused to recognize any boundaries in foreign lands and, in their thirst for something new, placed a new world beside the old one, each rebelled against each at home too, and found a way to express his superiority and to lay between himself and his neighbour his personal infinity. Each once more conquered his homeland for himself by overwhelming it with his architectural ideas and refashioning it into a house that was a feast for the eyes. When one contemplates how cities are built in the North, one is impressed by the law and the general delight in lawfulness and obedience. One is led to guess at the profound equality and subordination which must have reigned in the souls of all the builders. But what you find here upon turning any corner is a human being for himself* [einen Menschen für sich] *who knows the sea, adventure and the Orient; a human being who abhors the law and the neighbour as a kind of boredom, and who measures everything old and already built with envious eyes. With the marvelous cunning of his imagination, he would like to rebuild all of this anew at least in thought, put his hand to it and his meaning into it—if only for the moments of a sunny afternoon when his insatiable and melancholy soul does feel sated for once, and only what is his own, and nothing foreign, may appear to his eyes.*

—The Gay Science
(trans. Walter Kaufmann)

1. Good and Bad Taste of Architects

In *Das Philosophenbuch,* Nietzsche describes the world of fixed concepts in terms of a cover-up of the metaphorical character of so-called "proper expressions." To this end, Nietzsche repeats metaphors so stereotyped in their reception that they are no longer recognizable as metaphors. Nietzschean repetition, which also juxtaposes commonplace metaphors to entirely new ones, revitalizes and re-evaluates received or concealed figures by exposing all of their shortcomings. At the same time, Nietzsche's new use of metaphor revitalizes language by engaging in the work of the poet: he effects a transmutation of the norms of thought and action; he transforms the slave into a free man, "reality" into a dream. Through this metaphorizing play, he in turn becomes a metaphor—of life and of life's artistic power:

> With creative pleasure, the intellect liberated from servitude throws metaphors about pell-mell and displaces the limits of abstractions . . . it speaks only in forbidden metaphors and in unheard-of conceptual combinations in order to respond creatively to the impression of the powerful intuition of the present by thus destroying and ridiculing old conceptual borders.[1]

To describe the hierarchical system both of the concepts of ordinary language and of science—in other words, "well-made" language—Nietzsche uses architectural metaphors, following, it seems, tradition. But Nietzsche's originality lies in accumulating metaphors, in substituting one for another, juxtaposing to a stereotyped image a totally new figure, thereby inciting a re-evaluation of traditional metaphors at the same time as he ridicules them. From the architecture of the hive to that of the prison cell, passing through the Egyptian pyramid, the Roman columbarium, the Tower (of Babel), the fortress, a spider's web, a simple arrangement of beams—such is the metaphoric itinerary which Nietzsche follows. The genealogical reading interprets each of these fantastical architectures as symptoms of the health or sickness of their builders; all construction, in effect, is the expression of an internal architecture, that is to say of a certain hierarchization of instincts, of a subordination of the multiplicity of instincts to the strongest instinct which then serves as a provisional center of perspective. The "strength" or "weakness" of the will is the expression of the greater or lesser domination of one instinct over the others. Only the hypothesis of the will to power permits one to decipher, behind different architectural metaphors, the "good" or the "bad taste" of architects, the weakness or the strength of their will:

> Pride, victory over weight and gravity, the will to power should render themselves visible in a building; architecture is a kind of rhetoric of power, now persuasive, even cajoling in form, now bluntly imperious. The highest feeling of power and security find expression in that which possesses *grand style.* Power which no longer requires proving; which disdains to please; which feels no witness around it, which, without being conscious of it, lives on the objections raised against it, which reposes in *itself*, fatalistic, a law among laws: *that* is what speaks of itself in the grand style.[2]

Which "taste" then do architects, conceived as metaphors of the conceptual system, reveal?

a) The Hive

The *beehive* is the first construction which figures the conceptual edifice; it is a traditional metaphor used to describe serious, busy, preoccupied work. It is a metaphor which also frequently intervenes to contrast instinctive work, in its perfection, with human work, which remains intelligent but defective.[3] For Nietzsche, on the contrary, the metaphor is destined from the beginning to inscribe scientific work within life, to annul the opposition between the speculative and the practical,[4] the intellectual and the instinctive: concepts are products of an instinctive metaphoric activity much as honeycomb is produced by bees. The hive, as a geometric architectural ensemble, symbolizes the systematic ordering of concepts. The perfection of this architecture at the same time proves that it is the work of instinct. The "beauty" of the edifice is thus not unmotivated; it is at once the symptom and the mask of a primordial deficiency, which motivates the whole construction. This deficiency testifies to the necessity and productivity of the work: just as the bee, in order to survive, constructs cells and fills them with the honey it has gathered outside, so science constructs a formal and empty architecture into which it puts the totality of the world. The comparison of the scientific edifice, crowded with magnificence, with that of little cells excreted by a miserable insect, is designed to deride science's claim to reduce the world to its own measure—the presumption of science, which takes metaphors for essences.[5] Science can never explain the world; it can only describe it according to metaphorical schemas which remain human, all too human. Science is a pure "system of signs" (a semiology), a mythology, a world of fictions. It shares its pedigree with ordinary language, which it merely extends. It proceeds from the same metaphoric activity, and from the same materials, as ordinary language, building itself on concepts that it simply multiplies and renews:

> It is always constructing newer, higher levels, shaping, cleaning and renovating the old cells.[6]
>
> Knowledge "interprets," "introduces a meaning"; it does not "explain" (in most cases it is a new interpretation of an old interpretation that has become incomprehensible and that is now only a sign).[7]

The only advantage that science retains over ordinary language is that it "better" describes the "world," which is to say that it better describes us to ourselves, in a more systematic, a more refined, and a more disguised way. It eliminates any too apparent anthropomorphism in order better to obscure its metaphoric nature and make its interpretations seem like truths.

> The image of the world therefore becomes more and more true and complete. Naturally it is only a *mirror reflection*, a clearer and clearer reflection. The mirror itself is in no way completely foreign nor without relation to the essence of things, but it has also slowly emerged as an essence of things in the same way. We see an effort to render the natural mirror more and more adequate; science continues the natural process. Thus things are reflected in a purer and purer way with the progressive liberation from that which is too anthropomorphic. For a plant, the whole universe is a plant; for us it is human.[8]

That science must dissimulate its metaphoric character is symptomatic of its indwelling weakness; it cannot acknowledge its perspective as perspective without being destroyed by the very acknowledgment itself. Its systematicity allows science to dominate the world by enclosing it within the narrowness of its concepts, which in turn allows it to protect itself from the world by dissimulating it. Just as the bee makes honey by endlessly gathering nectar from flowers, so science turns the individual away from himself, from his own metaphoric powers, and forces him to seek his spoils outside, to go searching for truth in his hive:

> *Our* treasure is where the beehives of our knowledge stand. We are always on our way thither, being born winged insects and honey gatherers of the mind, having really but one desire at heart—'to bring home our spoils'.[9]

If the "individual," however, is susceptible to the injunctions of science, it is perhaps because he is not sufficiently strong to be able to affirm his own perspectives. The deficiency of science is correlative to that of the scientist, "objective" because he does not have in himself any instinct strong enough to dominate the others and to impose its own evaluations. The poverty of his internal architecture leads him to take refuge in a "cabin" not far from the tower of science that protects him and nourishes him. The metaphor of the hive therefore has an overdetermined meaning, one richer and more revealing than it seemed to harbor at first glance. The implications contained within it are made explicit in other metaphors which complete and modify it.

b) The Tower, the Bastion, the Fortress

The hive is also a tower, a protective bastion, a fortress. But because of its size, the hive is unsuited to symbolize the protection which science offers. So Nietzsche juxtaposes the metaphors of the tower and of the fortress, rather than the more common metaphor of the rampart.

This slight displacement not only revitalizes the old and more or less stereotyped metaphor, but also shows that it is not simply a matter of protecting oneself against external dangers: the supreme danger is life. And it is necessary to defend oneself against everything which, within oneself and outside of oneself, affirms life. Man needs to barricade himself, to isolate himself, to protect his constructions from the violence which other powers, wielding more impressive ensigns, might advance against them. Defenses must be established against the lie, against myth and against art, against all that would openly proclaim a cult of appearance, of surface, of fiction, that would dare to acknowledge scientific perspective as such—that which could reveal that scientific truths are also of a human, all too human measure, that "reality," the "true world," is only a dream and a fiction. The tower and the fortress are shields against the enemy, and also a means of cutting oneself off from life. These metaphors reveal that artistic activity, creation of forms, construction of a world in the image of man, is also will to power (although Nietzsche has not yet forged this hypothesis in *Das Philosophenbuch*); they express a conflict between enemy powers, one of which aims to affirm life, the other to deny it.

Thus the "greatness" of science sinks to miserable proportions; what is left is a purely fictitious mask intended to frighten and deceive. The fortress, the tower, and the bastion, deconstructed by a rigorous philology, are thus transformed into a mass of planks, supports and beams to which the weak cling in order to survive. The vitality of science's function is the measure of its "bad taste," its "lack of modesty"; in this strange architecture which man builds with his own resources no empty space remains, no room for the smallest fantasy:

> It tries above all to fill up this exaggerated framework to a monstrous degree and to arrange within it the entire empirical world, that is to say the anthropomorphic world.[10]

This is a monstrous filling up, which suggests that the tower of science is closer to a tower of Babel than to a fortress; having the same origin as ordinary language, the language of science distances itself more and more from the "music of the world," from a "natural language" which would "properly" name things as God did on the day of creation. Science possesses an artificial language comprising abstract signs and figures, genuine enigmata which represent more men's passions and conflicts than the essence of things:

> The domain of science has expanded and the towers of Babel erected by the sciences have multiplied in a monstrous fashion.[11]

The conservation of the human species is achieved therefore through the erection of a new, regular, and rigid world, at the cost, however, of driving divisions between, and effecting a separation from, the world and life. Indeed, the rigidity of the construction mimes that of a skeleton; it is only by being always already dead in life that man survives.

c) The Egyptian Pyramid and the Roman Columbarium

Thus the hive, the tower, and the fortress rearrange themselves according to a geometric, pyramidal structure, the order of which is analogous to that of Spinozist deduction. This new architecture proves that one was indeed able to build with concepts a hierarchized world: to file everything under rubrics, to assign everything to a specific place, to constitute a legal order, that of the rational and the reasonable. The pyramidal order imposes itself as the "true" order and opposes itself to the fluctuating world of impressions and the dissimulating world of appearances. The pyramidal order is the metaphor for the intelligible world of essences serving as models and norms:

> In the realm of these schemas something is possible which could never have succeeded in the midst of first intuitive impressions: the construction of a pyramidal order according to castes and degrees, the creation of a new world of laws, privileges, subordinations, delimitations, a world which is henceforth opposed to the other world, the one of first impressions, the one that seems the surest, the most general, the most known, the most human, and thereby the most regulating and imperative.[12]

The pyramidal order conforms to the rigid order of a skeleton; eight-sided like a die, it is the order of the *Egyptian pyramid*, containing the *mummification* of impressions, for which it serves as the tomb.[13] But from this metaphor Nietzsche must shift to that of the *Roman columbarium*, since mummification[14] implies that the figure of the corpse remains: the pyramid is a noble tomb; life, even though in impoverished form, is still present there. The *Roman columbarium* preserves only the ashes of the dead, just as the concept preserves the "residue" of metaphors. Ashes represent the total effacement of any effigy, the volatilization of any singularity. To conserve only life's ashes is to reduce differences absolutely. It is the ultimate equalizer, the ultimate injustice. Thus science is a "sepulcher of intuitions," but it is also the tomb of the scientist and even of the full range of the affirmative powers of life. The remedy against this impoverishment doubles, in fact, as poison: it gives the strong a bad conscience, seduces them with the honey of abstractions distilled within the hives of knowledge. The divinized idea is a frightening and castrating Circe, whose mode of operation is ruse; divested of any sensible apparel, dressed in tattered finery, in rags, she might evoke repulsion. But man is precisely attracted by "nudity," by purity, by the call of the great void, the call of nothingness, God, Being; man places the hollowest concepts at the apex or the base of his architecture: by a movement of reversal peculiar to the viewpoint of the weak, the top becomes the bottom, and the bottom the top, thereby topping off the whole process which has placed the end at the beginning. By putting God at the beginning and at the end, this anti-aesthetic disposition depreciates life and makes it ugly. The world it creates is the reflection of its own deficiencies.

And so the columbarium ends up burying its builder and destroying itself. If God is the foundation of the edifice, then this edifice is destined to be demolished. The magnificence of the architecture hides its foundations in metaphoricity—a sensible becoming which moves like running water:

> Just as the Romans and the Etruscans divided the heavens by rigid mathematical lines and, in a space marked out as in a *templum*, conjured a god, so every people has above it such a heaven of mathematically distributed concepts and, in accordance with demand of truth, it understands from then on that each conceptual god can be sought nowhere else but in *its* sphere. Here one must admire man for his powerful architectural genius, which manages to erect on moving foundations, as on running water, the escalation of an infinitely complicated conceptual dome.[15]

The stability of the edifice is therefore illusory. It floats without support, at the whim of chance: the base of the pyramid is made up of dice. Produced to deny becoming, the conceptual system in fact rests upon it and is, like it, a game of chance. The parts of the construction are not fixed: one only has to change perspective, throw the dice again, in order to transform the initial metaphors and, along with these, the façade of the architecture. The conceptual norm, which imposes itself as necessity, is a pure convention bound to a particular perspective, that of a life which can only survive by veiling its own perspective:

> Whereas every metaphor of intuition is individual and without equivalent and is, therefore, always able to avoid denomination, the great edifice of concepts displays the rigid regularity

> of the Roman columbarium and exhales [*ausatmen*] in its logic that severity and coldness which is proper to mathematics. He who would be impregnated with this coldness would have difficulty believing that the concept, made of bone and eight-sided like a die, and, again like a die, movable, is nothing but *the residue of a metaphor,* and that the illusion of the artistic transposition of a nervous excitation into images is, if not the mother, then at least the grandmother of every concept.[16]

The ensemble of the edifice is therefore a "game", a "toy" which, however, cannot be broken with impunity. The absolute rule of the game is that only under penalty of exclusion will it not have been taken seriously.[17]

The game of concepts, like the political game it produces, camouflages the balance of the powers which compose it:

> In this dice game of concepts, one calls "truth" the use of each die according to its designation, according to the precise counting of its points, to the formation of accurate rubrics and to the strict refusal to transgress the order of castes and series of classes.[18]

d) The Spider

Because this splendid and cold architecture rests on an illusory base, because it is made of the same material as that which it would shelter and protect, because it covers up the death of its inhabitants and the death of all life, the columbarium must undergo metamorphosis into a spider's web: the Spinozist geometric order is, finally, an arachnoid order. (Nietzsche is making a play here on the phonetic analogy between *Spinne* and Spinoza.)[19] The architecture of concepts is absorbed within the network of the spider's web; this net must be fine enough to be carried along with the moving waters on which it rests and, at the same time, solid enough not to be dispersed by the slightest breeze. The analogy, moreover, allows the construction of concepts to arise from man himself, just as the spider makes its web from its own substance.

Thus, mockery of mockeries, the hive is but a spider's web, the useful work of the bee is assimilable to the harmfulness of the spider; a "harmfulness" which arises not from bad intentions but is rooted in necessity.

The metaphor of the spider is spun out around the origin of a whole series of images: the image of the text as fabric, mask, clothing. It also serves as a symbol of castration.[20] Like a true vampire, the spider sucks the fluid from the flies it has attracted into its web in the same way the concept disfigures life, rendering it pale, sad and ugly, because, like a man frenzied with starvation, the concept takes nourishment from life. Feeding on life does not in this case give life. It is only the simulacrum and the ghost of life; the rags it wears, full of holes like the spiders web, are the symptoms of its own deficiency. The concept, which vampirizes an already anthropomorphized life, only has the appearance of life. Man takes from the world only what he has already deposited there; he feeds on his own substance which he then throws up in the form of concepts like the spider its web.[21]

Thus the joy of knowledge is procured by recognition; it reflects the security which narcissistic absorption in and of the world provides. But the regularity of the web he has woven assures man, in an illusory way, of the objectivity of the world he has created for himself:

> Man is only conscious that he is awake due to the rigid and regular web of concepts.[22]
>
> In his architectural genius, man rises far above the bee; the bee builds with the wax it collects from nature, man with the much more fragile material of concepts which he must make out of himself.[23]

The metaphor of the spider allows the demystification through ridicule of the teleological proof of the existence of God: God may be the architect of the world, but he is also only its supreme spider. Spider-man metaphorically transposes his crafty causality onto Nature and solemnly calls God the craftsman who produces the world. God, a product of the spider, metamorphoses himself into a spider, weaving intelligible models whose sensible trait would be a painted, and badly painted, copy:

> . . . As if there existed in nature, in addition to leaves, something else that would be "leaf," a sort of originary form [*Urform*] according to which all leaves would be woven, sketched, outlined, colored, crumpled, painted, but by awkward hands, to the point that no example would be correctly and surely rendered as faithful copy of the original form.[24]

Reversal of cause and effect, of beginning and end, is one of man's fundamental errors:

> The 'highest concepts', that is to say the most general, the emptiest concepts, the last fumes of evaporating reality, they place these at the beginning *as* the beginning . . . thus they acquire their stupendous concept "God" . . . The last, thinnest, emptiest is placed first, as a cause in itself, as *ens realissimum.*[25]
>
> And he himself [the God of the Christians] so pale, so weak, so *décadent,* even the palest of the pale have been able to master him, the master metaphysicians, the conceptual albinos. They had spun their web around him for so long that, hypnotized by their movements, he himself became a spider [*Spinne*], a metaphysician. Now he has begun to spin the world out of himself *sub specie Spinozae.* He transformed himself into something even paler and less substantial, became an "ideal," became "pure spirit," became *"absolutum,"* became "thing in itself" . . . *Decay of a God:* God became "thing in itself" . . .[26]

In a general way, the metaphor of the spider is associated with that of a haggardness characteristic of phantoms, a sickly pallor which shows the concept to harbor hatred of life and death of desire, but which also signifies that castration is caused not by "bad will" but by necessity: the creation of a "world of the ideal" is the only ruse which those whose life is impoverished to the extreme can practice to stay alive.

> Insects do not sting out of malice, but because they too want to live.[27]
>
> The activity of knowledge is comparable, in the end, to that of the spider spinning its web, hunting its prey and sucking it dry; what it seeks in return for its art and activity is to live and find satisfaction: and this is also what we want when we try to capture suns or atoms, to hold them fast and to record them in some way; it is a detour which leads us back to *ourselves,* to our needs.[28]

To transform the world into fixed metaphors is to uncover, behind the mask of metaphysical rags, a nihilistic will, the legacy of a life which is afraid of life, which is afraid to be seduced by sensuality because it does not possess sufficient strength or vitality to support its own intoxication—which preaches renunciation not because it lacks desire, but because it could never satisfy the senses it renounces. The metaphor turns on the fear of the senses which it interprets as an ideal. In its name, philosophers, like Ulysses's companions, plug up their ears to block out the sound of the sirens;[29] for them all music is seduction, deviation from the straight path. But once their ears are plugged, deafened, they no longer hear the musicality of the world they deny. However—and this remains its most dangerous characteristic—the world of the ideal is more seductive than that of the senses. The new philosopher should reveal the poison which lies hidden at this juncture, and expose the system of desires to which it corresponds:

> *Ideas* are worse seductresses than our senses, for all their cold and anemic appearance, and not even in spite of this appearance: they have lived on the "blood" of the philosopher, they always consumed his senses and even, if you will believe us, his "heart." These old philosophers were heartless; philosophizing was always a kind of vampirism. . . . Do you not sense in the background, for a long time concealed, a vampire who, having begun by sucking out the senses, is left in the end with the mere skeleton and clatter of bones? I mean categories, formulas, *words* (for, forgive me, what Spinoza left behind—*amor intellectualis dei*—is mere clatter and no more than that: what is *amor,* what *deus,* if there is not a drop of blood left in them?). In sum: all philosophical idealism to date was something like a disease, unless it represented, as in Plato's case, the cautiousness of a dangerously overabundant health, the fear of *over-powerful* senses, the prudence of a prudent Socratic. Perhaps we moderns are merely not healthy enough *to be in need* of Plato's idealism.[30]

Spinoza, the exemplary example of the spider-philosopher, only continues the lineage inaugurated by Parmenides and then perpetuated by Plato: Parmenides, who rejected the variegated world of becoming for the sake of Being—that hollowest idea, emptiest of all, a metaphor emptied of sense, of blood.

2. Saturnalia

Of poetry I will say now that it is, I believe, the sacrifice where words are the victims. We use words; we make them the instrument of useful arts. We would not have anything human if the language in us had to be completely servile. Nor can we do without the efficient relations which words introduce between men and things. But we deliriously tear them away from these relations.

—G. Bataille

So, among the metaphors of metaphor, the most symptomatic and also the richest is that of the fortress as spider's web; it is the architecture of "bad taste" which houses those who are unable either to build dwellings for themselves or to forgo a place or sense of security. It is therefore necessary that they expel from their bustling city, which is ruled by a spirit of seriousness, any party which attempts to play with their architecture, to take it apart, to deconstruct it, to substitute for it another, original in style, conceived in defiance of the measure of commonplace concepts. A new construction, which deconstructs itself to the benefit of yet another: thus Nietzsche eliminates the metaphors he proposes by juxtaposing them in turn with other "unheard-of" metaphors; thus Heraclitus' Zeus, like any artistic force, constructs and deconstructs everything in innocent playfulness.[31]

The metaphoric instinct, which in conceptual and scientific activity is repressed or manifest only in a sublimated and masked way, finds free expression in other domains—in the lie, the dream, myth, and art: there, owing to that overabundance of life which allows it to *will* illusion, it dares to affirm its perspective and recognize the mask as mask. Repressed in one place, the instinct which drives man to make metaphors manifests itself elsewhere via displacement: it is indestructible because it remains coextensive with life itself. But sometimes life presents itself for what it is—evaluating, lying, artistic—and sometimes it veils itself because it is not strong enough to follow through to its own end. It only aims then to vanquish power, to domesticate strength or vitality as reducible to "sublime deformity." The living who truly live can announce their truth on "more brilliant ensigns":

> This instinct . . . is in truth not subdued and is barely tamed. It seeks a new domain and another conduit for its activity and finds these in *myth* and above all in *art*.[32]

They therefore *will* confusion, the return to the archaic life of dream and childhood and the liberation from the slavery to which the rigid web of concepts submits them; what they *will*, in other words, is to play with the "serious":

> He [artistic man] continually confuses the rubrics and cells of concepts by introducing new transpositions, new metaphors and metonymies: he continuously establishes his desire to endow the present world of man's waking state which remains

so confusedly irregular, so incoherent, with an eternally new form, full of charm, as in the realm of dreams.[33]

Such a will endangers science, because it betrays the fact that without the conceptual fictions which imprison us behind rigid bars, we would not be able to distinguish between being awake and dreaming: "reality" rests on a regular coherence[34] which passes itself off as a necessity. "Reality" and "appearance," wakefulness and dreaming, seriousness and play: these are among the oppositions undermined by the strategic generalization of one of any two opposites: "But Heraclitus will always be right in this, that being is an empty fiction. The 'apparent' world is the only one: the 'real' world has only been *added as a lie.*"[35] Metaphysical fictions are "supplements"[36] appended to life, as though life were missing something, as though it were not, on its own, a power of affirmation without negativity. These fictions are necessarily produced by a type of impoverished, deficient life, which projects its own impotence in the place of desire, which it thus transforms from a purely affirmative force into a lack, an emptiness to be filled. Henceforward, it proves necessary to fill this emptiness with the creation of a fictive world, that "other world" which must be conceived as "purely" positive: the world of the absolute, the real, the true, analogous to the neo-reality projected by psychotics. Measured against this imaginary world, the "real" world becomes "apparent," relative, fluctuating, full of negativities. A cleavage comes to be introduced between the two worlds. The delirious production of the ascetic ideal thus achieves its meaning: "Man knew that something was lacking; a great vacuum surrounded him. He did not know how to justify, to explain, to affirm himself. His own meaning was an unsolved problem that caused him suffering."[37] The meaning harbored by the ascetic ideal is truly non-sense. But it was accepted by men; they consented to take "fictions" for "realities," because they benefited from the exchange (in the sense that Freud speaks of deriving benefit from illness[38]): they were able to *will*, even if what remains to be willed is only nothingness.

Pascal's thought: "If an artisan were sure to dream every night, for twelve hours, that he were a king, I think he would be almost as happy as a king who would dream for twelve hours every night that he were an artisan,"[39] is an aphorism which, as interpreted by Nietzsche, metaphorically resumes and states *en abîme* the relationship which Nietzsche establishes in *Das Philosophenbuch* between concept and metaphor. This thought undermines the opposition between dreaming and being awake by distinguishing them only according to their duration. The continuity of being awake is introduced by the conceptual coherence which transforms habit into necessity. The dream is moreover the fulfillment of a wish: which is to say that the waking state, which is simply a coherent dream, is a fiction that responds to human needs: the artisan who, in his dream, takes himself to be king, accomplishes the same as his wide-awake counterpart who, through unconscious metaphoric activity and scientific work, becomes king of the universe.

Being king is a happy dream, in which one takes delight by overlooking the metaphorical nature of the concept. The king's nightmare of being a mere artisan corresponds to the disillusionment of the man who, upon recognizing that his kingdom is but a phantasmatic product, finds that he is incapable of bearing the truth: he remains as happy as if he were the king of the universe. For him, truth is but a "bad dream."

The artisan's dream corresponds to the daytime programming of a people stimulated by myth: this ongoing daydream produces unceasing wonder. On this station, man is king of the world: he projects himself into the world in the place of the divinity; for him the world is a masquerade of the gods.

The king's dream is comparable to the waking state of the thinker disenchanted with science. In the dream—and in myth and art—the artisan transforms himself into a king, and the king into an artisan; the end of the reign of concepts brings about the true Saturnalia[40]: the end of the order of castes and interdictions, the mixing up of rubrics, the temporary interchange of slave and master. The "natural" and the "social" orders are transgressed, and thus they are revealed to rest not on any necessity, but on simple conventions and metaphors.

When a poet makes a tree speak like a nymph, he guarantees, through this transgression of the natural order, that there are possible orders of experience and expression beyond the simple order our habits have forged. In granting a plant speech[41] the poet shows that an absence of words only conceals, alongside our own equally metaphoric language, another system of metaphors "proper" to the plant.

To represent a god in the guise of a bull abducting some mortal transgresses a sexual interdiction and desires an illicit confusion of species. In this guise, sexuality can only be satisfied by disguising itself. Divinity, as the metamorphosis of a bull, remains a simple metaphor.[42]

To place a goddess on a chariot next to a mortal (Pisistratus) is wilfully to confuse the human and divine orders.[43]

Through this lifting of interdictions which art and myth accomplish, everything becomes possible. Nature, far from being reduced to ashes, is magnified. Nature doubles as art, playing with itself, constructing and deconstructing worlds; incessantly casting metaphors it plays at tricking man. To carry out this game, it must be strong enough to will illusion and to mask appearance and surface. This taste for mystification, which indwells the metaphoric spirit, is revealed—for example in the theater—whenever man feels sure enough of himself, with nothing to fear from transgression.

> The intellect, that master of dissimulation, is liberated and discharged from its slave's work only for as long as it can deceive without prejudice; only then can it celebrate its Saturnalia.
>
> This framework, with its monstrous planks of concepts to which the needy one clings his whole life long in order to save himself, is, for the liberated intellect, no more than scaffolding and a plaything for his most audacious works: and when he breaks it, reduces it to pieces, only to recompose it ironically by joining together the most divergent pieces and separating the most proximate ones, he shows that he has no need of this expedient born of indigence, and that he will henceforth follow out not concepts but intuitions.[44]

The more instinct is tamed, the greater will be the debauchery. Authorized licentiousness denies that daily life is also only dream and phantasmagoria and supports the habitual deceptive world in its normative rigidity. However, if there is a path that leads from the waking state to the dream state, there is no bridge between the dream and the world of concepts. The concept can serve as a metaphor for intuition, but intuition cannot double as a metaphor for the concept: whence the necessity, if one must give it verbal expression, of multiplying metaphors; but silence remains a more suitable language.

> From these intuitions no straight path leads to the land of ghostly schemes and abstractions. The word is not made for them, man either becomes mute when he sees them, or else he only speaks in forbidden metaphors and through unheard-of conceptual combinations in order to respond creatively, by thus destroying and ridiculing old conceptual barriers, to the impression of the powerful intuition of the present.[45]

Thus, as early as *Das Philosophenbuch,* Nietzsche distinguishes and opposes two types of man:

1. The rational man, insensitive to art, who dominates life through his preparedness, prudence, and regularity, led by the abstractions which protect him from misfortune—without, however, procuring happiness for him. He essentially aspires to be liberated from suffering. Exemplary example of this idiosyncrasy: Spinoza the Stoic. The latter remains, in his misfortune, a masterpiece of dissimulation. The nobility of his soul is only an act.

2. The irrational man, a happy hero, liberated from all deficiency because he only takes for real a life disguised as appearance and beauty. This type of man, thanks to art, is happy and more alive than the other, accepts joy and suffering as the two conditions of his love of life. He also suffers more; lacking "memory" he does not learn from experience. The prototype of this man is the pre-Socratic Greek who is able to disguise the ugliness of the world by projecting an overabundance of life onto things which he thus embellishes:

> This disguising, this denial of deficiency, this burst of metaphoric intuitions and above all this immediacy of illusion accompany all the externalizations of such a life. Neither the house, nor the gait, nor the apparel, nor the clay pitcher betray the fact that necessity invented them; it seems that in them should be expressed a sublime happiness, an Olympian serenity and in some way a playfulness with the serious.[46]

Translated by Peter T. Connor and Mira Kamdar

NOTES

1. *Das Philosophenbuch: Le livre du philosophe* (Paris: Aubier-Flammarion, 1969), pp. 196, 198. (Page numbers refer to the German text of the bilingual Aubier-Flammarion edition.)

2. *Twilight of the Idols*, "Expeditions of an Untimely Man," trans, R. J. Hollingdale (Penguin Books, 1968), par. 11, p. 74. Cf. also *The Gay Science*, pars. 280, 283, 290.

3. Marx, for example, also employs this metaphor: "A bee, by the construction of its cells of wax, confounds more than one architect. But what primarily distinguishes the worst architect from the most skillful bee is that the former constructs the cell in his head before carrying it through in wax." *Capital*, Pt. 1.

4. Cf. *The Birth of Philosophy in the Age of Greek Tragedy,* "Science and Wisdom in Conflict," par. 6: "the false antinomy of the *vita practica* and *contemplativa* is Asiatic. The Greeks understood that better."

5. *Das Philosophenbuch,* III, 1, p. 182.

6. Ibid, III, 2, p. 192.

7. *The Will to Power,* trans. W. Kaufmann (New York: Vintage Books, 1968), Book 3, 12 (parar. 604). Translation modified.

8. *Das Philosophenbuch,* I, 102, pp. 108 and 110. Cf. also I, 102 and 76. Nietzsche's texts on science as semiology and symptomatology are innumerable. The most important are: *Das Philosophenbuch,* 50, 76, 78, 80, 94, 100; *The Gay Science,* pars. 112, 121, 246, 373; *Beyond Good and Evil,* par. 21; *Twilight of the Idols,* pars. 4, 6, pp. 79–82 and 88–89 (in Hollingdale's translation, *op, cit.*); *The Anti-Christ,* par. 57.

9. *The Genealogy of Morals,* trans, F. Goffling (New York: Anchor Books, 1956), "Preface," I: 149. Translation modified.

10. *Das Philosophenbuch,* III: 192.

11. *Beyond Good and Evil,* trans, W. Kaufmann (Vintage Books, New York 1966), par. 205. Here Nietzsche takes up the biblical metaphor, already reiterated by Leibniz, in order to reevaluate it. For Leibniz, it was a question of constructing a scholarly language, univocal and universal, which would put an end to the diversity and equivocality of natural languages: "For it depends upon us to fix their meanings, at least in some scholarly language, and to come to an agreement to destroy this tower of Babel" (*New Essays concerning Human Understanding,* Book III, chap. 9). By taking up this same metaphor but applying it to science, Nietzsche effaces the opposition between artificial language and natural language, common language and scientific language.

12. *Das Philosophenbuch,* III: 182, 184.

13. Cf. *The Will to Power:* "What a mummified error surrounds the word 'abstraction!' As if this consisted in omitting a thing and not rather in underlining it, blazoning it, emphasizing it. Thus all images, all forms, are born in us through a crude schematization."

14. The metaphor of the pyramid is a parodic repetition of the Hegelian metaphor for the sign given in the *Encyclopaedia:* "The sign is a certain immediate intuition which represents a content quite other from that which it has itself; the pyramid in which a foreign soul is transported and preserved." Cf. the commentary which J. Derrida gives of this passage in "The Pit and the Pyramid: Introduction to Hegel's Semiology," in *Margins of Philosophy,* trans. A. Bass (Chicago: Chicago University Press, 1982), pp. 82–83: "The sign, as the unity of the signifying body and the signified ideality,

becomes a kind of incarnation. Therefore the opposition of soul and body, and analogically the opposition of the intelligible and the sensory, condition the difference between the signified and the signifier, between the signifying intention (*bedeuten*), which is an animating activity, and the inert body of the signifier . . . Hegel knew that this proper and animated body of the signifier was also a *tomb*. The association sōma/sēma is also at work in this semiology, which is in no way surprising. The tomb is the life of the body as the sign of death, the body as the other of the soul, the other of the animate psyche, of the living breath. But the tomb also shelters, maintains in reserve, capitalizes on life by marking that life continues elsewhere. The family crypt: *oikēsis*. It consecrates the disappearance of life by attesting to the perseverance of life. Thus, the tomb also shelters life from death. It *warns* the soul of possible death, warns (of) death of the soul, turns away (from) death. This double warning function belongs to the funerary monument. The body of the sign thus becomes the monument in which the soul will be enclosed, preserved, maintained, kept in maintenance, present, signified. At the heart of this monument the soul keeps itself alive, but it needs the monument only to the extent that it is exposed—to death—in its living relation to its own body."

From this metaphor Nietzsche retains the idea that the presence of life is maintained in the tomb, and that this monument serves to safeguard life against death. But while the metaphor of the pyramid in Hegel presupposes the opposition of the signifier and the signified (a discontinuity marked at the level of the *Aesthetics* by the fact that the pyramid there is the symbol of symbolic art, and no longer the symbol of the sign, as was the case in the *Encyclopaedia*), it is introduced by Nietzsche precisely with the aim of deconstructing the whole system of metaphysical oppositions. Thus this metaphor is itself erased by those which precede it: no metaphor could ever be *the* sign of the sign, the *proper* sign of the sign.

15. *Das Philosophenbuch*, III: 184.

16. Ibid.

17. Aristotle had already seen society as a game of checkers where each piece could move only according to predetermined rules under penalty of being disqualified from the game: πόλιζ is a game in which the players take a number of the opponent's pieces. The squares on the checkerboard were called "cities" and the pieces "dogs." The one who has no definite place in the game, the tyrant, is analogous to the gods or to the beast. Cf. *Politics* I. 2, 1253a: "From these considerations it is evident that the *polis* belongs to the class of things that exist by nature, and that man is by nature a political animal. He who is without a *polis*, by reason of his own nature and not through some circumstance, is either a poor sort of being, or a being higher than humanity. He is like the man of whom Homer wrote in denunciation: 'Clanless, lawless and hearthless is he.' The man who is stateless by nature at once plunges into a passion for war; he is in the position of a solitary advanced in a game of checkers." Cf. also J. P. Vernant,

"Ambiguité et renversement, sur la structure énigmatique d'Oedipe-roi," in *Échanges et communications, mélanges offerts á Claude Levi-Strauss* (Mouton, 1970), in particular p. 1275, where he alludes to Suetonius: "The *polis* is also a kind of game in which the adversaries take each others' pieces, which are placed as in chess on squares marked off by intersecting lines. These delimited squares were called, not without humor, cities, and the pieces of the opposing sides were called dogs." Once again, then, Nietzsche takes up a traditional metaphor, the city as game, only to call into question the very idea of play by generalizing the notion and deleting the opposition between game-playing and the serious.

18. *Das Philosophenbuch*, III: 184.

19. Cf. *Beyond Good and Evil*, par. 5, where the geometric construction of the *Ethics* is likened to a shield behind which the sickly Spinoza takes shelter: "Or consider the hocus-pocus of mathematical form with which Spinoza clad his philosophy—really "the love of *his* wisdom," to render that word fairly and squarely—in mail and mask, to strike terror at the very outset into the heart of any assailant who should dare to glance at that invincible maiden Pallas Athena: how much personal timidity and vulnerability this masquerade of a sick hermit betrays."

20. Cf. Freud, *New Introductory Lectures on Psychoanalysis* (Norton, 1964), Lecture XXIX ("Revision of the Theory of Dreams") where the spider is interpreted as the symbol of the phallic mother.

21. Cf. the fourth of the *Untimely Meditations*, section 5.

22. *Das Philosophenbuch*, III: 194.

23. Ibid., p. 186.

24. Ibid., p. 180.

25. *Twilight of the Idols*, 'Reason in Philosophy,' par. 4.

26. *The Anti-Christ*, par. 17.

27. *Human, All Too Human*, "Mixed opinions and Maxims," par. 164. Cf. also pars. 153 and 194.

28. *The Will to Power*, II, 114 (1881–1882).

29. Cf. *Beyond Good and Evil*, 230, where Nietzsche applies the same metaphor to the seductive song of the "metaphysical bird-catchers": "to see to it that man henceforth stands before man as even today, hardened in the discipline of science, he stands before the *other* nature, with intrepid Oedipus eyes and sealed Odysseus ears, deaf to the siren songs of old metaphysical bird catchers who have been piping at him all too long, 'you are more, you are higher, you are of a different origin!'"

30. *The Gay Science*, 372. Cf. also *Twilight of the Idols*, "Reason in Philosophy," 1, and "Expeditions of an Untimely Man," 23; in *The Birth of Philosophy*, truth is said to dwell, since Parmenides, in a castle of spiders' webs, in the company of a philosopher who is as bloodless as an abstraction: "The spider wants the blood of its victim, but the Parmenidean philosopher precisely hates the blood of his victim, the blood of the empirical reality he has sacrificed."

31. "And thus, like the child and the artist, the eternally living fire plays, constructs, and destroys, in its innocence, and this game is the game which eternity plays with itself. Sometimes the child throws away the toy, but he quickly seizes it back, in innocent caprice. But from the moment he constructs, he knots together, joins and shapes, finding his rules in an inner law and order. Only the aesthetic man has this view of the world, he alone receives from the artist and from the construction of the work of art an experience of polemic and of plurality, inasmuch as it can include both law and right—the experience of the artist as one who stands above the work and is at the same time in it, contemplating it and operating in it—the experience of necessity and play, of conflict and harmony, inasmuch as they must be coupled for the production of the work of art." ("The Birth of Philosophy in the Epoch of Greek Tragedy.")

The notion of play, fundamental for Nietzsche, implies successive constructions and deconstructions of worlds, without having to take recourse to any negative force. It allows Nietzsche to set up an economy of the death drive, akin to the way Freud sets up the hypothesis. Freud, when trying to prove the necessity of some principle which would lie beyond the pleasure principle, takes as his first example the child's none-too-innocent game. But the text goes on to reject this example, judging it hardly probing enough to justify anything beyond the pleasure principle. See *Beyond the Pleasure Principle*, Standard Edition, XVIII: 1–64

32. *Das Philosophenbuch*, III: 194. This "other conduit" can be compared to the Freudian metaphor of sublimation, which is also one of detour.

33. Ibid. For the metaphoric writing of dreams and art as a return to the archaic, cf. *Human, All Too Human*, II: 194: "*The dream*. Our dreams, when they exceptionally happen to be complete and perfect (usually the dream is a botched work) are symbolic sequences of scenes and images equivalent to the narrative language of poetry: they transcribe our experiences, our hopes, and the circumstances of our lives with such insistence and poetic precision, that the following morning we are always astonished at ourselves when we recall our dreams. In our dreams we consume too much artistic material, and this is why we have so little left during the day."

Cf. also "*The Logic of Dreams*. . . . The old aspect of humanity lives on in us in our dreams, for it is the basis upon which higher reason developed, and is still developing, in every human: the dream restores us to distant states of human culture and gives us a means by which to understand them better. Dream thought is so easy for us now because, during mankind's immense periods of development, we have been so well drilled in just this form of fantastic and cheap explanation from the first, best idea. In this way dreaming is recuperation for a brain which must satisfy by day the stricter demands made on thought by higher culture." See *Human, All Too Human*, trans. M. Faber and S. Lehmann (Lincoln, Nebraska: University of Nebraska Press, 1985), par. 13:

Cf. also *Untimely Meditations*, IV, 4, and *Beyond Good and Evil*, 193. Each of these conceptions, of the dream, of art, and of the relation between them, is very close to that of Freud. Freud himself in the *Interpretation of Dreams* (VII, B, "Regression"), quotes Nietzsche when he wants to show that dream analysis can lead us to knowledge of an archaic heritage, innate to everyone. Cf. Standard Edition, V: 549.

34. Cf. *The Gay Science*, 54: "I suddenly wake up in the midst of this dream, but only to the consciousness that I am dreaming and that I must go on dreaming lest I perish. . . . Appearance is for me that which lives and is effective and goes so far in its self-mockery that it makes me feel that this is appearance and will-o'-the-wisp and a dance of spirits and nothing more—that among all these dreamers, I, too, who "know," am dancing my dance; that the knower is a means for prolonging the earthly dance and thus belongs to the masters of ceremony of existence; and that the sublime consistency and interrelatedness of all knowledge perhaps is and will be the highest means to *preserve* the universality of dreaming and the mutual comprehension of all dreamers and thus also the *continuation of the dream*."

35. *Twilight of the Idols*, "Reason in Philosophy," 2. Cf. also *Beyond Good and Evil*, 34.

36. For Spinoza, also, the fictions forged by knowledge of the first kind are "supplements" added on to Nature by the demented. Nature, as complete and infinite totality, lacks nothing, but man's delirium, due to his truncated, mutilated, and lacunary knowledge, makes Nature delirious too: here again man projects his own impotence. Nature then appears as a blind force, capable on occasion of opposing divine law, and the miracle would then be a special intervention by God in the interests of man, authority within an authority, to complete a natural deficiency. The ignoramus, therefore, introduces a fictive opposition between nature and God, who becomes a transcendental power, a stopgap for human lacunae. Cf. in particular chapter VI of the *Tractatus Theologico-Politicus*, where Spinoza shows that natural causes are never *lacking*, but one believes in miracles because one *omits*, either through volition or ignorance, certain circumstances: "and if anything is there [in the scriptures] set down which can be proved in set terms to contravene the order of nature, or not to be deducible therefrom, we must believe it to be foisted into the sacred writings by irreligious hands." (trans. Vloten and Lahd, *Opere*, Nijhoff, 1882, I: 454).

For Nietzsche, as for Spinoza, the fiction implies that one separates Nature from its own powers, and that one falsifies the nature of desire.

37. *The Genealogy of Morals,* III, 28. Cf. also *The Will to Power* (ed. Kaufmann), par. 574: "Senselessness of all metaphysics as the derivation of the conditioned from the unconditioned. It is of the nature of thinking that it thinks of and invents the unconditioned as an adjunct to the conditioned; just as it thought of and invented the "ego" as an adjunct to the multiplicity of its processes; it measures the world according to magnitudes posited by itself—such fundamental fictions as "the unconditional," "ends and means," "things," "substances," "logical laws," "numbers," and "forms."

38. Cf. *Human, All Too Human,* II, 302: "So-called 'real reality.' " "The poet, when he describes the different kinds of craft . . . pretends to know these things in depth, and to be *wise* about them: even better, if he goes on to explain human actions and destinies, he behaves as if the entire web of the world had been spun and unfolded in his presence; in this sense he is an impostor. And an impostor who deceives a gathering of ignorami, wherein lies precisely the reason for his success; these people respond to him with a eulogy of his genuine and profound knowledge and induce him generally to imagine that he knows things just as well as the expert, the one who does them, indeed as well as the great spider of the worlds himself. So the impostor ends up being sincere and believing in his own veracity. Sensitive people even tell him to his face that he possesses the supreme truth and veracity; this is in fact because they are weary of reality, and they welcome the dream of the poet as a release, a night beneficial to the head and to the heart. What this dream shows them then seems of greater value because they experience, as we have said, a greater benefit: and men have always believed that the most precious appearances were the truest, the most real."

Cf. also *Das Philosophenbuch,* III: 174 and 175, and *The Gay Science,* 59, 57: "That mountain there! That cloud there! What is 'real' in that? Subtract the phantasm and every human *contribution* from it, my positive friends! . . . There is no 'reality' for us—not for you either, my positive friends!"

39. Quoted in *Das Philosophenbuch,* III: 194.

40. *The Gay Science* also has an air of celebration following upon a long period of enslavement: "gay science, that signifies the saturnalia of a spirit who has patiently resisted a terrible, long pressure, patiently, coldly, severely, without submitting, but also without hope, and who is now all at once attacked by hope, the hope for health and the intoxication of convalescence. . . . This whole book is nothing but a festival after long privation and powerlessness." (Preface to the Second Edition of *The Gay Science.*)

41. Aristotle said to speak to say nothing was to be similar to a plant. Cf. *Metaphysics,* 1006–1010.

42. Cf. Ovid, *Metamorphoses,* Book II, chap. 17.

43. Cf. Herodotus, *Inquiries,* Book I, par. 60.

44. *Das Philosophenbuch*, III: 196, 198.

45. Ibid., p. 198.

46. Ibid. Nietzsche's texts on the Stoics are numerous. Apart from the admirable paragraph 9 of *Beyond Good and Evil*, a genuine chef-d'oeuvre of deconstruction where all the Stoic themes are taken up to be reevaluated and genealogically interpreted, we should quote *The Will to Power:* "I believe that Stoicism has been misjudged. The essence of this temperament (and this is what it was before philosophy monopolized it) is a certain attitude towards pain and representations of displeasure; a certain *weightiness*, a certain *force of pressure*, a certain inertia intensified to the extreme in order to attenuate pain; the *rigidity* and the *coldness* serve as artifices, as anesthetics. Principal end of the Stoical education: to destroy *facile emotionality*, to limit more and more the number of objects worthy of our *emotion;* to consider as despicable and of little value most of the things which move us; hate and hostility against emotion, even against passion as though this were a disease or something shameful; to focus on all the ugly or painful manifestations of passion. In sum, *petrification* as a remedy for pain; henceforth to award this statue all the high attributes of the divine and of virtue. What does it matter if one kisses a statue in winter, when one has become insensate from the cold? What does it matter if one statue kisses another statue? When the Stoic attains the state he aspires to (usually he *brings it along with him*, and this is the reason he chooses this philosophy) this state has the *compressive force of a bandage* which induces insensitivity. This way of thinking repulses me greatly; it underestimates the value of *pain* (which is as useful and favorable as air), the value of *emotion* and of *passion*, and in the end one has to say: everything which happens is good, I wish for nothing else; *we no longer seek a remedy for any pain* because we have killed all sensibility to pain. This is expressed in the form of a religion, as the total acceptance of all divine acts (for example in Epictetus)."

Cf. also *Beyond Good and Evil*, 211, 227, 188, 44, 21, 198; *The Genealogy of Morals*, II; *The Gay Science*, 109, 306, 359.

6

Ecce Homo or the Written Body

Rodolphe Gasché

I

Of the body—the body proper—we can speak only improperly.[1] So it will not only be necessary to talk about it in metaphors, but also to develop the discourse *of* the body, by a process of substitution, as a chain of figures in which the figure of the body itself will represent only one figure amongst others. Wishing to speak of the body, we can therefore only speak of quite other things, to the point where we might ask ourselves if the body does not consist precisely in those other things, in that grouping of initially heterogeneous elements. In which case the body would be dependent on a certain confusion, because it is always more or less than a body properly speaking.

This is what emerges from a text such as Nietzsche's *Ecce Homo,* an autobiographical text (but one whose deviation from the genre should be noted), a text which also functions as a self-constituting corpus, thus as a text in which the constitution of a body [*corps*] is gradually worked out, of Nietzsche's body, or more precisely of a body in which Nietzsche's name ('Nietzsche') forms an essential trait in as much as it is—momentarily—the unitary trait, if not the unifying trait, or *trait d'union* ("hyphen"). In *Ecce Homo,* indeed, the body, or rather one body, becomes readable through a chain of metaphors which are seemingly as foreign one to another as, for instance, the book entitled *Daybreak,* a sea animal, the sun, the self or the name of Nietzsche. How can a body, a unified body, be constituted from the starting point of these metaphors, such diverse metaphors? If each metaphor represents an image of the body, it is, at the same time, only one of its traits, so that assembling these traits constitutes the body in question. It is in fact the Aristotelian question: what makes man "one" (*hen*)?—a unity on which the very name of man is founded (the denomination: man),[2] a question which should be introduced here in order to examine the principle which justifies the term 'body' for the set of metaphors in question. Certainly they are not the result of that contradiction of which Bachelard says in *The Psychoanalysis of Fire* that it is through contradiction "that we most easily achieve originality." He goes on to say "When it is directed towards objective knowledge, this need for originality *over-estimates* the importance of the phenomenon, *materializes* slight differences, ascribes *causes* to accidents, just in the same way in which the novelist imagines a hero endowed with an unlikely number of special qualities and portrays a willful character through a series of inconsistent actions."[3]

But although these metaphors, in Nietzsche, are not the result of contradiction, it remains that there are clear pretensions to originality, and that these are embodied in the metaphoric chain of which we are speaking. Now, since the self of the signatory who seems to unify, to gather together the chain of metaphors (for a moment, at least), is taken up and reabsorbed by the chain itself, the question of the unifying principle is raised over and over again. The impossibility of enclosing or of closing up the question once and for all represents perhaps the major reason why we cannot talk properly about the body proper. If the organizing principle of the metaphors for the body is abolished (or is represented) in the very chain which it is supposed to totalize, then the need to keep going back to a new unifying trait opens up the discourse *of* the body to the infinite importation of metaphors which are always foreign, always improper. The impossibility of preventing the unifying trait from tumbling into the series which is to be unified bears witness to disequilibrium as an essential mark of the body, and whose first effect is its impropriety. This amounts to saying that the body does not properly belong to anyone.

The body is thus characterized by this tendency to disintegrate into heterogeneous images which, when assembled coherently, formed for a moment a unified representation. The improper side of the body, its impropriety, also entails a temporal aspect peculiar to the body, that is to say its nature as event, its "momentaneity." The body only exists for the duration of an instant—before it is again split up into its singular representations. This will have at least two consequences for Nietzsche: on the one hand the will to repetition of the divine moment in which a body was born (which thus refers back to the intimate relationship between the body and the Eternal Recurrence); on the other hand the fixing of the moment, and of property, at the risk of seeing them turned to stone as memories, or again, as we shall see, as a handful of diamonds. In this way the body, which only really exists *in statu nascendi*, discovers the side of itself which is death.

From then on, *more than one* register will govern the thinking of the body.

Let us begin then by unfolding the metaphoric chain in which, as we were just claiming, the body is caught. Emphasizing in *Ecce Homo* the affirmative character of his book *Daybreak*, Nietzsche writes as follows:

> The whole book contains no negative word, no attack, no spite—it lies in the sun, round, happy, like some sea animal basking among rocks.
>
> Ultimately, I myself was this sea animal: almost every sentence in this book was first thought, *caught* among that jumble of rocks near Genoa where I was alone and still had secrets with the sea. Even now, whenever I accidentally touch this book, almost every sentence turns for me into a net [*wird mir . . . fast jeder Satz zum Zipfel*] that again brings up from the depths something incomparable: its entire skin trembles with tender thrills of memory. The art that distinguishes it is not inconsiderable when it comes to fixing to some extent things that easily flit by, noiselessly—moments I call divine lizards—but not with the cruelty of that young Greek god who simply speared the poor little lizard, though, to be sure, with something pointed—a pen. (p. 290)[4]

Without claiming to exhaust this passage, let us stress a few points: these three things, the book (*Daybreak*), the sea animal, and Nietzsche, may be substituted one for the other. What may be said of one is equally true of the others. The same thing is to be found under the skin of the book as in the bodies of the sea animal and of Nietzsche. The book, in fact, contains sentences like "ends" or "tails" (*Zipfel*) which allow you to bring some memory up from the depths. The book thus seems like a collection of ends or tails. Now this is equally true of the body of the sea animal and of Nietzsche himself basking among the rocks, sharing secrets with the sea. Nietzsche tells us that this book is distinguished by its art of fixing things that easily flit by, that is the moments, the instants which he calls "divine lizards." But lizards cannot be caught. You can barely get hold of them, they escape almost immediately, leaving you with their tails in your hand. The sea animal and the book, like Nietzsche's body, are thus nothing more than a set of broken tails, of lost tails, of dead tails. Like that other body which is largely made up of a single tangle of snakes, the medusa (a jellyfish). In this way the lizards represent "divine moments" flitting by noiselessly; after they have gone all that remains is an end, a tail left in your hand, which allows you to recreate them in memory. In order to fix them, to stop them, to catch hold of them, of their moment of presence, you must know how to use an instrument which, like the blade of a knife, cuts the vanishing moment from its full presence leaving only, to use a term from Rousseau, "commemorative signs."[5] Of course, the instrument is not the spear of that young Greek god, in whom we recognize the Apollo Sauroktoros of Praxiteles,[6] but an instrument no less steely, that is the point of a pen. The bodies of the book, the sea animal, and Nietzsche are thus constituted by work, by an operation of the pen which consists in fixing divine moments, of gathering together under a quivering skin a set of sentences, or tails, or phalluses, which are only ever commemorative signs of the lost actuality of that presence of a whole body. Nevertheless, in spite of, or rather because of, the cut-off, dead, and petrified nature of these instants which make up the body, this is a body which "lies in the sun, round, happy, like some sea animal basking among rocks." Paradoxically, it is that operation of the pen, fixing a set of moments by depriving them of their full momentariness which results in the body as such: a happy pile of dead moments. And what was said of each individual sentence, that it is presented as a lizard's cut-off tail, is valid for the book, for the corpus of aphorisms, for the whole body. For Nietzsche's body itself is no more than a petrified divine instant, formed, like the book, of phrases carved in granite. It is itself no more than the product of the action of a steely point which fixes that body in its momentary nature. So it is not surprising that the body only appears as one metaphor among others, caught in the chain *book, sea animal, sun*, etc. The body, like the book, is the effect of the pen: it is a fixed moment. But what does fixed mean? To what extent is fixing a property of the body? Where it appears as petrification, does it merge with the very momentariness of the body? This is what we must try to elucidate by moving to another level.

Speaking of *Human, All Too Human*, Nietzsche writes: "*Human, All Too Human* is the monument of a crisis" (p. 283). And again: "*Human, All Too Human*, this monument (*Denkmal*) of rigorous self-discipline with which I put a sudden end to all my infections . . ." (p. 288).

A monument then; insofar as *Human, All Too Human* is an event marking a close, an end. Now, a sudden beginning may equally give rise to monuments. This is the case with *Zarathustra*, with that monument which, Nietzsche tells us, occupies a place apart among his works ("Among my writings my *Zarathustra* stands to my mind by itself," p. 219). *Zarathustra*, indeed, put apart in this way from the rest of Nietzsche's works, is the monument erected in honor of that divine moment when Nietzsche was first struck by the idea of the Eternal Recurrence. The place where the revelation occurred was, according to Nietzsche, "a powerful pyramidal rock not far from Surlei" (p. 295). This rock itself represents the idea of the Eternal Recurrence inasmuch as, by its resistance to the elements, to the work of time, and to decomposition, it recurs ceaselessly as a new instant, as an original beginning. So the idea of recurrence appeared to Nietzsche like a petrified rock, the Eternal Recurrence being, in addition, nothing more than a pyramidal block resisting time. This contrasts, however, with what Nietzsche reports in *Ecce Homo* concerning the months preceding the encounter with the rock at Surlei:

> If I reckon back a few months from this day, I find as an omen a sudden and profoundly decisive change in my taste, especially in music. Perhaps the whole of *Zarathustra* may be reckoned as music; certainly a rebirth of the art of *hearing* was among its preconditions. (p. 295)

So a radical change in his appreciation of music precedes the event at Surlei, and also the erecting of *Zarathustra* as a monument. The rock, the pyramidal block in itself does not utter a sound; it is voiceless. So if the whole of *Zarathustra* may be reckoned as music, it is something like a symphony of rocks (silent in themselves), a symphony which would make the stones dance as petrified divine moments. Notwithstanding the fact that stone is already an affirmation against time (as decadence), already a petrified formula for the affirmation of that instance in which the temporality proper to the Eternal Recurrence erupted into the temporal continuum, it must still be reconstructed into a symphony which, once again, liberates the incidental idea of the Eternal Recurrence from its stony straitjacket. The music in question is pyramidal music, for it is important that the petrified product of the incidental moment is not just any rock, but a shaped block, like the pyramidal block at Surlei. This is perhaps even clearer in the following passages from *Ecce Homo* which refer to the *Gay Science:*

> What "highest hope" means here—who could have any doubt about that when he sees the diamond beauty of the first words of *Zarathustra* flashing at the end of the fourth book? (p. 293)

And, in "Why I am so Wise," explicitly with regard to *Zarathustra:* "Those who have eyes for colors will compare it to a diamond . . ." (p. 234). A diamond, the hardest of stones and literally invincible, is a cut stone. Nietzsche represents Zarathustra, or the idea of the Eternal Recurrence which strikes him at Surlei, as durable stone, finely cut, resistant to the vicissitudes of time. The diamond which is *Zarathustra* will repeat for all eternity what happened to Nietzsche at the site of that other indestructible stone, the pyramidal block not far from Surlei. Petrified signs of divine moments.

Further support for this interpretation comes from what Nietzsche says about the nature of his words, in particular at the end of the third book of the *Gay Science*. It is here that the relationship between the originary moment and the petrification of that moment becomes clear: "or when at the end of the third book he reads the granite words in which a destiny finds for the first time a formula for itself, *for all time??*" (p. 293). Granite words then, phrases formed out of hard crystalline material corresponding to the formulation of a destiny which is articulated for the first time *and* for all eternity! The event, the "incidental" moment, is so fleeting that it must be hewn to suit its divine nature in durable material in order to hold it, to fix it. It is only in this way that the instant will appear as that which resists the time of decadence. The instant when continuous time is suddenly, sharply broken by a time foreign to that temporality, must be slipped into a durable atemporal material so that the instant may repeat itself, becoming eternal outside time as the recurrence of that divine moment.[7] That which appears in *Ecce Homo* as a topography is the philosophical landscape, marked by the eruption of the eternal, of the untimely (*Un-Zeit*), into historical time; as a landscape of monuments it is a landscape of "fragments of the future."

It is clear that the petrified moment also disguises the specific nature of the moment, which is the "incision" of a divine time into continuous time. The moment is indeed caught in stone, and petrifaction cannot be the true destiny of the moment. In comparison with the essence of the divine moment, the stone in which that moment is embodied is no more than, as Nietzsche says, the "ugliest stone" (p. 309). So it will need a divine artist, a sun god, Apollo in fact, the sculptor god, to intervene and cut the stone to match the divine nature of that which it contains. To cite aphorism 541 of *Daybreak:*

> *How one ought to turn to stone*—slowly, slowly to become hard like a precious stone—and at last to lie there, silent and a joy to eternity.

Otherwise it would be necessary to release the divine moment from the stony straitjacket in which it is imprisoned. This is what Zarathustra says: "O men, in the stone an image is sleeping, the image of images! Alas, that it has to sleep in the hardest, ugliest stone! *Now my hammer rages cruelly against its prison*" (p. 309). The hammer strives to set free that image of images, the divine moment, from its prison, first by shaping the stone to match that which it disguises, second by attempting to extricate the moment from the stone itself, so that the latter may recover its original nature. By wielding this hammer Nietzsche succeeded, at least once, in making the stone dance. Relating in *Ecce Homo* how he played with the instrument "man," Nietzsche writes as follows:

> How often have I been told by the "instruments" themselves that they had never heard themselves *like that*—most beautifully perhaps by Heinrich von Stein,[8] who died so unpardonably young. Once, after he had courteously requested permission, he appeared for three days in Sils Maria, explaining to everybody that he had *not* come to see the Engadine. This excellent human being, who had walked into the Wagnerian morass with all the impetuous simplicity of a Prussian Junker . . . acted during these three days like one transformed by a tempest of freedom, like one who had suddenly been lifted to his own height and acquired wings. (p. 227)

So the body represents a petrified divine instant, fixed by a quill or cut in stone by the artist's instrument. The body merges with the divine moment; it is but the other side of it. In Nietzsche, it is the type, the *Typus*, which corresponds to a life, to a *fatum*, to a body which, as the Eternal Recurrence cuts into it, are transmuted into stone so that they might last beyond the vicissitudes of temporal decadence. Image, image of images, model, etc., the Greek *typos* comes from the term *typtein*, which means, among other things, to cut. The type is then indeed the cut stone,[9] a stone which encloses the image of images and whose form matches that image: a precious stone, then. So *Ecce Homo* is nothing other than the attempt to constitute a body for oneself, by writing oneself in granite words, by fixing the divine instants of a life, sparkling, like precious stones; it is nothing other than the effort to erect oneself as a monument by fixing oneself with the steely point of a pen. For Nietzsche himself, Nietzsche as body, is nothing other than an event, an instant in which an untimeliness outside time erupted into the time of decadence, and in which, in order to last, it had to turn to stone. This applies equally to *Ecco Homo* in which Nietzsche's written body will form an instant, a supplementary monument in that topography which makes up the book and in which is inscribed the divine moment when the idea of the Eternal Recurrence erupted in Nietzsche's body. And so, in the last analysis, Nietzsche, his body, will have been no more and no less than an articulation of that idea which he conceived—the Eternal Recurrence itself.

II

In order to think the type-body, the cut or written body, the printed body, we shall turn our attention to another metaphorical network in *Ecce Homo*. Let us begin, for example, by taking a look at what Nietzsche says to us when he is at his lowest ebb physically, in the declining years of his life. That moment coincides with a general exhaustion (*Gesamterschöpfung*) which explains the deterioration of all his organs. That exhaustion, in fact, should be understood as a weakening of the self as totality or whole. The general exhaustion is the sign of a loss of self as totality. Now, this morbid state, one of extreme weakness, a state which also corresponds to an aberration of the instincts, is, according to Nietzsche, a preparation for a refining of the organs, inasmuch as the illness is at once the culmination of decadence and an interruption of that decadence. It is then that Nietzsche acquires "that filigree art," that skill in *grasping* both properly and figuratively, that touch for *nuances*, which, in the end, will permit him to take himself in hand and make himself healthy again. "I took myself in hand, I made myself healthy again: the condition for this—every psychologist would admit that—is *that one be healthy at bottom* [daβ man im Grunde gesund ist]" (p. 224). With those fingers and that filigree art Nietzsche will reassemble the exhausted organs, organizing them into a new totality which corresponds to being healthy at bottom, in other words to what Nietzsche calls "the nethermost self" (*das unterste Selbst*), and which coincides (although this cannot be demonstrated here) with the name, or the type, of Zarathustra.

But that reorganization, that reassembling of the parts of the body, merges with an arithmetical operation. So we shall turn our attention briefly to that mathematical level. Nietzsche in fact *calculates* his "self", that on which the totality of his body is founded. From the outset, Nietzsche posits himself as being a totality *at bottom*, that is to say, at bottom a totality; and taking away the fact that he is a decadent, he gets to the opposite of decadence, that is to say, health. "Apart from the fact [*Abgerechnet*] that I am a decadent, I am also the opposite" (p. 224). So it is already no longer Nietzsche's totality which suffers from a general exhaustion, for by means of this little operation of subtraction, Nietzsche has already got himself back in hand. He writes: "As *summa summarum* ["overall"] I was basically healthy" (p. 224). This is understandable, inasmuch as *summa summarum* means *apart* from decadence, but also and equally means *despite* decadence—in that health, at bottom, allows making use of decadence, transforming it into a means for health.

Let us briefly outline the calculation of the *summa summarum*. The first condition of the reconstitution of its totality is complete isolation. In complete independence the subject is able to guess what is good for him, *sich zu erraten*, and to thrive, *wohl zu geraten*. This thriving, indeed, this *Wohlgeratenheit*, becomes the necessary condition for performing the calculation in question. Nietzsche tells us about the person who is thriving:

> He has a taste only for what is good for him, his pleasure, his delight cease where the measure of what is good for him is transgressed. He guesses what remedies avail against what is harmful; he exploits bad accidents to his advantage; that which does not kill him makes him stronger. Instinctively, he collects from everything he sees, hears, lives through, *his* sum [*seine Summe*]: he is a principle of selection, he discards much. (p. 224)

Now a sum (*une somme*), the arithmetical product of an addition, is also (in French) the title of certain books which make a general summary of the various parts of an area of knowledge. So the body as sum(mary) is also a book which constitutes this abridged body. Thus the book-body belongs to what Nietzsche elaborates under the heading of a language of signs (a semiotics). However, for the moment let us simply keep in mind that the sum of the body is the result of a selection, of an elimination (subtraction) of many things. The only things selected to go into the sum(ma) are of the sort that can be summarized in one's own sum. This only occurs on condition of including in the sum(ma) only things which are not marked "personal."

> He is always in his own company, whether he associated with books, human beings, or landscapes: he honors by *choosing*, by *admitting*, by *trusting*. (pp. 224-5)

The sum of the body is completed with a set of quite heterogeneous elements. The body is everything at once: books, men, landscapes, but homogenized by the intermediary of the index *me* or *mine*. These pronouns or possessive adjectives make a dividing line between a good and a bad *proximity* to things. For inasmuch as the calculation of his own sum is, according to Nietzsche, the same as a spiritual gestation, "any kind of stimulus from the outside has too violent an effect and strikes to deep." In order to keep to one side everything which could turn us aside from our task, from our giving birth to ourselves as our own type, Nietzsche appeals to Russian fatalism, which consists in slowing down all our reactions as much as possible, to the point of not reacting at all. This is how we withdraw from the continuum of time: slowly hardening until we become a precious stone, until we give birth to our body as something completely *mine* which belongs to no one, to be exact not even to me, which is the body of our most buried *self*—such as, for instance, Zarathustra. But in the enumeration of the elements which are part of the sum(ma) of the body, we must also gather in what seems initially to belong rather to the surroundings favorable for becoming oneself, that is to say, the choice of climate, diet, and recreation. Now, with regard to diet, for example, it soon becomes clear that it can be reckoned healthy when the food is easy to digest, when it is not foreign to *me*, when on that account, it can be classified as *mine*. One should note here that food which is mine can be digested quickly so that the body, the body of the *self*, proves, in Nietzsche, to be a metabolism which recycles itself at great speed. This body is not constituted by assimilating what is *mine* in order to store it up; but in such a way that, by the rapid rejection of what has been incorporated, it is no more than a movement of assimilation *and* expulsion. Nothing more. Only on that condition will it be granted "mobile feet." The relationship between elements classified as *mine* and the body as a rapid metabolism becomes clear during the discussion, in *Ecce Homo*, of the question of favorable place and climate.

> The influence of climate on our *metabolism*, its retardation, its acceleration, goes so far that a mistaken choice of place and climate can not only estrange a man from his task but can actually keep it from him: he never gets to see it. (p. 240)

It also follows that this body, characterized by its need for a rapid metabolism, is not sedentary, but moves about at an accelerated tempo in an appropriate topography. Thus:

> *Sit* as little as possible; give no credence to any thought that was not born outdoors while one moved about freely—in

> which the muscles are not celebrating a feast, too. All prejudices come from the intestines. The sedentary life—as I have said once before—is the real sin against the holy spirit. (p. 239–40)

But before suggesting that these various aspects (choice of food, place and climate) are not simply the conditions of possibility of a body with a rapid metabolism, nor simply the determining factors of the *tempo* of the metabolism, but that they are also metaphors serving to describe, by means of certain traits which are peculiar to each of the various instances, the body (and, to be more exact, the spirit) itself, we shall pause for a moment on another metaphor, that of the body as *instrument*.

> Now that the effects of climate and weather are familiar to me from long experience and I take readings from myself as from a very subtle and reliable instrument . . . I reflect with horror on the *dismal* fact that my life, except for the last ten years, the years when my life was in peril, was spent entirely in the wrong places that were nothing short of forbidden to me. (p. 241)

The body is played, like an instrument, by the effects of climate, weather and place: they determine its *tempo*. That instrument is, however, also a book asking to be read. That is what allows us to go on to what Nietzsche says about his choice of amusements.

> In my case, every kind of reading belongs among my recreations—hence among the things that liberate me from myself, that allow me to walk about in strange sciences and souls—that I no longer take seriously. (p. 242)

Why are books a form of recreation for Nietzsche, why does he not take them seriously? Because Nietzsche is himself his own book, because his writing is the writing of his body. The first reader of the book-body, of the type-body, Nietzsche cannot take an interest except in books which he already considers *his*.

> Otherwise I almost always seek refuge with the same books—actually, a small number—books *proved to me*. (p. 243)

These books which are already proved to him are books *always already* signed by Nietzsche—more precisely, the names of the authors are all pseudonyms for Nietzsche. As much by what they demonstrate as by the names of their authors, these books are already a part of the text of the written body. These books do not slow down the accelerated metabolism of the written body. On the contrary, this body will easily assimilate and dispose of them, retaining the one fact that the books are not foreign to it but are always already itself.

So to calculate his sum also means, to have space for everything in his body. "Nothing in existence may be subtracted, nothing is dispensable" (p. 272). But everything which enters this body must be marked with the index *mine*. Even the contradictory, the opposite will enter into the composition of this body provided that they are *my opposites, my contradictions*. So this writing-body, this book-body, or type-body bears witness to a dionysiac affirmation insofar as it is the field where opposing forces do battle. Or again, in other words, it is a work of art. We suggested that climate and place, diet, etc., are not only the conditions of the body's elaboration, but that they are equally a part of it. They are a part of it inasmuch as they are metaphors. Take for instance the passage in *Zarathustra* which is cited at the end of the chapter "Why I am so Wise": "Gone is the hesitant gloom of my spring! Gone the snowflakes of my malice in June. Summer have I become entirely, and summer noon . . . " (p. 234). These seasons are in fact metaphors for seasons. They are seasons which have become *mine* (and are, for that reason, marked with a possessive adjective or pronoun). It is they that make up, one might say, the matter of the body, insofar as this body—a rapid metabolism—stores them only in order to expend them, borrowing from them that movement which, as metaphor for the changing seasons, becomes the circulation of metaphors of (in) the body. The writing-body, then, is a metaphorical metabolism, the metaphorical set of transformations which take place within an organism *and* the set of metaphorical transformations which constitute a body.

III

One cannot help noticing that Nietzsche describes himself as distinguished by traits (*Züge*), as being *ausgezeichnet*, as being remarkably *marked*. In "Why I am so Wise" Nietzsche enumerates some of his traits. This is the last of them:

> May I still venture to sketch one final trait of my nature that causes me no little difficulty in my contacts with other men?

> My instinct for cleanliness is characterized by a perfectly uncanny sensitivity. (p. 233)

This final trait, which concerns cleanliness (*propreté*), is a trait which is Nietzsche's very own (*propre*). The cleanliness in question further implies that the traits which distinguish Nietzsche's body are proper traits, and that this is quite different from other men's bodies which are constituted by improper traits (traits both improper and unsuitable). One could even say that the difference between Nietzsche's body and that of his contemporaries is that Nietzsche possesses a body made up of proper traits or a body of signs, as we shall see. This body excludes any pathological trait:

> There is no pathological trait in me; even in periods of severe sickness I never became pathological; in vain would one seek for a trait of fanaticism in my character. (p. 257)

In the same way he excludes all "traces of struggle," " any trace of tension" (p. 258), etc. That leads us, in accordance moreover with the sign of propriety, to make a distinction between two kinds of traits: "signs of healthy instincts" (*Zeichen gesunder Instinkte*) on the one hand and, on the other, those of decadent instincts. The healthy instincts which characterize Nietzsche testify that his body has a different origin. Difference is inscribed in a comparison with men honored as the *first*, whom Nietzsche considers as non-men: "When I now compare myself with the men who have so far been honored as the *first*, the difference is palpable" (pp. 256–7). A privilege, a *Vorrecht* is associated with this other origin of Nietzsche's body, the privilege of having the supreme finesse which is necessary in order to discern all the indications of healthy instincts. Nietzsche is distinguished then by signs, by indices of healthy instincts: their traits characterize him as a body of signs (*ausgezeichnet*). In this capacity he possesses "a subtler sense of smell . . . than any other human being before me" for the signs of the ascent and decline of instincts. But what is the relation in fact between a body of signs and the subtle sense in question? Nietzsche writes as follows:

> My instinct for cleanliness is characterized by a perfectly uncanny sensitivity so that the proximity or—what am I saying?—the inmost parts, the "entrails" of every soul are physiologically perceived by me—smelled. This sensitivity furnishes me with psychological antennae with which I feel and get ahold of every secret: the abundant *hidden* dirt at the bot-

> tom of many a character—perhaps the result of bad blood, but glossed over by education—enters my consciousness almost at the first contact. If my observation has not deceived me, such characters who offend my sense of cleanliness also sense from their side the reserve of my disgust—and this does not make them smell any better. (p. 233)

One can already recognise here a first difference between the two systems of signs: the healthy signs are those of a clean (*propre*) and transparent body, while the signs of bad instincts bear witness to the abundant dirt hidden at the bottom of these bodies. That dirt seems to stand in opposition to the nature of the sign itself; in that it is an obstacle to the transparent clarity, the weightlessness, of the sign, that body will not yet have become a body of signs, in fact, a body at all. Or, again, as long as there is still something at the bottom (dirt, in that it is hidden), the body will not be a true body of signs. The bottom is the result of a process of sedimentation, of things which have not yet become light and transparent. Nietzsche, for his part, lays claim to a perfect transparency, and his body moves in a limpid, diaphanous element:

> As has always been my wont—extreme cleanliness in relation to me is the presupposition of my existence; I perish under unclean conditions—I constantly swim and bathe and splash, as it were, in water—in some perfectly transparent and resplendent element. (p. 233)

This holds equally true for mountain air: air, like water, is a clear element in which a body of signs can move about. Here there is no longer occasion to speak about a sedimented bottom; everything is transparency and weightlessness.

In addition to this subtle sense for dirt-encrusted depths, he has a sense for healthy instincts. This second sense is associated with an operation of distinction or respect, or *Auszeichnung:*

> To this day I still have the same affability for everyone; I even treat with special respect [*ich bin selbst voller Auszeichnung*] those who are lowliest: in all of this there is not one grain of arrogance or secret contempt. If I despise a man, he *guesses* that I despise him: by my mere existence I outrage everything that has bad blood in its veins. (p. 258)

It remains to analyze the interrelationships between these healthy signs, indeed to draw the map of the signed body. In view of our development concerning the body's gathering in of all around it, we can now have an idea of the contradictory aspect of the traits which make up its texture. They are opposed one to another. The opposing traits are organized on a hierarchical basis. Nietzsche, in a passage which one would need a separate paper to elucidate, suggests that "the organizing 'idea' that is destined to rule . . . one by one, trains all *subservient* capacities before giving any hint of the dominant task, 'goal,' 'aim,' or 'meaning' " (p. 254). First of all let us note the relationship between the trait and the whole, as a subservient trait in the service of the whole. This trait is developed in a certain order, and in such a way as to engender the whole. Here already one notices a certain order of rank among the traits. But this comes out more clearly in what follows:

> For the task of *revaluation of all values* more capacities may have been needed than have ever dwelt together in a single individual—above all, even contrary capacities that had to be kept from disturbing, destroying one another. An order of rank among these capacities; distance; the art of separating without setting against one another; to mix nothing, to "reconcile" nothing; a tremendous variety that is nevertheless the opposite of chaos—this was the precondition, the long, secret work and artistry of my instinct.

This order of rank among opposite terms keeps them at a distance one from another. Each new trait which becomes part of the composition of the body of signs contributes to spacing that body out (and making it lighter). Distance, as the condition of possibility of the hierarchy, prevents the body from returning to chaos. Spacing, the preventing of chaos in this body of signs, is all the more urgent in that it takes a vast sum of traits to give form to the *type* corresponding to the revaluation of values. By inscribing a set of contradictory traits in the body, organizing them in such a way that they form a new hierarchy which literally excludes nothing, the type-body already represents on the level of the body a first re-evaluation of values. The incorporation of so many traits within the type-body in fact transgresses the model of the individual hitherto prevailing, in such a way that the written body is a transgression of the volume of what it is customary to call a subject. Spacing by distance between the traits of the writing-body, of the type-body, paradoxically characterizes this body as plenitude (*Überfülle*).

There is a certain category of elements of the signed body which we have not yet mentioned. If Nietzsche, in *Ecce Homo*, can write that "Plato employed Socrates as a sign language (*Semiotik*) for Plato," we might suspect that names can function as traits, as signs *par excellence* for the written body. Before establishing this proposition, let us first analyze the way in which Nietzsche, in *Ecce Homo*, deals with names in general; let us read the following passage:

> Philosophy, as I have so far understood and lived it, means living voluntarily among ice and high mountains—seeking out everything strange and questionable in existence, everything so far placed under a ban by morality. Long experience, acquired in the course of such wanderings *in what is forbidden*, taught me to regard the causes that so far have prompted moralizing and idealizing in a very different light from what may seem desirable: the *hidden* history of the philosophers, the psychology of the great names, came to light for me. (p. 218)

Philosophy, for Nietzsche, is bound up with the names of philosophers; philosophy, for Nietzsche, is a history of names. He can be observed to be more concerned with philosophers, with their names (their types), than with their teaching.[10] For Nietzsche, philosophers' names already contain in some way their entire philosophy. These names evince a force, a power which is not to be underestimated. One name can repress another, one name can hide another, so that Nietzsche has to take more than one name into his protection, more than one name being threatened by a greater one: "My artist's taste vindicates the names of Molière, Corneille, and Racine, not without fury, against a wild genius like Shakespeare . . . " (p. 243). The vindication of these names, it can already be sensed, is explained by the relationship which these particular names entertain with that of Nietzsche himself. These names are a part of Nietzsche himself; more exactly, they coincide with a certain genealogy of his. One word only with regard to that genealogy; speaking of his reading, Nietzsche writes: "It is a small number of old Frenchmen to whom I return again and again" (p. 243). Nietzsche, by means of this genealogy, bases himself in the Latin origins of French culture, in what he calls "the strong race." The names, however, which should interest us the most here, are those of Schopenhauer and Wagner. What we have said about the names of the old Frenchmen is equally true of these names: they are in collusion with the name of Nietzsche. This is most clearly seen in the case of Voltaire. *Human, All Too Human* was originally dedicated to Voltaire; this is what Nietzsche writes about it in *Ecco Homo:*

> Voltaire was above all, in contrast to all who wrote after him, a *grand seigneur* of the spirit—like me—the name of Voltaire on one of my essays—that really meant progress—*towards me.* (p. 283)

Clearly it is Nietzsche's strategy to bind himself, to bind his own body to all these names: already the second edition of *Human, All Too Human* no longer bears the name of Voltaire. Nietzsche substitutes his proper name for Voltaire's, he reappropriates once again his writing for himself; but that is only possible if Voltaire has always already been another name for Nietzsche. That names may be substitutes for other names, is in fact what may be read in the case of the names of Schopenhauer and Wagner. Nietzsche, in *Ecce Homo,* speaks of *The Birth of Tragedy* as a "practical application to *Wagnerism,* as if that were a symptom of ascent" (p. 270); and he continues thus:

> In this respect, this essay was an event in the life of Wagner: it was only from that moment on that Wagner's name elicited high hopes.

The event then is the linking of two names, that of Nietzsche with that of Wagner. It is an event in the life of Wagner insofar as that linking elevates the name of Wagner. Nietzsche gives us to understand, however, that that connection was a mistake on his part, just as Wagner was not an ascending sign. There remains, however, the problem of knowing how a liaison between the two names had been possible. First of all let us note that the *Birth of Tragedy* was a "practical application of Wagnerism." The effect (like the fascination) of that work, that is to say, the timely effect which it enjoyed at the period, was a *zeitgemäßes* effect. So the critique which Nietzsche gives of the *Birth of Tragedy,* a critique which works towards ridding it of the name of Wagner, intends to free that book of its timely aspects, by showing that that work was untimely even when it first appeared.

But let us get to what makes the liaison between the names of Nietzsche and Wagner possible. Nietzsche provides a first explanation in the following manner:

> I think I know better than anyone else of what tremendous things Wagner is capable—the fifty worlds of alien ecstasies for which no one besides him had wings; and given the way I am, strong enough to turn even what is most questionable and dangerous to my advantage and thus to become stronger, I call Wagner the great benefactor of my life. That in which we are related—that we have suffered more profoundly, also from each other, than men of this century are capable of suffering—will link our names again and again, eternally; and as certainly as Wagner is merely a misunderstanding among Germans, just as certainly am I and always shall be. (p. 250)

The bond between Wagner and Nietzsche is such that Nietzsche can turn to his advantage that which was most questionable and dangerous in connection with the name of Wagner, the name of decadence *par excellence*. It is in this way that Nietzsche, being healthy at bottom, knows Wagner better than Wagner knows himself. Moreover what Nietzsche recognizes in the life of Wagner is pain, what might be called an *untimely* suffering. It is this untimely suffering, in fact, which is at the root of the relationship between the two names. That the suffering which Nietzsche attributes to Wagner is no more than his own suffering can only be justified insofar as Wagner is only another name for Nietzsche.

> That the two Untimely Ones distinguished by the names of Schopenhauer and Wagner contribute much to the understanding of, or even to the formulation of the proper psychological questions about, these two cases, I should not wish to assert—excepting, as seems fair, some details. (p. 280)

Let there be no misunderstanding about this suffering which makes the union of these names possible: it is not the suffering of the man, Wagner, that is to say, of the empirical Wagner. It is more a question of an untimely suffering, of a trait which distinguishes Nietzsche. Notice the turn of the phrase cited: The UNTIMELY are distinguished (*abgezeichnet*) by the names of Schopenhauer and Wagner. These names have nothing in common with their empirical support. Nietzsche continues:

> What I was fundamentally trying to do in these essays was something altogether different from psychology: an unequaled problem of education, a new concept of self-discipline, self-

> defense to the point of hardness, a way to greatness and world-historical tasks was seeking its first expression. (p. 280)

What can be read in the following passage is that the suffering which binds together the names of Wagner and Nietzsche has nothing to do with Wagner himself, nor with his music:

> A psychologist might still add that what I heard as a young man listening to Wagnerian music really had nothing to do with Wagner; that when I described Dionysian music I described what I had heard—that instinctively I had to transpose and transfigure everything into the new spirit that I carried in me.

So the names substituted for Nietzsche's traits, for the traits of his spirit, are names which are borrowed and reinterpreted, transposed and transfigured. Nietzsche:

> The proof of that, *as strong as any proof can be,* is my essay on *Wagner in Bayreuth:* in all psychologically decisive places I alone am discussed—and one need not hesitate to put down my name or the word "Zarathustra" where the text has the word "Wagner." The entire picture of the dithyrambic artist is a picture of the pre-existent poet of *Zarathustra,* sketched with abysmal profundity and without touching even for a moment the Wagnerian reality. (p. 274)

Several things may already be emphasized: the relationship between names, an interpretation of the other's name according to one's own instincts, is a transfiguration of reality. Wagner, as a name for Nietzsche, in no way designates the Wagnerian reality. The union of names is the translation of oneself into another name; it is, in so many words, the production of a mask. In addition, since the borrowed name has nothing in common with the true bearer of that name, the translation of one name into another coincides with the transfiguration of something timely into something untimely. And as these names which make up the body have acquired an untimely status, they can be exchanged in a rapid circulation, not for a proper name: Nietzsche, for instance, but for a name which is indeed a name for Nietzsche, but which does not bear any relation to the Nietzschean reality. For, as Nietzsche said, the name of Wagner *or* Zarathustra can easily be substituted for that of Nietzsche. So the name of Nietzsche ("Nietzsche") turns out to be as fictive as the name of the protagonist of the fiction *Zarathustra*.

If Nietzsche can claim that he projected his own traits onto the name of Wagner, it is because these traits are those of the fictive Nietzsche.

> The pathos of the first pages is world-historical; the glance spoken of on the seventh page is Zarathustra's distinctive glance: Wagner, Bayreuth, the whole wretched German pettiness are a cloud in which an infinite mirage of the future is reflected. Even psychologically all decisive traits of my own nature are projected into Wagner's—the close proximity of the brightest and the most calamitous forces, the will to power as no man ever possessed it. (p. 275)

It is Nietzsche who is the mirage which is thus projected onto the names of Wagner and Schopenhauer, but it is Nietzsche only inasmuch as he is an untimely mirage, inasmuch as he is a fiction. The traits of Nietzsche, his proper traits, and those of his type, are projected onto something (Wagner and Nietzsche) which is primarily only an accidental reality. That reality gathers in traits which are fundamentally foreign to it:

> This is the strangest "objectivity" possible: the absolute certainty about what I *am* was projected on some accidental reality—the truth about me spoke from some gruesome depth. (p. 275)

The projection of one's own traits, of oneself as a future type, presupposes an absolute certainty about what one is. But one can only be what one is by projecting proper traits onto an accidental reality: what one is can only be objectified after an alienating projection. Hence the necessity of recuperating that alienated self, the obliterated name.

"Schopenhauer and Wagner or, in one word, Nietzsche" (p. 277). It is true that the fact of tying his name to that of another implies distinction. Nietzsche writes: "I honour, I distinguish by associating my name with that of a cause or a person: whether pro or con—it makes no difference to me" (p. 233). Distinction is at the same time creation of a sign for oneself, for one's own body. This creation is, however, an alienation, and afterwards the proper and originary name must be restored. Nietzsche tells us this about Wagner, about his relationship with him:

> What reached a decision in me at that time was not a break with Wagner: I noted a total aberration of my instincts of which particular blunders, whether Wagner or the professorship at Basel, were mere symptoms. (p. 286)

So employing names, particularly timely, proper names, in order to make a body of signs for oneself, also represents an aberration of the instincts in that healthy instincts are directed at the untimely. Even Nietzsche's proper name ("Nietzsche") does not fulfill these conditions. This name does not represent a final solution, for "Nietzsche" remains the name of a timely being. However that may be, the supplementation of oneself by foreign names cannot be avoided in the constitution of oneself as body. When for instance Nietzsche attempts, in the *Untimely Ones,* to develop a concept of self-discipline and self-defense as a world-historical task, he puts forward the names of Wagner and Schopenhauer knowing that he is essentially concerned with constituting himself. It is not enough simply to know precisely who one is before being able to project oneself onto the names of others; projection, on the contrary, is a part of the process of recognizing what one is:

> Broadly speaking, I caught hold of two famous and as yet altogether undiagnosed types, as one catches hold of an opportunity, in order to say something, in order to have at hand a few more formulas, signs, means of language . . . Plato employed Socrates in this fashion as a sign language for Plato. (p. 280)

In this way other types, or their names, become the means, the signs needed to make oneself a body of signs, or even in order to recognize what one is (for in writing the *Untimely Ones* Nietzsche did not yet know fully who he was). It is only by making use of Schopenhauer and of Wagner, in a manner which was without the slightest relation to their reality, that Nietzsche succeeds in knowing by these formulas, signs and means, what he is. But not the real, empirical Nietzsche, rather the fictive Nietzsche.

> Now that I am looking back from a certain distance upon the conditions of which these essays bear witness, I do not wish to deny that at bottom they speak only of me. The essay *Wagner in Bayreuth* is a vision of my future, while in *Schopenhauer as Educator* my innermost history, my *becoming,* is inscribed. Above all, my promise! (p. 281)

The relationship between this sign language and the fictional articulation of a body is indisputable. In fact, if, as has been suggested, Nietzsche's name ("Nietzsche") is the other name for Nietzsche, the real name ("Nietzsche") being opposed to the fictional name "Nietzsche" (there is a connection to be explored between the relationship between the two sides of the name: Nietzsche, and what Nietzsche tells us in *Ecce Homo* about his dual descent), then that fictional name "Nietzsche." which is the name of all the other names (Schopenhauer and Wagner on this occasion) is separated from the Nietzschean reality just as much as the name of Wagner used by Nietzsche no longer had the slightest relation to the reality of Wagner. The fictional name "Nietzsche" is a name as untimely as the other invented names. And that is not all. As all these names are fictive, they have to enter into an organic exchange and so constitute the rapid metabolism whose play is that of a perfectly transparent body of signs.

Nietzsche: "I do not know any other way of associating with great tasks than *play:* as a sign of greatness, this is an essential presupposition" (p. 258).

This play of the body will become unrestricted play from the moment when the names which institute the typical body have lost all relation to, all memory of, the reality which they used to designate. Let us say, from the moment when the "dirty depths" have been completely eliminated from the names. This is the reason why the process of projection and substitution does not come to a stop with the restoration of Nietzsche's proper name. Let us remember that in order to re-substitute his name for those of Wagner and Schopenhauer, Nietzsche owed it to himself to make his name into fiction. Now, that fictional name "Nietzsche" is still reminiscent of the real name, and hence of the Nietzschean reality, of its timeliness. This is the reason why the already fictive name of Nietzsche has to give way to names engendered by "real" fictions, as in the case of Byron's Manfred, with whom Nietzsche identified in his youth, and as it is above all the case with the names of Zarathustra and Dionysus. Here we possess names which are entirely free of their "dirty depths." It is these entirely fictional names, then, which will have to assume the task of instituting the typic body, the type-body. This body, then, is nothing other than a sum of names, which are fictive, fictional, circulating, continually being exchanged. In other words, it is a text-body. In the case of Nietzsche there is no proper body save the fictional body of a body entitled, for instance, *Zarathustra*. Now, Zarathustra is Dionysus, Dionysus representing the other name for Zarathustra. But Dionysus is the name for whom?

Always lacking a name, the typic body, made up from a multitude of names, remains, finally, nameless.

"Being new, nameless, hard to understand, we premature births of an as yet unproven future . . ."[11]

Translated by Judith Still

NOTES

1. This paper was given at the conference on "Body and Gesture" organized by the Centre International de Sémiotique et de Linguistique (Urbino, 12–17 July, 1976), and published in *Documents de Travail* (Urbino: Centro internazionale di Semiotica e di Linguistica), No.57 (1976).

2. " . . . the fact that a thing is itself is the single reason and the single cause to be given in answer to all such questions as 'why the man is man, or the musician musical,' unless one were to answer 'because each thing is inseparable from itself, and its being one just meant this.' " And again: "In the case of all things which have several parts and in which the totality is not, as it were, a mere heap, but the whole is something beside the parts, there is a cause; for even in bodies contact is the cause of unity in some cases, and in others viscosity or some other such quality. And a definition is a set of words which is one not by being connected together like the *Iliad,* but by dealing with one object. What, then, is it that makes man one; why is he one and not many? " (Aristotle, *Metaphysica,* in *The Works of Aristotle,* Vol. 8, tr. W. D. Ross (Oxford: Clarendon Press, 1928), 1041a 15–20 and 1045a 5–15).

3. G. Bachelard, *The Psychoanalysis of Fire,* tr. Alan C. M. Ross (London: Routledge and Kegan Paul, 1964), p. 80.

4. All quotations from *Ecco Homo* are from F. Nietzsche, *On the Genealogy of Morals and Ecce Homo,* ed. Walter Kaufmann (New York: Random House, 1967). Page references are given in the text.

5. J. J. Rousseau, *Dictionnaire de Musique, Oeuvres Complètes* (Paris: Furne, 1835), 3:744.

6. Cf. for instance, Pliny, *Natural History,* Book 34: 70.

7. The whole meaning of *recurrence* in Nietzsche depends, in fact, on the determination of that nature of the recurring which is the *moment*.

8. Indeed, *Stein*, in German, means "stone."

9. For the problem of type, of typography, of the relationship of this to autobiography, see the remarkable work by P. Lacoue-Labarthe, *Typographie* in *Mimesis. Des Articulations* (Paris: Aubier-Flammarion, 1975).

10. Cf. for instance *Die Philosophie im tragischen Zeitalter der Griechen*, in Nietzsche, *Werke in drei Bänden* (Munich: 1954), Vol. 3.

11. Nietzsche, *The Gay Science*, W. Kaufman (New York: Vintage, 1974), p. 346.

7

Friedrich Nichte

Laurence Rickels

Martin Heidegger Weg
(Todtnauberg street sign)

According to recent cultural rereadings, the idea of childhood belongs among the effects of the printing press; the new standard of literacy summoned the pupil who, until he became a differentiating reader of print, was not yet an adult. As became increasingly clear the more he could be observed in his new habitat, this pupil had to be considered as something separate, as child. With the advent of printing-press culture, the child received a proper name and image that could be reflected even beyond death; not only was the child's portrait now painted, but even his place of burial was, from this time onward, marked and preserved. Only since the eighteenth century have there been special clothes, games, and even books designed just for children. In West Africa, where the advent of childhood today counts a late arrival, the miniature model of a chair is tied around a child's neck to offer the spirit of some ancestor a place of rest which will in turn keep the ghost with the child. And indeed the double but separate world of the child has always had only one available model and analogue: the temples and cities of the dead where even the accoutrements and utensils of everyday life were miniature replicas constructed out of impractical materials.

According to Philippe Ariès, in the eighteenth century the new focus in the work of representation in mourning covered not some image of the living person but the moment or monument of his individual death. "Children were the first beneficiaries of this new desire for preservation," but not because they had benefited from any decrease in infant and child mortality, as Ariès miscalculates in assigning the advent of childhood to the child's increased chances for survival. The decrease went into effect nearly a century after the invention of the child, who thus attained ontological status too soon, only in time to deliver a massive occasion for mourning. The gap between the invention of the child and the era of its expected survival thus frames the onset of a certain history of the unmournable death of the child.[1]

The apotheosis of the printing-press child shadowed by death is the beautiful soul, who is always also a niece. In Goethe's rendition, the beautiful soul, who attains as her prime identifying mark the almost supernatural status of niece, is in turn reincarnated by her own niece who, all agree, is the true beautiful soul. The beautiful soul, eros in Kant, is, according to Friedrich Schlegel, a coquette and, according to Otto Weininger, a woman who has introjected a man's soul, devoured a man's corpse. In Kant, Schiller, and Hegel the discourse on the beautiful soul faces toward eros while pressing back annihilation: the beautiful soul ultimately attains and retains nonbeing, "an empty nothingness."[2] The beautiful soul in *Wilhelm Meister's Apprenticeship* occupies, as supreme leftover, the position of perennial mourning. In a culture where a high rate of infant mortality, including infanticide, is the norm, the beautiful soul would be the first to go. In the new culture of *Bildung,* however, she survives the various severe childhood illnesses that correspond to her basic inclement health. Kept artificially or supernaturally alive, she buries and mourns even her well-constituted siblings; she alone remains behind to argue with her uncle about the upbringing of her nephews and nieces. The avuncular structure that attends the death cult of the child has not yet come into focus, though the specter of the niece has been sighted in certain cases. Flaubert's niece Caroline, for example, who covered over her namesake, the corpse of the sister Flaubert could not mourn, embodies a circuit of unmournable loss which becomes in many other cases the rule. In the corner of every secret transmission of the legacy or corpse, the niece was there.

According to Freud, every scene of legacy transmission—such as the survival of Moses's religion through what Freud also calls tradition—remains an instance of transference. Transference reanimates the original, infantile rapport with the parents, *imagines* of the parents that lie buried in the adult. Freud also calls these childhood *imagines,* carried within each individual, "clichés" that, over time, are repeatedly "reprinted."[3] The control of the mechanism of transference, Freud would henceforth believe, guarantees a successful analysis. It is by taking over the controls of the press that the ego, according to one of Freud's analogies, tells the id what to like and what not to like (*SE* 20:92). But the "control" of transference remains out of reach; Freud later rephrases his most fervent wish as the dread hope that telepathic transference of thoughts might one day be brought under man's remote control (*SE* 22:55).

As the internal resurrection of originary object relations, transference also requires introjection.[4] These introjected relations, exploited in hypnosis (hence the "uncanniness" of hypnosis according to Freud), are disinterred and put to rest in the course of analysis: although, Freud adds, even following an otherwise successful analysis, scars and phantoms frequently remain.[5] Ever since the invention of childhood—of an unconscious—the annihilation of the remainder is, as such, impossible, unthinkable. At the same time, however, the fantasy of annihilation directs that transfer of introjection, which ends up as melancholia. Even during the two-year term of healthy mourning, the bereaved must, according to Karl Abraham, temporarily introject the deceased so as to safeguard the departed against the "threat of annihilation." Once the frenzy of sadistic vengefulness and self-torture has subsided, the encrypted object can be expelled from its hiding place and released into the outside world. In melancholia, of course, this release is held back; the "threat of annihilation" is greater since more closely encountered. The melancholic's wish remains the incorporation of his love objects: "In the depths of his unconscious we find the tendency to swallow, to annihilate the object."[6]

The threat of annihilation that always attends the disposal of a corpse can also appear, as in the case of one of Freud's near-telepathic dreams, alongside the arrival of two nieces in mourning (*SE* 18:198). According to Jones, the niece belongs to the first pieces of the kinship puzzle that Freud, in his own early childhood, summoned premier psychoanalytic insights to interpret: doubled through the inclusion of step-relations, the family he would interpret proffered Freud a childhood structured from the start by an avuncular complex. Born an uncle, Freud's first playmates and object-choices among his peers in age were his own nephew and niece, John and Pauline Freud. The niece was later offered to Freud in marriage, allegedly to encourage replacement of his unprofitable intellectual pursuits with more practical ones.[7] The offer of the niece represents a recurrent temptation, which Freud would always resist, to enter the death cult shaped by melancholic annihilation. Abraham argues that the incestuous attachment to cousin or niece is the libidinally impoverished choice of the melancholic—the melancholic conceived, that is, as one who mourns his lost libido. According to Abraham, in those families in which such intermarriage occurs, perennial bachelors abound; to marry the niece, for example, is tantamount to not marrying at all. And yet the niece in particular is granted special powers by Abraham; in the marriage between uncle and niece the latter rules absolutely.[8]

Though Freud withstood the temptation to submit to the niece, the Pauline episode nevertheless belongs to his most profound erotic fantasies; according to Jones this episode rehearses and repeats Freud's first experience of love in adolescence as well as, of course, his infantile rape fantasy concerning Pauline. This primal fantasy had been one of gang rape conducted together with John. It was talk of corpses and name effacement, however, that prompted Freud to recognize the reincarnation of his rapport with John in his relation to Jung. Freud discovered the mechanism of transference only to the extent that he recognized in his own friendships, for example with Fliess and then with Jung, the phantom presence of John. Fliess and Jung were thus the reprinted *imagines* or clichés of his early rapport; indeed, as Freud puts it in his case, they doubled as *revenants* (*SE* 5:483).

In addition to being, obviously, a way of sleeping with the person at hand, the dead faint which invariably followed Freud's recognition of John in Jung also represents, according to Freud, either self-punishment for a death wish or identification with a corpse (*SE* 21:182–83). But the only corpse around in time to be covered by both Freud and John was that of Freud's little brother Julius, who died in infancy when Freud was not yet two years old. Freud's relation to John was always played out with regard to this corpus and citational prop. When John returns on a visit to Vienna at age fourteen, he and Freud improvise for an audience of children a dramatization of the Julius Caesar story (*SE* 5:424). Freud again delivers the citation in a letter to Fliess by leaving out what he would always keep inside: "My heart is in the coffin here with Caesar."[9]

Freud first formulated the theory of Oedipus as an Oedipal theory of grief. In a letter to Fliess, dated May 31, 1897, Freud writes that mourning for dead parents is a vulnerable undertaking precisely because the son has, at one point, harbored the wish that the father depart, the daughter that the mother do the same. Identification with the deceased is described at this time as hysterical adoption of the symptoms of the ailment that disposed of the parent. Yet it was the death of little Julius that Freud commemorated by toppling from a chair. This fall, this enactment of an ancient interpretation of *Trauer*, or mourning—*Trauer* bearing etymological association with falling, dropping, or casting down—leaves behind on Freud's jaw a permanent scar. The "open wound" of melancholia, which Freud first conjures in his correspondence with Fliess—and which thus lies alongside Freud's only open reference to Julius's passing[10]—and then also applies in "Mourning and Melancholia" to describe the way unmournable loss impoverishes the ego, remains the most vulnerable point of articulation of Freud's corpus: even doubling as an uncanny harbinger of Freud's cancer.

Freud fell for Julius while trying to reach a certain box, or *Kasten*. As Stephan Broser has shown, the homonymic strands that ultimately combine to form *Kastration* were first collected in a series of boxes within boxes, which Freud began to confront at the time his younger brother departed and his younger sister arrived.[11] In one of Freud's telepathic dreams, the reappearance of the *Kasten* not only triggers Freud's recollection of his own fall and wound but even transmits this wound to his son, whose turn it had been, according to the dream, to stand, pale and mute, on top of the box (*SE* 23:127). In the lexicon of Freud's analogues, the trajectory of transmittable wounds is always first developed within a photographic *Kasten*. The analogy Freud uses to explain how, given the weakness of the infant's perceptual and psychic apparatus, early eidetic memories can nevertheless emerge in the adult is the somewhat delayed development of photograph out of imprint. The next image Freud develops to illustrate the displacement whereby that which was repressed in early childhood returns in some other place in the form of symptoms is that of a "repression scar" that blocks immediate outlet or gratification and thus makes symptom formation necessary (*SE* 23:126). One of the absurd dreams cited in *The Interpretation of Dreams* displays this displacing power of a scar which, in this dream, mars the dreamer's dead father: on the other side of dream, however, the scar had in fact been cut just the other day into the photograph the dreamer had taken of his young daughter (*SE* 5:426–27).

The *Kasten*—even the photographic *Kasten*, as Freud argues in his case study of a female paranoid (*SE* 14:269)—holds the place of the mother, who in turn places into the river between life and death the little box or casket (*Kästchen*) that also bears Moses to his foster parents (*SE* 23:11). In his revision of the story of Moses, however, Freud chooses, as always, the third casket, the one bearing death.

Freud's association with Moses was such that his essay on Michelangelo's Moses even appeared anonymously because, as Freud asked, "Why disgrace Moses by putting my name to it?"[12] Freud's identification with the Moses name also embraces a certain tradition of German authorship that always returned to Moses. Before he, like Moses, perishes in view of the promised land, Faust recognizes his death in the form of "the rhyme-word . . . death."[13]

When in *Moses and Monotheism*, Freud's final work and testament, this rhyme-word returns as the double of a name, Freud calls on Goethe for support of controversial claims regarding the name and identity of Moses. Freud notes that Goethe advanced in early essays a singular interpretation of the character and fate of Moses: in the essay "Israel in the Desert," for example, Goethe had already assumed the murder of Moses by the Jews. Moses, the legendary father of the Jewish people, was, says Freud, in fact their resented stepfather, a conclusion Freud reaches by emphasizing—as had Goethe before him—that Moses's speech was marked by a speech impediment, a stutter, from which evidence Freud curiously concludes that Egyptian was probably Moses's native tongue. Goethe, by contrast, had concluded that since Moses's every word was confounded by a stutter, Moses was destined to concentrate on deeds (*Thaten*)—concluded, in other words, that, in this case, the stammer gave rise to the deed.[14]

In proving his claim that Moses was an Egyptian who used the Jews as carriers of the shortlived Egyptian monotheistic religion devoted to Aten, Freud shows that, even in name, Moses was plainly Egyptian. Moses, meaning "child," is itself the detachable, suffixal form of Egyptian patronyms; Freud attaches to this child a rhyme with the German word for death—*Tod*—when he speculates that Moses's name was originally Thotmoses. Though Freud hesitated before signing his own name alongside that of Moses, just as he waited till the end of his life to declare Moses to be Thot, already in his anonymously published essay on Michelangelo's statue, his writing on Moses had been guided by rhyme-words of death: Freud's every insight into the statue's significance had been prompted by Henry Thode, and his method of inquiry by Morelli.

Though Freud first brings up the stammering attributed to Moses only to dismiss it as referring simply to Moses's Egyptian accent, stammering, it turns out, gets pressed into service in place of the annihilation of name and legacy. Since Jahweh was, according to Freud, the proper name of the "uncanny" primitive desert deity worshipped by the Jews in Aten's stead, the interpretation of Jahweh as a stammer significant of the Mosaic prohibition against naming or representing God arises, in Freud's reading, upon the return of Aten within the religion of Jahweh. But Aten returns only to the extent that Moses's speech impediment returns. In Adonai, Freud accordingly detects a stammered variant of Aten.

> If it is not merely by chance that the name of the Egyptian Aten (or Atum) sounds like the Hebrew word Adonai and the

> name of the Syrian deity Adonis, but if it is due to a primaeval kinship of speech and meaning, then the Jewish formula might be translated thus: "Hear, o Israel our god Aten (Adonai) is a sole god." (*SE* 23:25)

The boomerang-like return, as Freud puts it, of Moses's legacy was cast by the primal father, whose assassination the murder of Moses repeated. The primal father was the native speaker of what Freud, following Karl Abel, calls primal words: the oldest roots of words referred to two contrary meanings. Stammers, metatheses, lapses, and the like refer back to and derive from the original antithetical meanings of words. Every word was originally indissociable from its antithetical stammered variant; to this day slips of the tongue, which make use of opposites, demonstrate that both a given meaning and its contrary still inhere in every word. Over time, the primal word that meant at once strong and weak, for example, or "strongweak," split off into two words differentiated by a slight modification in sound. As the twofold meaning of *sacer* still attests, the primal word is doubled by a death wish which achieves only through the stammer the stereo broadcast it anticipates. Through *fort/da*—the stammering differentiation that irrupts within the primal word "o"—the young child recuperates loss and separation by reversing their administration. The broadcast of death wishes covers over separation with the simulation of some terrible control the child exercises over all transit between life and death. *Fort/da* thus holds the magical place of the name. In this name game can even be discerned a stammered variant of Freud's own name.[15] The stammer that mutilates the name also preserves it; the stammer is the name's internal support system. And yet, among the examples Freud cites in "On the Antithetical Meaning of Primal Words" is the word pair *stumm/Stimme* (mute/voice), which, through his association of *Stummheit* with death in "The Theme of the Three Castles," indirectly assigns to death a kind of voice, a stammer.

To push back the avuncular complex which Jung recycled, Freud passed out rings. With each ring Freud rehearsed *Moses and Monotheism* by ringing up *Nathan the Wise*. The ring parable in *Nathan the Wise* allegorizes monotheism in terms of inheritance of the patronym: hard-pressed to keep his promise that each of his sons be the sole heir, a father copies and multiplies his unique ring, which remains original only insofar as it is henceforth found missing. This loss or abandonment of the original ring promotes what Freud analyzes in *Moses and Monotheism* as the "spiritual progression" from the maternal relation, which is always verifiable through the senses, to paternity, which chooses or adopts to the extent that the patronym is in turn adopted. And yet, *Nathan the Wise* closes by embodying the terrible return of the discarded blood bond. It is not so much that Nathan's daughter is disclosed to be an adopted orphan—this shift only confirms the progression of the parable. But the adopted daughter also attains the status of niece. This revelation cannot be contained but doubles on contact until everyone in its range has been united within one avuncular blood line—everyone but Nathan.

1977 saw the publication of the memoirs of Nietzsche's niece. According to its dust cover, *Zarathustra's Kinfolk* focuses on a love story, "a love story in the shadow of the great tree."[16] The Nietzsche family tree (*Stammbaum*) shadows the niece's incestuous attachment to a young man who, as her anxious parents rush to enlighten her, is her half brother: he also becomes, by dint of this intervention, the gentile stepson of his Jewish father. The revelations summoned by the niece animate Nietzsche's nephew, her supernatural counterpart; the Jewish stepfather remains displaced with respect to the avuncular complex that excludes him.

Every avuncular complex covers an unmarked grave. Enter the genealogist or ghostbuster who, consonant with Foucault's injunction, must look "in the most unpromising places, in what we tend to feel is without history."[17] It is always the very bottom of the process of handing down legacies that must be explored and sounded. The autobiography of Nietzsche's niece takes a walk across the night of nihilism, in the course of which Nietzsche and Freud, though both crying uncle, must meet.

By taking Nietzsche's school days at Schul-Pforta as her focus for the abbreviated images of the biography she centers around Nietzsche's Lou affair, the niece confirms Nietzsche's own inclination to include himself only in Pforta-graphs. The picture taken in Lucerne, for example, in which Lou brandishes the whip over Paul Rée and Nietzsche, can be seen as covering the range of Pforta. Nietzsche remains at the horse's end of the long haul of *Wiederholung*, of a repetition that reaches back to Rossleben, literally the "stallion's life," where Nietzsche's father attended the theological seminary, and forward to the photo-finish: Nietzsche, without a name, locked in embrace with the whipped horse.

Schul-Pforta, literally the school portal, served as aperture for the development, or *Bildung*, of Fichte, Klopstock, Novalis, Ranke, and the Schlegel brothers. At the other end there arrived, following Nietzsche, not only the father of the niece but even, and at closer range, Wilamowitz. At this end the niece receives from her father

Nietzsche's essay on the institution of Pforta: *On the Future of Our Educational Institutions* (*Bildungsanstalten*). The portal, we learn in this essay, embraces and proffers access to the cultivation of the mother tongue, though only to the extent that it can regulate what Nietzsche calls *Bildungstriebe*, *Bildung*-drives. The students at Schul-Pforta, called Pförtner, "gatekeepers," are accordingly trained to assume guardianship of the mother tongue and to superintend its course: "*Bildung* begins with the correct gait or tempo of language." Schul-Pforta is, according to Nietzsche, the "womb" of *Bildung;* as such it launches and regulates the flight and tempo of the "genius" of every Pförtner. The *Bildung*-drives must proceed, under control, in stately flotation, or else the mother tongue will die while a "glittering phantom" of *Bildung* emerges before the gates of the institution; like that uncanny guest, nihilism, it waits at the portal.

While within the gates of Schul-Pforta, Nietzsche designed a satellite society of letters, which involved two additional correspondents in the "mutual surveillance of the *Bildung*-drives." In this society, called Germania, Nietzsche and his correspondents exchanged, through the gates of Pforta, letters and manuscripts that were returned with appropriate emendations. Yet this sending and receiving arrangement, which regulated its transmissions through Pforta, the portal of the mother tongue, cast off all but its founding member and genius. Unaware that the group had already disbanded, Nietzsche ended up sustaining this postal procedure for over a year with himself as sole participant. Though the society had been designed to include two or more correspondents, the Pförtner Nietzsche nevertheless played this Pfort/a game singlehandedly on the threshold of a womb.

Nietzsche would find and found, around this womb, another society that, like Germania at Pforta, promoted through mutual superintendence the regulation and refinement of the *Bildung*-drives. This society—the Trinity—was commemorated in the Lucerne photograph: in Leipzig, Nietzsche, Lou Salomé, and Paul Rée together attended a performance of *Nathan the Wise* to inaugurate their writing team in the ensuing exchange and emendation of separate takes on the Nathan problem. For Nietzsche this problem could be simply put: he was looking for an heir, a disciple to inherit and promulgate his thought. Though he was the acknowledged "father" of Rée's first book, Nietzsche turned around his reception of the "Réealism" of this book at the same time that he judged his own early work no longer equal to reflections he was now conceiving under the new rubric of Eternal Return. Even as the three of them were planning to live together in a major university town, where Nietzsche would pursue studies aimed at elucidating and promoting the doctrine he was intent on handing down, it became increasingly clear that only Lou was to be Nietzsche's pupil, indeed his heiress. As Nietzsche confided to Lou in a letter drafted in December 1882:

> Back in Orta I conceived the plan of leading you step by step to the final consequence of my philosophy—*you*, as the first person I took to be fit for this. Oh, you cannot suspect what resolve, what determination, this took. As teacher I have always done much for my students . . . but what I meant to do *here, now,* given my continuing physical deterioration, went beyond everything earlier. A protracted building, building up! . . . I thought of you as my heiress.

During his single encounter alone with Lou in Orta—which he moreover commemorated by coining the expression "Orta-weather" to describe any particularly fine moment in terms of their special bond—Nietzsche first elaborated to Lou the Eternal Return of the Same. But Nietzsche's forecast was not quite accurate. Only when, after some delay, no reply to his letters to Lou was forthcoming did Nietzsche realize that he had put her off right from the start, and that the Trinity founded in Orta had, for some time already, retained only Nietzsche as correspondent.

Suspicious of the wedding ring of recurrence that Nietzsche had eagerly bestowed on her, Lou, looking back on the bond established between them in Orta, discovered a relentless return of discarded sensuality that continued to return in each of her post-Orta relationships until, in her relation to "father" Freud, this return subsided before its definition:

> Just as Christian (like every) mysticism passes into crude religious sensuality right at its highest ecstasy, so can the most ideal love become sensual again in its ideality precisely by the power of the great tensing of sensation. A disagreeable matter, this revenge of the human element—I do not like those feelings where they reconverge in their circulation, for that is the junction of false pathos, of lost truth and integrity of feeling. Is this what is estranging me from Nietzsche?[18]

Just as Lou found Orta-weather suspect, so she also suspected that the doctrine of Eternal Return turned—by recycling repressed feelings—on defective mysticism. But according to the logic she already embodied, her rejection of Nietzsche's legacy only guaranteed its transmission. Even as described in her commentary on the Orta afternoon, the bond established between Nietzsche and Lou in Orta takes the form of a cycle which, at its apogee, links Nietzsche, through Lou, to Freud. Though she castigated Nietzsche's conceptions of Eternal Return even before he published them, composed them into a body, Lou—the father of Zarathustra as Nietzsche saw her—nevertheless doubled as secret bearer of the doctrine of Eternal Return.

The speculations which found their rebound in *Beyond the Pleasure Principle* were first released in the argument between Lou and Freud, in February 1913, over her poem "Life Prayer"—which Lou presented to Nietzsche, and which he himself set to music and continued to praise in *Ecce Homo.* When next Freud discloses to Lou, in a hushed voice, his discovery of the primal father alongside notions that would comprise *Beyond the Pleasure Principle,* she at first rejects the revelation, just as she had rejected the Eternal Return of the Same that Nietzsche, similarly in a hushed voice, had sought to hand down to her. Thus when it comes time to give an example of repetition compulsion in *Beyond the Pleasure Principle,* Freud inserts the return of the phrase "Eternal Return of the Same" into his example of the lover "each of whose love affairs passes through the same phases and reaches the same conclusion. This 'Eternal Return of the Same' . . ." (*SE* 18:22).

"It was known that as a girl she had kept up an intense friendship with Friedrich Nietzsche, founded upon her deep understanding of the philosopher's bold ideas," Freud reports in his Lou eulogy: "This relationship came to an abrupt end when she refused the proposal of marriage which he made her. . . . It was in Vienna that long ago the most moving episode of her feminine fortunes had been played out. In 1912 she returned to Vienna in order to be initiated into psychoanalysis. My daughter, who was her close friend, once heard her regret that she had not known psychoanalysis in her youth. But, after all, in those days there was no such thing" (*SE* 23:297–98). Lou would claim on occasion to be "more Freudian" than Freud himself; indeed she was "more than Freud" by having always been, already with Nietzsche, in the Freudian system. She returns the Eternal Return to the psychoanalytic model when, upon receiving it from Nietzsche, she interprets it as the return of the repressed. And she eventually returns the Eternal Return to Freud in person, to have it analyzed and to have her interpretation confirmed. And even Nietzsche returns to the psychoanalytic model, as when, in *Ecce Homo,* he suggests that, since he could not brook the thought of his mother's and sister's return, the Eternal Return would have to be selective or not be at all. Indeed, as he put it, the whole maternal German side of his family posed the "deepest possible objection to the doctrine of Eternal Return."[19]

Freud was unable to come to terms with Nietzsche, to acknowledge any debt whatsoever to him, and what continues to attract our attention is that Freud's resistance seems so strong. In this context Lou is herself the return of the repressed. Lou was the link between Nietzsche and Freud, their only link, Freud claimed upon her death. This link even comes full circle: when Freud included her in the secret committee, Lou finally accepted the ring she had refused in Orta. Is Lou caught between Nietzsche and Freud in a tug of war, or is she holding the end of the line? Does Lou play *fort/da* with both of them, or is she herself the *fort/da* bobbin of each of the men, whose homosexual link—witness Freud's extraordinary jealousy of Nietzsche with regard to Lou—she would, then, guarantee? Lou is the messenger sent by Nietzsche to Freud, bearing the doctrine of Eternal Return which she thus rescued from that degeneration of Nietzsche's name which in 1977 is embodied by his niece. A certain fear of contagion nevertheless accompanies this transfer. Although Freud's citation of Nietzsche's doctrine amounts to that insemination of Freud's corpus by Nietzsche which could only be accomplished by Lou, the father of Zarathustra, the very place of insemination is meticulously sealed off. It is within the context of a repression and of Freud's theory of repression that "the Eternal Return of the Same" is situated and contained in *Beyond the Pleasure Principle.*

The primal father was the superman, Freud corrects the teacher; Nietzsche placed in the future what belonged to the past (*SE* 18:123). Every father leaps out of the past to become the superego, the phantom over-and-out man. But there remains another phantom authority, which Freud allows in the midst of his discussion of such uncanny phenomena as Eternal Return of the Same and return of the dead. Though he hastens to emphasize that this contrast does not hold the two mechanisms apart, Freud nevertheless offers another opposition. Uncanny experiences, Freud has already established, occur whenever repressed infantile complexes are reanimated through some current impression. Or, he now adds, they occur whenever long-overcome (*überwundene*) primitive convictions suddenly seem to receive new confirmation. The animistic convictions of primitive cultures have not been left behind by modern man but are in a precarious state of *Überwundensein.*[20] The uncanniness of the double must also be charted back to a surmounted era of mental development. This ancient source of the uncanny's double aspect is still current, Freud advises Jung, in the belief of many primitive peoples that the placenta is the baby's brother or twin which must, accordingly, also be fed and cared for "—which naturally does not last long."[21] Thus Freud postulates as part of the phylogenetic program that every child is born alongside a sibling who cannot be kept alive.

In uncanny experiences that confirm surmounted convictions, it is belief in the material reality of a certain idea—the belief in doubles or ghosts, for example—that has returned. Freud stresses, however, that it would press repression beyond the bounds of its definition to claim that this too belongs to the return of the repressed. The ghost hails from the tribal past, from childhood, but not from a childhood complex that can undergo repression. The dead, child and savage alike believe, return as ghosts and vampires. Such a belief is not repressed but is "overcome" only to return whenever seemingly confirmed. One's tribal past, including infantile or archaic beliefs associated with mourning, comes in, like a ghost, under and over the threshold of repression. In taking cognizance of the exceptional status of belief in ghosts, Freud touches on the wound of interminable mourning. Freud could never fathom why mourning should be so painful even as it provides prosthetic replacements for each lost attachment.[22] With what may be Nietzschean pathos, Freud summons the great overcoming as well as, already secretly scarred over, the *Überwunde*, the superwound which, in occult settings, exercises the kind of control that is otherwise the superego's prerogative.

Freud puts the *Übermännchen* in its place, in Nietzsche's past, and leaves it there. There remains, however, a telepathic call to be put through. In an aside in his case study of Schreber, Freud noted that Nietzsche's hymn "Before Sunrise" manifested Nietzsche's longing for his father. Shortly after his father's death, Nietzsche received a close-call from the father's ghost:

> In the church I heard organ sounds like those at a funeral. As I looked to see what the cause might be, a grave suddenly opened and out steps my father in a shroud. He hurries into the church and soon returns with a small child in his arms. The grave mound opens, he climbs in and the cover sinks back down onto the opening. At the same time the organ sound falls silent, and I awaken.—The next day little Joseph falls ill, convulses and dies within a few hours. Our grief was unbounded. My dream had been completely fulfilled.

In the dream the phantom father withdraws with an unidentified child, the double of the dreamer. Awakening, Nietzsche finds himself still here, while the younger brother, as it turns out, soon goes. In yet another telepathic dream, Nietzsche foresaw the death of his grandfather, also a double of the dreamer. He is able to receive these signals of impending death, Nietzsche writes in *Ecce Homo*, because he is his own double. It is the double's departure that doubles Nietzsche and installs in him telepathic reception.

Pfort/a must be played with doubles at the threshold of a double aperture—the "father womb."[23] As he first passed through its gates, Nietzsche also already called this place of double occupancy "Mother Pforta:"

> Seeing Pforta shining forth, I felt I recognized in it more a prison than an alma mater. I proceeded through the gate. My heart overflowed with sacred sensations: I was lifted up to God in silent prayer and profound peace settled over my spirit.

Behind the gates Nietzsche first conceived, in essays on Fatum, the doctrines of Eternal Return and amor fati (*Vati*).

Pforta holds the place of the parents Pfort/a would hold in place. Nietzsche celebrated not only Lou as his "double" and "sister brain" but also his typewriter as prosthetic part and portrait of himself. Lou accordingly occupies interchangeable places both with the problem of Eternal Return and with Nietzsche's typewriter. In a letter to his sister, Nietzsche complains that his typewriter, forwarded to him by Paul Rée, has arrived damaged, "like everything that people of weak character have in their hands for a time, whether typewriters, problems, or Lous."[24]

The typewriter is a Mystic Writing Pad or *Wunderblock* which, with its styluslike keys, rips into one surface—the typewriter ribbon or unconscious memory—so that another surface can be printed upon. This *Wunde-block* leaves a wound that blocks the emergence of one inscription so that imprinted text can emerge in some other place.

In a letter to Abraham dated May 4, 1915, Freud announces that he is having "Mourning and Melancholia" "typewritten" so that Abraham can receive a carbon copy: the "open wound" was thus typed. The death wish travels and etches the route of displacement between scar and symptom. The scar scratched into the photograph taken of a daughter ends up on the face of the phantom father. In an adjacent dream, the dead father makes a ghost appearance in his son's dream only because he, the father, does not know that he is dead. Freud anchors this paradoxical knowledge that does not know in a wish that went without saying in the dream: what the father does not know is that his son at one point wished him dead. The father is a phantom only to the extent that his son's death wishes, which animate him, go unacknowledged (*SE* 5:430–31).

The death wish gives rise to ghosts. As premier application of what Freud called the omnipotence of thoughts, the death wish accordingly corresponds to belief in and practice of magic. But that's not all: the modern technical media, Freud concludes, have their origin in the onmipotence of thoughts (*SE* 23:113). The death wish thus inaugurates a primal structure represented and run by death cults, including, to this day, the modern technical media. The death wish is effective only to the extent that it also opens up a joint account with—and shifts the balance to—the dead. The primal response on the part of the survivor is to project onto the animated image or corpse death wishes that come into focus up close as vampiric, but in the long shot, at the other end of mourning, as worthy of some ancestral spirit or friendly ghost.

What Freud discovered in *Totem and Taboo* was also discovered that same year by anthropology, though in some other place under the name of cargo cult. The cargo cult astutely interprets products of technology, in particular those in the service of telecommunication, as achievements of the dead. But even the cargo that dead persons have made for the living members of their tribe has been stolen by the white race which keeps all cargo for itself. To intercept some of these products of their dead, one tribe sets out paper reproductions of birds to attract the cargo-bearing planes flying overhead, much as in contemporary West Germany—though in this case the purpose has been muddled by ambivalence—bird silhouettes clutter every larger window. White men, who are the rulers of the realm of the dead—some tribes call it Australia—and who remain, via magic transmitter boxes, in constant contact with their phantom laborers even across vast distances, also keep to themselves the messages from the dead intended for the tribe. Because he stands at the switches of telecommunications, the white man is what Freud calls a "prosthesis god" (*SE* 21:92); that is, he is a god, according to the cargo cult, to the extent that he is living dead. Insofar as his sensorium consists only of devices that the dead build to keep in touch with the living, the white man controls a phantom zone he also embodies. According to Freud, every prosthesis represents castration by adding something on. Yet castration and death, says Freud, cannot be represented but only embodied—for example, by some dead person. Thus every point of contact between a body and its media extensions marks the site of some secret burial. The white god of the cargo cult holds the place of unmournable death. The underworld slave labor camp contains the mournable deaths which, from the cult of Isis to psychoanalysis, have always taken the dead father as model. Thus in Freud's Ratman case—where Freud first borrows the phrase "omnipotence of thoughts" from Ratman, who coined it to describe the efficacy of his death wishes—the dead father must pay, must slave for Ratman's every wish. Ratman's sister, who died in early childhood, is the rat at the controls of his cargo cult. In exchange for the total thought control her brother thus grants her, the rat never conveys to him the messages of the mourned dead. The mourned dead know Ratman's thoughts only to the extent that he does not know it; the dead, however, must slave for Ratman's every thought.

Nietzsche's dead brother installs in him a certain Pfort/a frequency that cannot be tuned out by the superegoistical broadcast—always an admixture, according to Freud, of early parental criticism and public opinion. But like Ratman, Nietzsche does not know that his Oedipalized past nevertheless knows his thoughts and watches for the chance to return. According to the cargo cult, on the day lines of communication with the mourned dead are restored, the believers must annihilate everything that would remind them of their former lives. Total annihilation thus greets the return of the mourned dead.

Following his break with Lou, Nietzsche struggled to keep his legacy distinct from association with the "Fritz and Lieschen game," the gift his mother bestowed on him.[25] Elisabeth brought about the Eternal Return of the Nietzsche name when, after having discarded it upon marriage, she appended it, calling herself Förster-Nietzsche (F.N.). Through her incestuous marriage to the patronymic, she vouchsafed the return of the name. And "Nietzsche," as the forgery *My Sister and I* has it, would be transmitted, from this point onward, through the portals of Elisabeth's "incestuous womb."[26]

Upon sealing the breach between Nietzsche and Lou, Elisabeth initiated the process whereby she would accede to the patronymic. A year after the dissolution of the Trinity group, Elisabeth, a recent convert to anti-Semitism—her latest "distraction"—paid Nietzsche back for his own distraction with Lou by entangling him in a frenzy of retribution against the former Trinity partners. "I belong to both of you with my warmest feelings"—Nietzsche had earlier written Lou and Rée to mark the end of their Trinity association—"as I mean to have proven through my departure more than through my *nearness,*" though one year later, under Elisabeth's direction, Nietzsche produced a second or simulated end to his affair with Lou, denouncing her now as "that scraggy, dirty, smelly she-monkey (*Äffin*) with her false breasts."[27] It was at this point, then, that Elisabeth dispatched the Nietzsche name, departing for South America to found together with her husband, the prominent anti-Semite Förster, Nueva Germania, a satellite society of the true fatherland, Germany having become, they felt, through increasing Jewish influence, a "stepfatherland."[28] And through the portals of the new Germania society, Elisabeth continued to advise her brother to dissociate his legacy from the likes of Brandes, Rée, and Lou, lest his thought end up a Jewish science. By now, at the very latest, Nietzsche knew that he had risked and lost his name. Did Nietzsche only now recast his legacy, handing down, in *Ecce Homo,* "dynamite" set to go off in the midst of "Zarathustra's kinfolk?" Is there not some relation of correspondence here—between Nietzsche's knowledge that the part of him that signed as his mother, that signed F.N., would live on, on the one hand and—on the other—his desire for the annihilation of the name?

Though the anticipated "birth" of his name would lead in the ensuing controversy over *Birth of Tragedy* to his being declared "academically dead," Nietzsche had interpreted as a good omen the circumstance that his name rhymed with that of his publisher Fritsch.[29] Once Nietzsche commences rhyming, Nizza and *Nichts* take on unsuspected value and force. A good deal of Nietzsche's thought was always born again within a zone of paronomasia or pun on his name. Nietzsche invites us to give a closer hearing to the enigmatic force of nomination at work, for example, in *Schopenhauer as Educator,* in the play on words "zwischen Ichts und Nichts" ("between I and nothingness") as well as in his Dionysian dithyramb beginning "Jetzt / zwischen zwei Nichtsen / eingekrümmt" ("Now suspended between two nothingnesses"). Though elsewhere in *Schopenhauer as Educator* Nietzsche characterizes "uncanny" deceptive speech as "stammering,"[30] it would in fact owe to stammering that he could not help but overhear the *Ich* in *Nichts*—or the *Nichts* in *Ich*—as a tension operating within his own name. And indeed, as Nietzsche everywhere makes clear, the genealogist philosophizes with a stammer. But does Nietzsche remain in some other place, or niche, which he reserved for himself, when unscrambling the stammering associations to which nihilism always owes it emergence, or does he in turn succumb to what Freud in a letter to Fliess called "philosophical stammering"?[31] Stammering juxtaposes "Nietzsche" to the *Nichts* and to the will to

Nichts or nihilism against which Nietzsche militated in identifying and attacking resentment, declared in the final section of *Genealogy of Morals* to be the only will on earth.

"The great nothingness," we read in Nietzsche, is also that which is nameless (*das Namenlose*). Though it has, in Nietzsche, no ontological status, existing as it does solely as negation of the other—like a parasite—without powers of affirmation, without voice or proper name, the will to *Nichts*—or *ressentiment*—nevertheless holds the place of the proper name, the place between self and otherness, between *Ichts* and *Nichts*. This place can be termed a principle, the stammer principle of the name: each time the name is cited, is called by name, it is made to stand alone and expressionless, on the one hand, while on the other, it attracts, through rhyming, a new context of similar names.[32]

The stammering of the Nietzsche name always drifted toward the maternal side, at once the greatest objection to the Eternal Return of the Same and the embodiment of life. When in a letter to Carl von Gersdorf, dated December 18, 1875, Nietzsche punningly inaugurated the adjectivalization and institutionalization of his name, he left his sister equal rights to this leftover; it is life together with Elisabeth that renders everything around him "wholly Nietzschean" (*Nietzschisch*). Already in a comedy written at age ten, Nietzsche envisioned his own apotheosis by Jupiter as independent of his sister: Elisabeth has been left behind weeping at her brother's grave while father and mother are raised by Nietzsche to heaven. And this arrangement, which also accords the parasite hosted by the patronymic the role of sole survivor and heir, continues to count late arrivals.

The dust jacket to *Zarathustra's Kinfolk* announces that the author—a certain Miss Sigismund—is none other than Friedrich Nietzsche's niece: Nietzsche's Nichte. Tucked inside this novel we find that:

> In this novel, any resemblance to real persons is by no means coincidental. Nietzsche's Nichte brings astounding things to light, things which hitherto had been guarded family secrets. What she divulges—about Nietzsche and his sister, about herself, her brother, and unusual sibling relations—she packs into an ingenious, delicate story which takes the curious reader into confidence and keeps him entertained.

Born twenty-one years after her uncle's death, Nichte was raised in close range of the most potent Dilet-*TANTE* of our time—her aunt

Elisabeth. And yet Nichte claims greater interest in what her aunt does *not* say ("was sie *nicht* sagt") than in what she does say (149). Within the conclave of ascetic priests, knowledge that does not know conducts secret assassination attempts:

> One day our German teacher asked me to give an oral report on Nietzsche, and after his remark "For you that really shouldn't be difficult" I agreed to do it. Then I dared to criticize the great man—his aloofness, his Zarathustra style, his animosity towards women, his lust for war, his arrogance towards petty virtues. And yet at the end of my contradictory talk I cited the lines:
>
> Yes, I know wherefrom I stem! (*Ja! ich weiß, woher ich stamme!*)
> Unsated like the flame
> I glow and consume myself
> All that I touch turns to light
> All that I leave behind to coals:
> Indeed I *am* a flame.
>
> —and afterwards I almost started sobbing, which is why I quickly had to take my seat. (139)

Nichte thus claims her place and, like Nietzsche himself, knows wherefrom she stems: from the stammer that attaches her to the *Stamm* which she mutilates while carving into it its secret name. Interpreting the destruction wrought by World War II as Nietzsche's legacy—the legacy of nihilism—Nichte concludes:

> The war—we hadn't yet gotten out of the habit of personifying it—had destroyed, bombed out, and annihilated (*zunichte gemacht*), and yet we could live, and like life, simply because we were there. (288)

The war, Nietzsche's alleged legacy, amounts, as personification, to another name of Nietzsche: "Nietzsche" has made everything *zunichte,* into nothingness, to naught—into Nichte. In 1977 Nietzsche thus lives on as Nichte, a distant relative of his mother. Nichte is that double of Nietzsche forged out of Elisabeth's Oedipalized past. Thus the double that Nietzsche was in turn was doubled—simulated and repressed. Nietzsche ended up double to the extent that he died within his own archives, within his sister's institution of the Nietzsche name. *"Die ewige Wiederkehr des Gleichen"* names the return of the double, at once the "same body" and the "corpse" (*Leiche*). In 1977 Nietzsche lives on not as the same—*gleiche*—name, but as its corpse, the *G-Leiche*.

Upon witnessing at the close of World War II the exodus of inmates from the neighborhood concentration camp, as they wandered about the streets of Weimar "like ghosts" and "dressed improperly" (287), Nichte comes to a conclusion. Watching her children vigorously sled down the hill dubbed "Death's Track," Nichte feels reassured about the capacity of her kind for survival. This could be the end of Kafka's *Metamorphosis* or a certain end of Nietzsche. In fact it is always only the beginning, the vigorous downhill slide of Nietzsche into Nichte.

NOTES

1. See Philippe Ariès, *L'enfant et la vie familiale sous l'ancien régime* (Paris: Plon, 1960) and Neil Postman, *The Disappearance of Childhood* (New York: Delacorte Press, 1982). Postman stresses the link between the printing press and childhood, arguing that the eventual decrease in infant mortality rates did not, as Ariès suggested, contribute to the establishment of childhood since the decrease went into effect only some time after the invention of the child. The citation from the midst of Ariès' discussion of funereal representation can be found in *Images of Man and Death*, trans. Janet Lloyd (Cambridge: Harvard University Press, 1985), 247

2. In *The Language of the Self* (Baltimore: The Johns Hopkins University Press, 1968), Anthony Wilden provides a genealogy of "the beautiful soul" from Goethe and Hegel to Lacan (pp. 284–293).

3. Sigmund Freud, *The Standard Edition of the Complete Psychological Works*, ed. James Strachey (London: Hogarth Press, 1960) 12: 100. Hereafter cited in the text as *SE*.

4. Freud borrowed the term introjection from Sandor Ferenczi, who introduced it in the course of discussing hypnosis and transference in terms of prior "introjections." See "Introjektion and Übertragung" in *Schriften zur Psychoanalyse*, ed. Michael Balint (Frankfurt: Fischer Taschenbuch Verlag, 1982), 1: 12–47.

5. See Derrida's "Télépathie," *Furor*, February 1981, 5–41. Freud addresses the scars that outlast a "cure" in *Moses and Monotheism (SE, 23: 77)*.

6. *Gesammelte Schriften*, ed. Johannes Cremerius (Frankfurt: Fischer Taschenbuch Verlag, 1982), 2: 70, 28.

7. Ernest Jones, *The Life and Work of Sigmund Freud* (New York: Basic Books, 1955), 1: 3, 11, 25.

8. *Gesammelte Schriften,* 1: 14–21.

9. March 27, 1895

10. March 10, 1897

11. "Kästchen, Kasten, Kastration," in *Confrontation* 8 (1982): 87–114.

12. Cited in Jones, *Life and Work of Freud* 2: 366.

13. *Faust* II: lines 11400–01. This history of German letters that conjugates authorship with the death of Moses commences with Luther in Stotternheim ("stuttering home"). Luther ended up sending the stammerer Moses to the gallows.

14. See Konrad Burdach, "Faust und Moses," *Sitzungsberichte der Königlichen Preussischen Akademie der Wissenschaft* (1912), 1: 358–403.

15. Derrida overhears this paronomasia of the name in *La Carte postale.*

16. Ursula Sigismund, *Zarathustras Sippschaft* (München: Franz Ehrenwirth Verlag, 1977). Subsequent page references are noted in text.

17. "Nietzsche, Genealogy, History," in *Semiotexte* 3, 1 (1978): 78.

18. Lou Andreas-Salomé, *Lebensrückblick* (Frankfurt: Insel Verlag, 1968), 242 n. 85.

19. *Ecce Homo,* 1: § 3.

20. In the third section of "The 'Uncanny.'"

21. See Freud's letter to Jung dated October 13, 1911.

22. See the final paragraph of *Inhibitions, Symptoms and Anxiety.*

23. From a poem Nietzsche composed in early childhood.

24. Cited in Rudolph Binion, *Frau Lou: Nietzsche's Wayward Disciple* (Princeton: Princeton Univ. Press, 1968), p. 104. Friedrich Kittler discovered that Nietzsche was the first philosopher to type. See "Nietzsche: The Mechanized Philosopher" (in this volume).

25. See Nietzsche's letter to Overbeck dated Christmas 1888.

26. *My Sister and I,* pp. 24ff.

27. See Binion 96, 97, 107, 109, 110.

28. H. F. Peters, *Zarathustra's Sister: The Case of Elisabeth and Friedrich Nietzsche* (New York: Crown, 1977), 61.

29. See Curt Paul Janz, *Friedrich Nietzsche. Biographie* (Munich: Deutscher Taschenbuch Verlag, 1981), 1: 474.

30. *Kritische Gesamtausgabe*, ed. Giorgio Colli and Mazzino Montinari (Berlin: Walter de Gruyter, 1972), Part III, vol. I: 345. The pun on "nothing" can be found on p. 349.

31. October 16, 1895.

32. See Walter Benjamin's "Karl Kraus." in *Gesammelte Schriften*, ed. Rolf Tiedemann and Hermann Schweppenhäuser (Frankfurt: Suhrkamp Verlag, 1977), II, i: 334–67.

8

Nietzsche Medused

Bernard Pautrat

Since this session is officially the introductory one to the colloquium, it would be appropriate to serve you with an aperitif, something to pique the appetite, to "fill the gap." I will indeed be speaking of a hole, concentrating on a hole—this is what interests me *at bottom*. And since chance has it that I have been put at the head here, I will also be speaking about a head. About a head, then, and a hole, which have something to do with one another. All this must seem a little mysterious, but it will, I hope, become clearer. Let me say, to indicate very quickly where we are going, that the hole in question will be the hole of truth, it being understood that truth is not only what comes out of the well, but also the well "from which it comes out," as much the one as the other and, in fact, both at the same time. The head winks in the direction of wisdom and philosophy, which are both a bit lethargic. Not just any head, but the one which Athena places on her chest as a third breast, to instill fear: Medusa's head, which she had severed. Wisdom begins with severance, with decapitation. I will speak, then, about this operation and this cleaving.

Should you want a philosophical translation of this, or simply something "a little more" philosophical, let us say that I will be inquiring into the rapport of philosophic discourse to truth, to the referent "truth," without which we couldn't define philosophy as such, nor the desire to philosophize. But this is a question we can't simply snatch out of the air, but which ought rather to be raised in the context of a particular text, provided that this text is organized

---

This essay was presented at the Collogue International de Cerisy-la-Salle in 1972, organized around the theme of "Nietzsche anjourd' hui?"

systematically around the hole of truth, the *point of truth.* I will set out therefore from Nietzsche's *Zarathustra,* and from this alone.

Before going any further, let me line up the points around which our itinerary will be organized, the various pins necessary to keep these shreds of discourse in place: these will be *truth, repetition, castration* and *desire.*

I would like to signal right away the very peculiar riddle which aroused in me the desire to ask of Nietzsche in particular, and of his *Zarathustra,* a question that could legitimately be addressed to every "author" and every text, a question concerning the rapport between truth conceived as the dominant referent of the philosophical and the internal structuring of the text which aims at it, or makes itself the "echo" of it. Among the various sketches for *Zarathustra* which have come down to us, several drafts and plans contain a persistent reference to a certain great thought which Nietzsche qualifies in several instances, metaphorically, as a "Medusa's head." One example: "In *Zarathustra* IV: the great thought as a Medusa's head: all features of the world harden, a frozen, mortal combat." Or again: "Seventh solitude:—in the end, 'Medusa's head.'"[1] These references are not altogether isolated instances: they can be found here and there throughout other fragments of this same fourth part of *Zarathustra.* The allusion is obvious: when Nietzsche invokes, in this precise context, the great thought, he can only be referring to that supreme thought of which Zarathustra is in principle the depository, the father, the owner, and the *porte-parole:* the thought of the eternal return.

The thought of the eternal return is (therefore) *a Medusa's head.*

First riddle. Since what we have here is clearly a metaphor in Nietzsche's discourse, in this fore-text which is a "plan," how does it function? Or, how can one compare a thought to a head, especially Medusa's head? A simple, naive and strictly mythological reply would be that Medusa's head is that which cannot be looked at, under penalty of being immediately *medused,* petrified, frozen, hardened unto death. This is the obvious meaning of Nietzsche's explanation of his expression: the effect of Medusa's head is to harden the world into a mortal combat; this is therefore also the effect of the thought of the eternal return. If this "thought" *is* a Medusa's head, it must produce these same phenomena of stupor and *rigor mortis.*

To displace the question a little: why *is* this thought a Medusa's head? We will leave this question, provisionally at least, suspended.

Straight away to a second riddle. This time it is a factual difficulty concerning the material of the actual text, and the real work which produced it. The episode with the Medusa's head was supposed to occupy, according to the plans which have been found, quite an important place in the fourth part of the book. Something happened—this "something" is perhaps not a thing, but this is what interests me—to prevent this episode from ever being written: at the appointed place, nothing comes to figure the emblem announced in the plans. A strange silence, very curious indeed: the element, the Medusa, which Nietzsche extracts without originality from mythology, presents a terrifying face, terrifyingly significant in that it stages death and rigidity born from the eye and the spectacular: it is that which one cannot see, which one cannot want to see, and even, whence its place and rank as an emblematic metaphor, the sign of that will to blindness by which one escapes petrification. The sign itself, then has vanished: a blind spot in the text, one no longer sees it. This does not necessarily mean that one doesn't see its traces, its vestiges on the sands of the text. In the end, however, it is literally no longer there. Medusa has literally disappeared. Stranger still: if Medusa (or her head, for it is up there that everything is played out) is in itself a terrifyingly significant object, then what it was meant to represent in discourse, that for which it was the metaphor, or that which was the metaphor for it, turns out to be an object as well, of a different nature perhaps, but highly significant with regard to *Zarathustra* and the structure of its narrative. For the thinking of the eternal return of the same is scarcely an indifferent point in Nietzschean "philosophy"; it is surely its most elevated or most buried point, and acts as its pivot: at least this is what Nietzsche himself says and writes from the time just after the mystical discovery of the "return" onward. Thus when silence descends, at the last moment, on Medusa's head in *Zarathustra*, what we are witnessing is quite simply capital mutilation. The thinking of the eternal return has therefore two claims to its *capital* rank: because it is like a Medusa's head, and because it is like the *summum* of Nietzsche's philosophy. The one goes with the other, probably.

One could always consider (though I leave the task and the responsibility to others) that the silence which befalls the Medusa, in Nietzsche's finished text, is insignificant, that it could without doubt be explained empirically and anecdotally and, moreover, that the metaphor of "Medusa's head" is so well worn and popular that it isn't worth wasting anybody's time over it. It suffices to know what "eternal return of the same" means, to have the specifically philosophical formulation of it, to know its dominant function in the order of the great Nietzschean doctrines (tragedy, will to power, ect., etc.). Undoubtedly so. Let me speak therefore for those who don't know what the "return" is, and who therefore have never believed in it. And let me suggest that the thought of the eternal return is completely missing from Nietzsche's system, even if its place is marked within it, that it is that which is absent, and that this absence activates, in a profound way, Nietzsche's text.

The eternal return does not exist as an articulated and developed thought anywhere but in *Zarathustra*, even if elsewhere it happens to be named. We can distinguish three kinds of text in which Nietzsche alludes to this great thought. Some letters and autobiographical fragments (*Ecce Homo*) set forth the revelation of how a thought can pass into a man and become consubstantial with him. This is articulated as: everything must return eternally. Then there are some attempts, in the *Nachlass*, at a scientific demonstration of the cyclical hypothesis, where it is a question of confirming, by the use of thermodynamics among other things, the scientific thesis of the universal and eternal circle of becoming. An endeavour which ended in failure, on Nietzsche's own admission. And finally *Zarathustra* itself, which is supposed to be the most developed staging of the thought of the return. It is known that the idea for such a book came to Nietzsche shortly after his experience at Sils, and indeed it is already present in *The Gay Science* and develops along the lines announced in the four "songs" in *Zarathustra*. It is this last form that Nietzsche wanted and chose in order to present the "content" of the specific thought that is the eternal return. One can claim, therefore, that *Zarathustra* is the text of the eternal return, and that the eternal return is the thought of this text (in whatever way one might interpret this proposition).

However, if the eternal return is there, in the text, the riddle comes precisely from the fact that it is not there: for what this thought says, what it "means," is never directly, positively presented in the form of a philosophical *thesis*.

The eternal return is, in theory, the hero Zarathustra's principal teaching: it is the *truth* which has matured in him, and for which he himself has to mature. It is his child, his own fruit, his product. But he is never is a position to give an exoteric statement of it. The mode of presentation of the eternal return is either the dream or the riddle, the responsibility for which is always left to others, dwarfs or animals. And each version which is given of it is immediately contradicted by the master of the return, who fails to see his truth in it, the truth he wants to transmit to his future disciples. It is in this way that the most simple and facile interpretation of the eternal return, the cyclical interpretation, the very one which Nietzsche seems to adopt in some of the fragments of the *Nachlass*, is rejected by Zarathustra, in the form of an "it is not that." The eternal return is not the simple *reiteration*, indefinite and yet definitive, of the same. The type of repetition which this expression must denote is not the periodical resurgence, as such, of that which is now present.

This reiterative version of the eternal return, however, is at the same time the most natural and the most developed. It has at least the merit of being the one and only version set forth in the text. So let us dwell a moment on this cycle and see how it is incompatible with the "true" thought of the eternal return. To think the cyclical and unlimited return of the same is first of all to posit that the same can return *as such*, without modification, at different moments in time, in other words now and an infinite number of times *in the future*, as if it were a matter of indifference that something, that its *identity*, should appear now, as opposed to some other, future moment in time. On the one hand, then, this supposes that time is merely an exterior, extrinsic, and indifferent determination which does not threaten the identity-to-self of all things (consequently, then, it is becoming itself which is found to be limited in its universal effect); and on the other hand, that time *has* a future, that something can be repeated in the future as it has been repeated in the past: the linear model of time, divided into a past, a present and a future, monodromous and monotonous, is not for one moment placed in question. It is as if the same thing were to come about repetitively and indefinitely, along one same thread stretched between a past eternity and a future eternity. The metaphysical representation which subscribes to the before and after, therefore, is not fundamentally upset.

But such an interpretation is incompatible with what Nietzsche has told us about his thought, because there is no identity of the thing with itself. And because time is not linear, it comprises neither before nor after: if everything returns eternally, the whole future is necessarily already a past, and the present is then at the same time a past *and* a future. And there is no need even for a memory to register that this present is eternally a past and a future. The cyclical version is thus a thinking not of difference—what Nietzsche wanted it to be, if we are to believe him—but of identity. In the eternal "coming back to the same," becoming would encounter its limit. Whereas the return has to be thought as a process of radical differentiation, of dispersion and selection in which difference is active. The tragedy of non-identity with itself, of the will to power as a differing of forces.

Thus the eternal return "isn't that either." This thinking of the identical is for the slow-witted. Zarathustra, and Nietzsche, will have none of it.

If one wants to think the eternal return in a radical and different way, one is reduced to conjecture. Since Nietzsche explicitly erects in his text a barrier against this first version, let us ask what it is that the return might be, and if at any moment it achieves articulation. It must be assumed that the eternal return is a thought of the non-identical, resting on a conception of time other than that of the before and after and of a present which would be identical to itself *now.* It must be admitted, to safeguard the philosophical coherence of the Nietzschean project, that each "thing" and each "moment" is at the same time its own infinite return, innumerable internal difference, infinitely repeatable and sublatable, affecting every thinkable identity, scanning it, rendering it immediately and infinitely other at every moment. An infinite dispersal of the moment, of the thing, of the now, which is like the punctual but never fully *enumerated* total of an infinity of sameness, simulacra of an unprecedented identicality which is endlessly assignable. Repetition on the spot, an explosion of everything at its source.[2] It is no longer a coming back to the same: there is no longer either a coming back or even an identity, wherever you turn. One can only now *will oneself* an infinite number of times, will that it comes back and has already come back an infinite number of times, and approach this strictly tragic difference through the game of "self-overcoming." From being an ontological thesis the return has become the experiential object for thought and life—a *Versuch.*

The arguments by which I am proceeding are perhaps Nietzschean: they are never made "by" Nietzsche, and our problem returns. Nobody ever *says* this thought. Not Nietzsche, not Zarathustra, not his animals. We could always just wait for someone to say it out loud in the body of the text, as Zarathustra does, but we would wait in vain. If one is reduced to conjecture, it is precisely because one feels a need, from the moment its enunciation is presented as imminent and fatal, that the eternal return be *stated.* But the statement is forever deferred: our need falls down a *hole.* A hole in the text around which everything is organized. The organs of the text must, in some obscure way, communicate with this hole. The object of *Zarathustra* is, then, a never-to-be-stated statement. Or, on the one hand, a false statement, on the other, no statement at all. Curious.

A textual hole.

If this hole is ever filled, it is by a false image of repetition, against which a double philosophical censure is at work: Nietzsche doesn't claim this idea as his own; he incorporates it into the narrative, delegates it to his fictions, but further takes care that it be denied by the one who, in principle, knows the answer to the riddle. But unless it is filled by Zarathustra himself, it will never be filled at all. There is no statement or image for the *other* idea of repetition. A double hole, if you will: for it must be said that repetition is intrinsically linked to that which slices into the identical, cuts it, cuts it again, to that which gashes it, *makes a hole* in it. On this point, where repetition stands in its immediate and irrepressible rapport to *castration*—conceived as that which makes a difference, determines through mutilation, posits an identity while necessarily cutting it—there is a complete mutism, a silence you can cut with a knife. Censure, a repeater alarm, works overtime: nothing overcomes.

Such is the paradox of Nietzsche's *Zarathustra:* it is headed by a hole, the most salient of holes, perhaps, but still a hole. It is, properly, a *decapitated text*.

But nothing says that this paradox doesn't obey its own logic, above and beyond the one from which we can leap out to denounce it. Let us suppose that there must be a logic of decapitation which alone can lift this contradiction of an eternal return thus shared between a "thinking" and a "thought," between an enunciation and a statement. A contradiction exists between the necessity of the enunciation and the impossibility of the statement: for the eternal return flees before enunciation and rejects the word, or, if it gives in to it, it is only to fade straight away into an ontological thesis.

This contradiction can be seen at work throughout the text of *Zarathustra,* insofar as the eternal return is certainly present in it, but always functioning only as an entity, a kind of theoretical object closed in on itself, jealously guarding its secret. It is an object of desire, or dread, which plunges Zarathustra into the throes of agony. One can neither state nor define its identity, but this identity must exist. At this level, in short, the thought of the eternal return, which everybody talks about as if they know what it is, seems like a truth, *the* truth: it has all the classic attributes. An illuminating sun whose midday of knowledge we await. A truth which has to be extracted from its silence and its darkness, which has to be ripened in itself. Zarathustra's whole phantasmagoria is ordered around the uncracked kernel of this thesis. Once again the great thought tips over to the side of identity and metaphysics, even into its discourse.

And the adequation between this form and the cyclical content we have just dismissed would be perfect: the paradox vanishes.

But just as the conjectural version began to weaken the certitude of the cyclical version, one gets the distinct impression (I shall point this out, without insisting) that the text, in spite of everything (in spite of the "author"?) immediately weakens this fantastic system of truth and revelation. Midday is relegated to a place outside the text, whereas it ought as well to be the object of an integral part of *Zarathustra*. Midday disappears like the Medusa's head. It is the same movement which cuts the head, that differs the midday, both only announced in the book; the same gesture brings down a double censure on these programmatic inscriptions.

A double censure which is still at bottom contradictory: it operates on the one hand against a thinking of the identical, incompatible with universal becoming, and on the other hand it prevents absolute difference from being articulated. On the one hand, its target is repetition as mimetic reproduction, on the other it is repetition as gap, cleft, and castration. We have, then, a logical difficulty, even if it appears right away that this double censure is *dissymmetrical*. For it operates once consciously, in the name of philosophical coherence, and once in the unconscious of the text, in its unwritten outside and against this outside, interrupting the narrative. So much so that the status of the different textual lacunae, which by combining and partially merging with one another situate the eternal return in the position of a hole, must be carefully delineated within a logical system which cannot simply be one of non-contradiction. And since we have touched on something like the unconscious, let us recall that "the unconscious, it seems, knows no contradiction."

Let us proceed, slowly and stubbornly. We can distinguish two agencies at work in the text, constantly at play in their juxtaposition: the agency proper to the narrative, where the drama is built up between Zarathustra and the great thought, an intra-textual agency, then, limited to "that which is written"; and another agency, not simply exterior, but comprising at the same time the text and its exterior, its surround and its margins, everything which is at play when the text begins and finishes writing itself: this time it is between "Nietzsche" (a new "character") and the great thought that something is going on, deciding on a beginning and end to the text. The agencies are dissymmetrical, one *watches over* the other, trying at least *in part* to control it: this is what we mean when we say that Nietzsche *meant to say* this or that in *Zarathustra*. But it is not certain that he said what he wanted to say: there are philosophical *lapses,* just as there are in all discourses.

What happens, then, in the first scene? The eternal return, insofar as it is *one* thought, a truth to be confronted, is *Zarathustra's fetish,* that which he wants as a comfort for his being, that on which he pins his hopes. Midday, the moment when this thought will be supremely established as rule, will be the triumphal advent of the fetish, of truth as fetish.[3] But Zarathustra *knows well* that the eternal return is a thought which reeks of death, and which must crush him, since it would claim, if it could, that there is no future, that there is at present nothing but the abyss, chaos, the threat of invasion. He knows this well (Nietzsche makes him know it), but he cannot prevent himself from wanting *not to see it;* hence the Orient where the truth will rise, comforting and generous. Thus the function of the fetish is precisely to cover over the gap left by the castration, and to erect a substitute—and why not a thought as a substitute?—in place of the missing penis, against the hole where sexual difference becomes immediately manifest. The thought of the eternal return as thesis of identity and identifiable thesis, arises as a fetish against the world of difference which *also* seeks to think itself in the eternal return. This "truth" is only there to cover the truth which opens its abyss in front of my face, and my thought: Zarathustra is connected, at one and the same time, to castration and to the fetish which underscores it by trying to conceal it. A contradictory situation, but thinkable in the unconscious logic of the fetish and the denial through which it operates.

This is Zarathustra's scene: it goes without saying that where the other agency is concerned, the one in which Nietzsche "watches over" the scene, Nietzsche cannot allow Zarathustra to want the fetish. He doubly deprives him of it, as we have seen, by means of a censuring, conscious or not, which in effect takes steps towards the *obliteration* of the fetish, placing the eternal return in its most terrible position, in its immediate rapport to castration and the risk of death. Under Nietzsche's gaze, only the anguish of castration survives, working the text over and carrying it through.

This is how we can move finally from a position of *desire* to a position in *reality,* a reality which would be the reality of castration, difference and repetition. The eternal return at this point is nothing but the terrible, deadly thought with which the whole world, Nietzsche and Zarathustra included, is engaged in mortal "frozen" combat. The great thought as a Medusa's head. The attitude grounded in reality must bring about, within the narrative, the staging of Medusa's head which is the truth of the eternal return. Thus the wheel will come full circle, and Medusa's head will not enter into the narrative, but will remain outside of the writing in the mode of an index. Hence the readable fall that occurs in the material of the written text, that is, in the first of the two agencies, can only be explained at the level of the second agency of the text. Everything takes place *as if* Medusa's head were engaged in combat with the "author" himself, who is above all an effect of the text, as though some censure were intervening to prevent his appearance. As if the eternal return could never look itself *in the face*, in any shape or form, neither Nietzsche nor Zarathustra, neither textual "character" nor textual "operator."

Getting back to Medusa's head and the fetish, we have just said that the eternal return never looks itself in the face. This is the same as saying that nothing can withstand the spectacle of castration, of difference as castration. Now Freud in fact suggests that the symbol of Medusa's head is a symbolism of castration, in a short text dating from 1922: "To decapitate = to castrate. The fear of Medusa is also the fear of castration, which is linked to a gaze." The child's gaze falls upon the mother's sex, which terrifies him. The anguish of castration is born exactly at the moment the child, who until then has refused to believe in the threat to his sex, confronts the spectacle of the maternal sex, with no penis, surrounded by hair. The Medusa's head signifies this spectacle. The head of hair composed of snakes, which art attributes to the Medusa, Freud interprets as the multiplication of representations of the penis, and proposes the following analytic rule: "The multiplicity of symbols for the penis *signifies castration.*" In the end, the petrification experienced by the spectator is to be understood as a defense erected *against* castration, a denial of reality in the form of an "I *have* a penis, the proof being that I am all stiff, I *am* a penis." Petrification is denial in the form of an erection.

Thus viewed, Medusa's head is entirely paradoxical, being at once an image of castration (open-mouthed, eyes bulging) and a multiple image of the threatened penis. At once, then, the head of the penis and decapitation. A head and at the same time *acephalous*. This contradiction can be traced even in zoological classifications which define "medusan" animals—another instance of the metaphor—as "invertebrate animals, of the acephalous kind, which live in the sea." The dreadful maternal ocean plunges you into the throes of agony. In French, *affre*, ("throes"), comes from the High German *eiver* ("harsh, bristling"). The Medusa, bristling with serpents, makes the spectator, who is threatened both in his reality and his desire, rigid with terror.[4] This seems a very paradoxical figuration, since Medusa's face conveys *castration and its denial at the same time*. And the *more* it conveys the denial, the *more* it affirms its *necessity*. Thus it follows a logic entirely incompatible with the syllogisms of consciousness.

Medusa's head is therefore at one and the same time the real and the desire, castration as real and the fetish which, in a manner of speaking, wishes that castration didn't exist. Now this logic of the unconscious corresponds exactly to the logic of the fetish as stated by Freud in his 1927 article *On Fetishism*. Freud explains that in fetishism two beliefs can co-exist, the important thing being the *splitting* of the two: one belief based on desire and the other based on reality. Freud then remarks that "in very subtle instances both the disavowal and the affirmation of the castration have found their way into the construction of the fetish itself . . . A fetish of this sort, doubly derived from contrary ideas, is of course especially durable."[5] The only interpretive problem posed by the fetish is how to make equal allowance for both the denial and the affirmation of castration. Which is to say that every fetish is a compromise formation, taking the form of an impure compromise: it is a *tragic sign*.

Medusa's head faithfully obeys the logic of the fetish, and in it reality prevails over desire; the acknowledgment of castration massively outweighs the disavowal, and the absence of the penis is read before the fiction of its presence. If we read the Medusa's head as a fetish, it would be the extreme example of a fetish in which castration is *almost* fully acknowledged, only to be filled in and obliterated by a number of substitutes: the serpents, the head itself, shining forth like a sun against the darkness of the abyss.

We have taken this long detour via the fetish and the symbolism of the Medusa's head because in the particular functioning of the "thought of the eternal return" we noted a certain number of contradictions, and because Nietzsche himself has suggested the comparison between the eternal return and the Medusa's head. What this detour should clarify, down to the details of their contradictions, is the rapport of the eternal return to "truth" as castration or reality, and to "truth" as fetish and object of desire.[6] Let us now come back to this rapport, return to it now in the ambiguous light of the fetish.

The determining characteristic of the eternal return is, as we have suggested, its status as a capital thought. Once can never posit something as capital, indeed initiatory; never with impunity, nor innocently. To place something "at the head," is to accord it the signifying position *par excellence*. The eternal return's extreme richness of signification comes from its being in this *place,* and not in another. From being at once the sun and the darkness of *Zarathustra,* at once Zarathustra's and Nietzsche's fetish and the destruction of every fetish. From being a compromise formation, undoubtedly of the most enduring kind, between the belief based on reality and the belief based on desire, in relation to castration. It is in these terms that I would like, in concluding, to take up the different textual elements I have identified in *Zarathustra,* in order to propose the beginnings of an interpretation.

The eternal return as Zarathustra's fetish: this is what emerges in the first agency of the text, where the eternal return is inflected as a gratifying thought, the anticipation of the ultimate solar moment, when "the sign comes." Midday, the moment which is dreamt of and desired and when the eternal return will step forth as the supreme and universal thought, shields the very reality of the eternal return, its reality as *threat*. The desire of being articulates itself against becoming and its incisive truth. In this scenario it is the fetish element which prevails; it is the denial of reality to the profit of desire which predominates in the compromise. And we can see how, from "outside" the narrative, Nietzsche, who knows all about becoming and its adherence to death, refuses to assume it in person, delegating to his fictional hero, Zarathustra, the work of blinding himself to the true meaning of the return. By the same score, and this is part of the nature of *any* fetish, it is clear that the acknowledgment of reality as against disavowal is also already present and operative in the functioning of the eternal return: Zarathustra *wants to blind himself,* but *cannot* do so totally. Whence the fact that death always accompanies the evocation of the great thought, and that Midday is absent from the text. If Nietzsche delegates to his fiction the trouble and desire of being, this is indeed "natural"—it is a continuation of the same movement of surveillance and censure—that he should deny him in the text the satisfaction of this desire which is a *phantasm,* and nothing but a phantasm. Nothing will ever fill it. What interrupts the narrative, what cuts it off *before Midday* is far from being a mere vagary of the pen. It is precisely in the play of the fetish, in the logic of the Medusa, that castration is already affirmed even as it is being denied. The more one affirms being and "truth," the more becoming and death flaunt themselves as a reality in the script of the text.

The eternal return then ceases to be the simple fetish of Zarathustra, it is the Nietzschean symbol for the face of the world, it is the Medusa's head. A variation on the same "object," with the same ingredients. Now what is peculiar to Medusa's head is that it does not look itself in the face, it effaces itself; or rather, its castrative effect must be attenuated, represented, mimed, played with. To the extent that the censure soon comes down on the head in question, decapitates the textual thrust, because the symbol is *too clear.* Writing would be medused by it. In this respect Nietzsche is in the same camp as anyone else, fictional or not: neither more nor less clairvoyant. What Zarathustra does not *want* to see, Nietzsche *cannot* see. Unless, perhaps, in painting. One will never see (one will never write) the mortal combat waged between the world and the Gorgon-thought. Though in a sense one sees only this. This combat, before becoming universal, can only be personal and singular, everyone's individually lived rapport to difference and death, one's *own* death necessarily inscribed in the law of the return. A combat between Nietzsche and his great thought. And if there is combat, it is surely because this thought is the coupling, in accordance with the splitting, of desire and reality, caught in the unending sway of denial and acknowledgment. This cannot articulate itself: it can only show itself, as in a dream, revealing itself as a complicated rebus which will activate all the censures and deactivate none, since they are all fundamentally contradictory. It can only ever repeat itself: write itself. An insane game, with an absent partner—absence itself.

Which thus guides the double, repeated writing: traces of Zarathustra, climbing and descending to the infinity of the text, without encountering anything which he would wish to keep: Nietzsche's hand, cast out upon the furtive reiteration of the narrative, in order not to meet up with what one cannot hold, retain, contain, sublate, signify: a death, multiple and instantaneous. Simply.

Translated by Peter Connor

NOTES

1. See Nietzsche, quoted in the French edition of *Ainsi parlait Zarathustra, Oeuvres philosphiques complètes* (Paris: 1971), pp. 422–423, and Edition de poche (Paris: Collection des Idées, 1972), p. 477.

2. In his *Saint-Genet*, in an acute analysis of the "Nietzschean strategem," Sartre interprets the eternal return in exactly the same terms: under the effect of the eternal return the real finds itself put into a "state of destruction," "the present tears apart." Cf. *Saint-Genet* (Paris: Gallimard, 1952), pp. 320–324.

3. It goes without saying that this problematic of the fetish is never explicitly formulated by Nietzsche, but his entire critique aimed at the fiction of "truth" could easily be understood in terms of the general concept of the fetish.

4. If one wanted to follow the metamorphoses of Medusa one would have to combine it with the cloacal sun, the putrid and maternal sun which rises and makes me rise. It leaves its mark in many texts, for example in some very "analytic" poems by Raymond Queneau, collected in *Chêne et Chien:* "The sun: Oh monster, Oh Gorgon, Oh Medusa, Oh sun," or again:

> I have seen, Oh source of my life!
> the solar wheel which blazes
> and I have seen the Gorgonian
> the noble head of Medusa,
> that face, ah! I recognize it,
> I recognize the awful [*affreux*] face
> and the gaze which petrifies,
> I recognize the awful smell
> of a hatred which terrifies,
> I recognize the awful feminine
> sun which is putrefying,
> there I recognize my childhood,
> still and always my childhood,
> infected source, dirty wheel,
> severed head, evil woman,
> Medusa who pulls your tongue,
> could it be you then who castrated me?

Chêne et Chien (Paris: Gallimard, 1937), pp. 69–72. Let's associate a little more: "If on this cool globe which bears us, combs shape hair according to fashion, what their teeth untangle is perhaps the silent trace of some quite other nature, that of the constellations, the galaxies, the comets, a streak of fire there where coldness has set out the order of our houses. On heads hair rustles, as foreign to the fixity of concerns as the most transparent Medusas bathed in light through the waves," Georges Bataille, "Chevelures," in *Oeuvres complètes (Paris: Gallimard, 1970), 1, 495.*

5. Freud, "Fetishism," in *Collected Papers* (New York: Basic Books, 1959), 5: 302.

6. If one wanted to find confirmation of the constant ties which link the eternal return and castration in Nietzsche's writing, one would have to read closely the chapter of *Zarathustra* entitled "On the Version and the Riddle," one of the places where the great thought is directly evoked. One finds here a very unusual staging of time in Zarathustra's speech: two paths (two eternities), one leading forth, one leading back, meet under the same gateway, which has two faces. This gateway is nothing but a hole

without matter, a limit internally shared. And this gateway is called Moment, that is *Augenblick,* that is, the wink of an eye. Hole, or eye which, by closing itself, can decapitate time, cutting it in two, just as the shepherd decapitates the snake with his teeth. All this amidst a concert of awful whining and groaning, with the dog barking, "bristling, his head up." This is the riddle for which, says Zarathustra, we must "find the word."

9

How the Fable Becomes a World

Peter Canning

The logos as reason, discourse, ratio, cannot and never could extricate itself from itself—logos—as story, mythos (fabulation) embedded radically, mythologically within language. The dream of a language free of any necessarily implicated story, of "free thought" liberated from linguistic-categorical constraints, of a perception and conception directed toward the "things themselves," the story of a pure reason, thought, or understanding no longer bound to reflect an unconsciously ventriloquized program—the dream of uncontaminated thought transparent to itself, undistorted in the utterance through language—this is the fantasy of a logos without logos. It is the dream of a language not always already dreaming and fabling. In every reason there is something mything, to be supplied by the act of desiring-imagining a conceptual scheme rid of desire and dream-distortions, rhetorically unbound.[1]

G. S. Kirk's construing of the logos in Heraclitus is so perfectly equilibrated in perhaps unintentional equivocation, it deserves a citation: "*Logos*, which is perhaps to be interpreted as the unifying formula or proportionate arrangement of things, what might almost be termed the structural plan of things."[2] Does the word "arrangement" (a fortiori: "formula") refer here to a subject's synthesizing act of perception and conception, or to an ordering of "things" by anthropomorphizing praxis, or to the "way things are" cosmically arranged, or all three? Is Heraclitus' logos the Kantian "transcendental schema" interposed between conception and perception, the "mediating representation . . . (which) in one respect must be *intellectual*, (and) in another must be *sensible*"?[3] Kant, in an untypically Heraclitean moment of concession to obscurity, calls the "schematism of our understanding, in its application to appearances and their mere form . . . an art concealed in the depths of the human soul."[4] It is in any case concealed in the depths of human *language* and linguistic consciousness.

It is likely that Heraclitus meant by logos something at once thought, spoken, reasoned, ordered, ordering, and already "in the nature of things," in the world. He advises "listening not to me but to the logos" (Diels fragment 50, Kirk trans.) that is "common" (Fragment 2)—common to all who speak the same language, who share a logos. For "Evil witnesses are eyes and ears for men who have barbarian souls [*barbarous psukhas*]." Kirk translates "souls that do not understand their language," but "barbarian" souls are ones that do not understand *Greek*—that is, the language of the logos. *Barbaros* means primarily "not Greek, foreign"; the *barbaroi* are "all that were not Greek, or did not speak Greek."[5] Jacques Derrida argued recently, in his seminar on "*Le national philosophisme*" (Paris: ENS, 1984–85), that nationalism is an inherent, perhaps inescapable tendency of all philosophizing in the name of a universal reason, enlightened understanding, a reason that would "transcend" nationalism. With all the best intentions, it is always one's own logos staking the appropriative claim for universality. All those who understand the logos are already Greek (or German, or French, etc.). They are *eo ipso* one of us. They speak our language, the language of enlightenment. *Barbaroi psukhai* are inevitably souls that do not reason by *our* logic. Nietzsche attempted to extricate himself from the automatic presumption of universal application for "our" categories (proposed as universals), not by disengaging from language(s) but by proliferating in them, by *multiplying perspectives*, and inventing the "soul as subject-multiplicity [*Subjekts-Vielheit*]."[6] That is, dodging metaphysical closure by assuming manifold positions, alternately or simultaneously, on and always within traditional fabulations.[7]

Perfectly aware that he is constitutionally dislocated within or without European positions and structures, Nietzsche resolves to denounce—in all cheerfulness—the conceptual regulations patterning European metaphysics from within: a metaphysics whose constructions continue those of theology by way of the "god in grammar," "owing to the unconscious domination and guidance by . . . grammatical functions" (*BGE*, 20).

But Nietzsche remarks at another instant, or in the same crisis of recognition and denunciation, that the (Christian) god sustaining the modern European metaphysical grammar has authored a set of stories and a plan—a "plot" relating to the future of Europe and the world, to the life of "this world." "To invent fables [*fabeln*] about a world 'other' than this one has no meaning at all, unless an instinct of slander, detraction, and suspicion against life has gained the upper hand in us: in that case we avenge ourselves against life with a phantasmagoria of 'another,' a 'better' life." (*TI*, "'Reason' in Philosophy," 6.) The metaphysics of Truth, of the true world beyond, concerns not only a concept but a "fable," a *story* of transcendence and salvation. It is a fantasy inhering in a discourse, subtending it and intricated within its conceptual infrastructure (European metaphysical grammar).

Fables consist traditionally of animal or human stories with satirical or moral purpose; or *Fabel* may refer to the *fabula* of a work of fiction and story-telling: the mythos, the plot or intrigue, action abstracted from the *sjuzhet* (the actual order of words in the narrative).[8] Finally, the semantic field of the direct European descendants of *fabula* comprises "fabrication" of various device: a lie, a wild or unbelievable story, a delirium. The semantics ranges from "story" to "lie" to fantastication of a lunatic tale. The verb-form in German, *fabeln*, is restricted to fancying and prevaricating, inventing a wild or delirious fiction, whether for entertainment or implicitly passing it off as truth—and whether one believes it oneself or not. In Latin, "*Fabulae!*" is an expression of disbelief and scorn. "Words!", *only* words, false or confused speech, phantasmagoria, *Schwärmerei*. The fact of speech, that it can be used to lie, is so much an inherency of language—and of other semiotic practices, each in their manner—that semiotics, the theory of signs, has been defined by Umberto Eco as "a theory of the lie," of "everything which can be used in order to lie."[9] But a sign tends to be inherently lying or deceptive as it pretends to or is taken for the value it stands for but is not in itself (signified, referent, interpretant, etc.). There is an inbuilt and irrecusable fetishism of the sign.

Obviously humans have every reason to want to try to separate truth from lying; they are ever anxious about the difference. Lies have extraordinary power—*la puissance du faux*—of taking effect in history. The lie may have an "effect of truth" in the sense that people so consistently act on and perpetuate it that it becomes true over time. Because of a special sign or marking, a child is rumored by a superstitious community to be possessed by the devil. It becomes demonized over time, undergoes an apprenticeship and becomes a witch or a sorcerer, trained to be possessed. Or, if the institutional practice of witchcraft is lacking—once the society becomes rationalized—the aberrant case is gradually criminalized or psychiatrized.

The "true" determination of identity and character (and event) by "false" opinion, subverting the alternative of true or false, will be accomplished by institutional implementation and performance of the opinion (fabulation). Banishment from the community for being "mad" reinforces or induces insanity. What could be more common and usual in all of human history than the creation of truth out of persistently fabulated and enacted falsehood? Ostracism or imprisonment for a crime not committed molds a criminal character in the spirit of revenge (cf. Kleist's "Michael Kohlhaas"). The example of raising a devilish child to be a witch may seem extravagant or anachronistic. But modern societies produce "delinquents" and "schizos" as well as the regular, normalized results of programming and conditioning. Fabulation is immanent to their procedures; it is the expression form "quasi-causing" or complicit with the content form which is the ritual enactment of the story-diagram.[10]

Foucault has argued that techniques of total "micro-physical" formation of a "displined" social being are immanent to bourgeois society. Hospital, school, factory, orphanage, juvenile detention, prison, army: each is set up to produce with precision engineering its specific product (even if that product is "the reject," the delinquent, or the "mad").[11]

Madness, it has also been argued, is molded from within a certain type of family matrix, "schizophrenogenic" (R. D. Laing). This is a controversial thesis, attacked from the right (responsibility for madness is to be induced from the personal history or genetics of the individual subject, without addressing the family or social order); and from the left (schizophrenia is immanent to capitalist society—its unusable, "unmarketable," ubiquitous, (in)visible, unsociable human (?) remainder, the one whose abnormality or deviation or "neurosis" cannot be marketed and who just "doesn't work." The family is thus an agent of the total network: Foucault; Deleuze-Guattari). But Laing's basic hypothesis is nevertheless sound, if under-determined. The family of a schizophrenic is not the cause, it is the co-producer which, as "agent of production and reproduction" (Deleuze-Guattari), selects and codifies the emerging pathology. It breeds into the developing child a delirious variant of the matrix-set of social mythoi and praxes. If instead of schizophrenizing, the child grows up to be a "normal neurotic" (functional) and winds up on the couch, the analyst may be privileged to hear an adult subject's version of "the neurotic's individual myth." That "myth" will more than likely be the tale of an upbringing in which the adult neurosis was constantly fed and bred into a developing character, gradually modeling its mode of existence and destiny as it internalized and self-subjected to the paradigm.[12]

The concept of "breeding and discipline," of *Züchtung und Zucht*, was perhaps first emphasized by Nietzsche, from whom Foucault took it up, relayed by Marcel Mauss, who had studied the *techniques du corps* in primitive and modern societies: techniques of breeding, training, and indoctrination, of encoding in mind and body the basic program of a society both at the level of "ideology" and at the "microphysical" level of the application of "knowledge" to bodies. Bodies and minds (and "souls") are taken as objects of disciplining to be bred and boarded within a "common matrix."[13]

Non-discursive institutional forms, "forms of content," cannot be isolated from the fabulation forms ("of expression") which subtend and sustain them as psychic ("soul") installations of the social matrix. When Nietzsche speaks of "breeding, discipline and punishment," he has also fabulation (and phantasm) in mind as their metaphysical and ideological supports, soul training. His critique bears not only on the European conception system, but on the phantasms installed within that system of logos as its underlying mythoi. He is beginning to underline a process of speech-actualization, not merely the speech that is an act, but that induces action—to make or break a world.

So when he claims that to fabulate another, true world, can mean nothing *unless* it is the "instinct of slander" (*Verleumdung*), he is remarking the *effect* of vilifying, nullifying "this world" on the morale and habits of its inhabitant subjects. The act of slander is a fabulative performance: "[wir] *rächen* uns am Leben mit der Phantasmagorie," we *avenge* ourselves on life with phantasmagoria (*TI*, loc. cit.). The (false?) affirmation of the "true" world, by implicitly or explicitly maligning this one, takes (fabulative-eventual) revenge against life and the "will to live." Which, as we know, is Nietzsche's thesis concerning Christianity. It is a centuries-long *soul-action* and institutional training in life-slander which prepares and initiates revenge (world annihilation). The ascetic ideal (which is its controlled form, non-suicidal) would thus have two "forms": form of expression = denial of this world in speech and thought, and meditation; form of content = annulment in practice of worldly life, withdrawal, meditation, non-participation (relayed by the secularizing Christian-capitalist layaway for future life, financial legacy, estate after life, etc.).

Nietzsche studied transformations and effects of *longue durée* and slow incubation. He insisted that "we Europeans" look critically to our millennial intentions. This is what he calls (in the same passage) having a "tragic" sense, being Dionysian. He knows the grammar god is all that is holding his own identity intact, his personal syntax. He senses that he (it) must fall apart in *sparagmos,* the breaking up of the subject-syntax and proliferation of his soul-identities (eventually signing himself "the Crucified," Dionysos, etc.). He anticipates the self-destruction of Europe after the Christian fabula has "died" or (as Lacan says) gone unconscious. There is no beyond or outside of fabulation: the only thing to do is to *counter-fabulate.*

His own fable explains "How the 'True World' Finally Became a Fable." The word "Fabel" has now altered its value from the verb form, *fabeln,* in the previous section, where it refers to the fabulation historically sustaining the fantasy of the True World. Here it is a question of the world's *becoming* a "Fabel"—at the end of the historical process, the history of Western metaphysics. In effect, the progression of Nietzsche's schema from (1) the true world existing for the virtuous to (6) the true world abolished—and with it the "apparent" one—actually spans and comprehends the historical-semantic spectrum of the magic word, most of it still (re)currently (re)active. At first the mythos or fabula of the true world is believed to be attainable, and is *practiced* as such. Nietzsche proceeds through the philosophical institutional history of the truth-world from Platonism and Christianity to its critical destruction by way of skepticism, atheism, positivism, and so on through to the present-day ultra-pejorative or *pessimus* (nihilist) position. It is not only a question here of the true world's becoming discredited as fabula: the truth itself is turning—in pursuit of itself—into a lie; it is no longer believable (practical) as an Idea (fabulae!). The truth as world (beyond) reduces, by degree and over time, to a fable, a vain signifier exposed and dis-covered void of significance. It no longer *works* as truth. It is impossible to accord priority in logical or historical time either to the unveiling of the lie in the heart of truth (the truth disclosing itself, disclothing itself as lie) or to the cessation of practice of truth—because they are the same process of unveiling and abandonment of which Nietzsche is both the (outside) reporter and (inside) active agent of demystification.

Eco writes: "If something cannot be used to tell a lie, conversely it cannot be used to tell the truth."[14] But in Nietzsche's version of European soul-history the sign of truth loses its sense of differential opposition to the lie, in its practical significance it turns into a lie, the fabulation is exposed—in the proceedings of a *history:* "The History of an Error" in its diachronic unraveling and devolution. In the beginning, the Fable is swallowed and remitted as truth. Is it "really" (i.e. already) a lie? Perhaps a certain reading of

Nietzsche would affirm this. But as long as the lie was practiced as truth, it had the truth it sustained and accorded itself, it was true, in effect. Or let us re-pose the statement: it was *real*, that world, *because* it consisted in fabulation and in institutional practice. It had real expression and content forms and substances, an *effect* of truth and of reality. It had the reality-form of its institutions. Nietzsche has recorded and co-operated the transvaluation of truth into a lie—simultaneously as observer and as culminating "subject" of the evolution of the tradition (Western metaphysics). History, through him as its enunciating subject, has pronounced judgment on the true world and given it the lie. He must confirm and complete that history and get over it (across the bridge), get it over with. This destiny comes to him as the rule and result of his cheerful "tragic sense," in its final dionysian reflex (*amor fati*).

As the section develops its emerging sense (its sense of emergency) and verges toward apparent closure (which is the closing of the Western European metaphysico-historical eon, life-time), its subject, the writing subject of Nietzsche, begins to split from and within itself into an ironic and trans-ironic spectrum of tonalities. The strain and stress in Nietzsche's tone is, too, a part of his message and its "intended" effect. It is one (among many) of his ways of feeling and expressing the "*Teufelslärm aller freien Geister*" ("pandemonium of all free spirits": paragraph 5). He almost completes the story thus (6): "The true world—we have abolished." (Note that "we," we Europeans as a group and relay-team of inter-subjects in history, have accomplished this act—there is no more "they".) "What world has remained? The apparent one perhaps? But no! *With the true world we have also abolished the apparent one.*" With the true world we have abolished the opposition between true and apparent, and thus the apparent in its difference. More profoundly, having lost the belief in truth, it will be impossible to continue to credit it (a lie) or its opposite—also a lie—unless the lie itself were to be recognized as truth (or real in effect)—which is almost already the case. Consider Nietzsche on "appearance":

> How wonderful and new and yet how gruesome and ironic I find my position vis-a-vis the whole of existence in the light of my insight. I have discovered for myself that the human and animal past, indeed the whole primal age and past of all sentient being, continues in me to invent [*fortdichtet*, from *dichten*, "to make poetry, to fabulate"], to love, to hate, and to infer [or "conclude," *fortschliesst*]. I suddenly woke up in the midst of this dream, but only to the consciousness that I am dreaming

> and that I must go on dreaming lest I perish—as a somnambulist must go on dreaming lest he fall. What is appearance for me now? Certainly not the opposite of some essence . . . Appearance is for me that which lives and is effective and goes so far in its self-mockery that it makes me feel that this is appearance and jack-o'-lantern [*Irrlicht*] and a dance of spirits and nothing more—that among all these dreamers, I, too, who "know," am dancing my dance; that the knower is a means [*Mittel*] for prolonging the earthly dance . . . to *preserve* the universality of dreaming and the mutual comprehension of all dreamers, and thus also *the continuation of the dream*." (*GS*, 54)

The dance will never be the same now doubled back into reflection of itself in Nietzsche's self-consciousness. His "knowledge" changes the nature of the dance if not its form; the waking alters the identity of the dreamer in and of the dream. Dancing, dreaming, fabling: so many figures of the ritual pattern and program of existence which must continue even (and especially) after the belief in it has gone, now that Nietzsche is waking up Zarathustra. The true world has vanished, but for him the apparent one remains, sustained no longer in belief but in dreaming the dream of which he is the waking, sleepwaking subject and medium. "(Noon; moment of the briefest shadow; end of the longest error; high point of humanity; INCIPIT ZARATHUSTRA.)" (*TI*, loc. cit.)

Zarathustra will pull us through somehow, over and across into the future. The truth and its opposite, the appearance, became *fabulae* when the true world lost its following, its producers and consumers. Plato's trans-world and the Christian after-life have collapsed. Plato had hypostatized and the tradition substantiated an entity which has now expired or is in its last gasp. There is no way out of this metaphysical dead end except, Nietzsche hints with histrionic hyper-irony, Zarathustra's way: the eternal return of the will to return eternally different in knowing I will always be this same difference, having received and forgotten this thought (identity) innumerable times already, having been before now and again about to complete "this thought" and go unconscious.[15]

The aphorism of the fable of the world (*fabula mundi*)—which is also traditional (what else can it be?)—has to be completed, or rather supplemented; otherwise it will never stop turning itself around in the void. After all, everything is gone now, abolished. All the worlds and truths we have slandered and negated. First "this world"; now the "other" one. They are all done in. And yet one might get just one wor(l)d in at the end. First, is absolutely everything gone? No. Nietzsche's word remains, and his alternative ending in continuation of the dream, awake. And something more, a kind of apollo-dionysian survival in a dream-dance of speech, fabulation (history). We may complete the fable by reversing it and continuing, rejoining it to itself, with values now reversed, giving it the sense it demanded all along. The true world has become a fable: the fabula becomes a world. A false world? A simulacrum world, perhaps? But who knows what a simulacrum truly is in itself, having no true self? No truth, no meaning? The only way to get (to) the truth is to make it fabricate itself, to perform it performing itself. Hence: the fabula shapes (itself) a world. But it has been making- and becoming-world (history) all the while. The task of evaluation is to *select* certain versions of "the fable" to come to be, to return. But the first "truth" of fabulation has always been that the human reality is performed and pre-formed continually—even if it threatens its own annihilation in negating the very essence of itself as falsehood and prevarication (pre-verification).

> The reputation, name, and appearance [*Anschein*] . . . of a thing, what it is worth [*die Geltung*]—originally almost always error and arbitrariness, thrown over things like clothing, and altogether foreign to their essential nature [*Wesen*] and even to their skin—all this grows from generation to generation, through belief in it, gradually to be a part of the thing and turns into its very body: what is at first appearance [*Schein*] becomes in the end almost invariably *Wesen* and *works* [*wirkt,* "is efficacious," underlined by Nietzsche] as *Wesen* . . . it is enough to create new names and likelihoods [*Wahrscheinlichkeiten,* "verisimilitudes"] in order to create in the long run new "things." (*GS,* 58)

In the aphorism previously cited from *The Gay Science* Nietzsche awakes "in the midst of this dream, but only to the consciousness that I am dreaming and that I must go on dreaming lest I perish." Instead of abolishing the apparent world, he maintains it by continuing to dream it. Can he do otherwise? Apparently not, for the dream shows itself consistent, if not identical, with his *Vorstellung,* his representations—even as self-reflecting substance awakening to consciousness of itself in the subject of Nietzsche. Why *must* he go on dreaming "lest he perish"—as though it were an ethical imperative, as though there were a choice? Appearance is "that which lives and is effective." To cease dreaming one's representations (perceptions) would be to stop living and *effecting*, for the dream carries the effect of reality.

It is not that "life is a dream," but that humans are always dreaming it through and into their perceptions. "What is appearance for me now? . . . Certainly not a dead mask that one could place on an unknown x or remove from it" (*ibid.*). The "x" refers here to the Kantian x, thing in itself, noumenon. The covering veil, the dream, does not obscure a hidden or transcendentally remote being; it is the being, the reality—now doubled with consciousness of itself as dream. A troubled, dangerous revelation. In the world-becomes-a-fable fable it is that transcendent thing (True World) that becomes "a consolation, an obligation, an imperative" in Kant. One *must* believe in it—in order to maintain it *in absentia* as the basis of a moral order (in Nietzsche's rendition of the Kantian ethics). But here in the *Gay Science* aphorism it is Nietzsche who "must go on dreaming" while knowing both that his representations are a dream and that there is no Other (True) World behind this (apparent, dreamt and dreaming) one. The "categorical imperative" has shifted its object, in transition from Kantian to Nietzschean conscience, from obligatory adherence to the transcendent order of truth (in the self-legislation of moral law by the transcendental subject) to active maintenance of the immanent dream as "that which lives" as long as the dreamer goes on dreaming.

The problem is no longer to divide reality from appearance. The dream is the imaginary enactment of a narrative, a fabula (the true world waking up as appearance). The question of the real has not defaulted, it has implicated itself into the subject's waking in the middle of his dream. The problem now is to decide, not whether the dream is true or false, real or apparent, but what effect it (dream-waking) has on the history of the subject. What is the object of the dream, what is its desire? The desire for the Truth produces the illusion of the Other World, the beyond, which threatens this one with extinction, first because "this" is not real but only apparent, and later because neither the true nor the apparent is real, and both deserve the annihilation—in thought, in deed—which is their due and destiny (real result of the discovery of their unreality). Whence the urgency of Nietzsche's counterfabulation, both here in the fable of the world-fable, supplemented by the two aphorisms from *The Gay Science*, and in the imperative of *Zarathustra:* "remain faithful to the earth, and do not believe those who speak to you of otherworldly hopes! . . . Once the crime against God was the greatest outrage, but God died, and these criminals died with him. To outrage the earth is now the most dreadful thing"; "back to the earth, back to the body, back to life" (Z, Prologue, 3, and "On the Gift-Giving Virtue", 2).

Is the "earth" then a reality exempt from the interference patterns of the dream-distortion, the *Entstellung* subverting *Vorstellung* from within? Is it the True Ground and foundation of existence, basis of the new ethics and ontology? Perhaps the fact that you can stand on it makes a difference . . . It is not a beyond, it is "here", there, *Da*. Yet what is its "meaning," the "meaning of the earth" of which Nietzsche (Zarathustra) speaks in the same passages? Is it anything more than the *promise* of the Hyperman coming over man "in the middle of his way between beast and overman"? (Z, "On the Gift-Giving Virtue," 3). Does the man promise to suppress himself in rolling over and surpassing himself? What possesses Nietzsche to think that the bridge will overcome itself without self-destructing and exploding "the earth," the body, the life? Zarathustra *commands* it, "be true to the earth," but Nietzsche already senses the futility of the order (countermanding the Christian contempt of the body, of earth)—it is only in becoming Zarathustra that he is able to give voice to an authority which is not his own but that of a "prophet."

In the midst of this perplexion of masks, persons, voices, wills, intentions, and desires, what ground do we stand on? Exposed to consciousness in the middle of a dreamlife consisting of the phenomena that appear to be, we can only insist on the division within the dream of a real (effect) from an unreal—that is, the ineffectual. As Nietzsche said, "God died," meaning he is no longer effective in history. Yet nothing is less certain than that the God-effect is finished with his death, as Nietzsche already sensed, since we—being his murderers—now have to bear the guilt for the crime (*GS*, 125). The crime of deicide is really that of killing the Truth, dissolving the True World by critical analysis. But the narrative continues, and the penalty for the crime of deicide will be paid, as it has since the first episode of the killing, by the deicidal race itself, the Jews. The narrative—it is still Nietzsche's story, with supplement—continues into history. The question whether "the Jews" really killed God, once by crucifying him or again by criticizing him (Jews and atheists), whether the event occurred in a historical reality, is utterly contingent on the question of the *effect* that the fable of the murder has in history—a real history, in continual revision and reconsideration of itself, problematic, doubtful, but real precisely at the plane of intersection between fabulation and event.

The event itself, *eventum tantum*, is always a "primal scene," ineffectual until re-marked and thus constituted afterwards (with its subject) as bound to recur continually. "The real always returns to the same place", says Lacan,[16] meaning the subject is bound to meet up with the trauma of the unbindable continually in the same place in his life-story—where there is a gap, at the origin. But Nietzsche's dream—awakening to itself—encounters the trauma of self-recognition of itself as the *arbitrary,* the appearance ("almost always error and arbitrariness") lived and taken for real in the absence of a Truth of the subject (the other realities are of other subjects taking various perspectives within Nietzsche's *Subjekts-Vielheit*). The trauma, unbindable in any stable network of signs, unanticipatable, is the primal scene of *awakening*—into a dream-language conscious of itself (*circulus vitiosus*).

The problem of the after-binding of trauma in psychoanalytic theory is complicated by the realization that the "event itself" has never been recorded as such (as image-impression) in any memory accessible to consciousness. It establishes its hold on the subject's desiring formations in fantasy-events re-presenting variations on the lost (never experienced) original which cannot remember itself except in re-enacting the scene in a history constantly reworked in new derivative formations. The event-phantasm consists therefore in a "structure of resonance" *between* two repetitions of itself.[17] It never has a first time until the second time, at which time the "first" can only be deduced as the prior repetition of the second which has already been bound in an anticipatory structure and continually reproduces itself—as difference (*différance*) and disguise of the lost original. The distortion (*Entstellung*) of the original is the original *effect* of traumatic recognition.

It always seemed undecidable to Freud whether the first time ever "really" occurred or whether it was somehow "inherited" as "archaic remnant" of a mythical event in the prehistory of the subject, an event of uncertain status and transmission (genetic?). Freud wrestles most openly with the "primal scene" / "primal fantasy" dilemma in the case of the Wolf Man. As we see in so many instances of human event-production, the "reality" must, can only, be located in structuration of every *future* repetition of an original that is not only in fact but "de jure" inaccessible. A future that is already past, "future past." The fantasy works (effects) like a promise that remembers itself even—and especially—in the absence of the subject's conscious recall. It promises—it is bound—to recur, to come back in variations both of its psychic representation of itself, and in the personal- and world-historical event. It always remembers the future (Cf. *GM*, Second Essay).

The Wolf Man's case focalized the problem of the "repetition of a missed encounter with the real" (Lacan), which figures itself in reproduction of a disguised, displaced version of the event-phantasm in its internal resonance. On the outside edge of the Moebius-stripped phantasm-event complex, the real would be the trauma that cannot itself be recalled or bound, because it does all the calling and binding—that is, the unconscious signifying system (*automaton*) is oriented in synchronic structure around the place of lack, the umbilicus of the dream-phantasm, which attracts the psychic excitations in their primary-process disposition and facilitation. It attracts the attention which it ultimately frustrates by eluding capture within the network, like a black hole which exercises infinite gravitational attraction but is itself invisible because no light can escape its gravitational field. It is bound to bind, it is the "gap itself." In human sex-death consciousness, its representative is the ontogenetic "origin," the womb from which the being emerges, but which forever after signifies a lacking something. The something-missing would be the phallus, hallucinated as "maternal phallus" in order to re-cover the (w)hole. The event of "seeing" the lacking phallus is called "castration," of which the primal scene (or fantasy) stages a variation in which the father supplies the missing link in coitus, in periodically losing and regaining his own organ. The phallus appears to disappear continually into the real gap.[18]

"The real bears [*supporte*] the phantasm, the phantasm protects the real." "The real is what always returns to the same place—to that place where the subject as cogitator, where the *res cogitans*, does not encounter it" (*Quatre concepts*, 41, 49). On the way to the encounter with the real—an encounter which is "undecidable" as to its status as phantasm or "historical event", as the necessary *re*-construction of the Wolf Man's "primal scene" made evident—"the subject cannot approach except by dividing itself into a certain number of agencies [*instances*]" (*Quatre concepts*, 51). These agencies can be thought of provisionally as actors or voices doing a *répétition* (rehearsal) "for the first time" in front of a live (and fascinated) audience. The subject watches and "identifies" with one or several of the actors. This moment, which is forever to recur in the life of the subject, is the constitutive moment of subjectivity. The subject is constituted as divided: one part, let us say, is always left there "with the real" that cannot be bound in subjection to the language it subjects, cannot be entered in a communicable memory, memory available for recall. It does the recalling, it, the *tuché*, the (missed) "encounter with the real" (*Quatre concepts*, 51). "Transference" re-lays and re-enacts elaborated versions and reversions, half-conscious fantasies, of the traumatic scene, "the event itself"; it perpetually renews the effort to bind the "memory"—which has never been conscious, because it is the moment of "splitting of the subject" into various conscious and unconscious agencies.

When during analysis the subject nears this immemorial and unbindable real, when "little by little remembering [*la remémoration*] substitutes itself for itself"—i.e., as it approaches the "original text" instead of continuing to recall and reproduce after-the-fact re-enactments ("screen memories") and revisions—"and approaches ever more closely a sort of focus, a center where any and every event would appear to have to deliver itself up [to the analytic process of curing by working through and getting over it]—precisely at this moment we see manifest itself . . . *the resistance of the subject*, which becomes at that instant repetition in act." (*Quatre concepts*, 51)

Now Freud uses the word resistance to cover anything that hinders the analytic cure, the working through—including, ultimately and most of all, the transference itself, that which makes the analysis possible. The analytic process is ultimately obstructed by that which made it begin to take effect, the hooking into and capture of the subject's desire by the analyst (who did "nothing to deserve it"). That transference drives the analysis on indefinitely, interminably. Actualization of all the past repeated missed encounters and re-enactments (of the phantasm which "covers" the real), it must be "analyzed" continually and indefinitely, interminably—as it is the very reason for the subject's continuing to come back for more.[19]

(In taking up the problem of the "European phantasm" [and Europe has spread to cover the world], in pretending to do "analysis" on a "history" [European] that is not localizable as such in space, time, or even text, much less presentable, one runs the risk [at the least] of having no subject to "recognize itself" in the analysis and to work through and out of its subjection. On the other hand, perhaps in its desire to know itself, the event selects subjects to wake up in the middle of our story.)

Lacan's reading of Freud consists of a series of breaks and twists, of Moebius strippings of the unconscious. If the unconscious real "is" itself the apparition of a disparition (see *Quatre concepts*, 33), the opening of a closure, or (as I am arguing) the interference pattern arising between a dream and its prior and subsequent enactment —and if the text too is a kind of dream in this sense of interfacing a world of thought with a world in deed—then the space between a text and its pre-text or impossible real outside future, that opening and threshold, must somehow establish itself in both fabulous time and "real time." Every fabulator has to show us at some moment something of the mutation, the break and twist, that the mutually induced event-phantasm is about to face, to surface and undergo, that the fabulation is about to undertake. There must be a connection with the real within a history self-divided between an elusive fact and a delusive narration. Every text has a program, an "interest"; it has to make us want to do something, to think or feel or act in some way. If the *referent* eludes us, the text will still show us its preference, its *preferents,* on the threshold of its unfolding, where it has been and wants to go, where and what it was and will become before and after text—on its continuous outside (eventual) and inside (fabulous-fantastic) edge. It will tell us where to go and what to do with it, where to put it in the real of history.

It is in the threshold space of his prefaces that Nietzsche approaches and anticipates Freud (primal scene) and Lacan (the real) in pursuing his own question of Truth—of the search, the "questionable" search for Truth ("What strange, wicked, questionable [*fragwürdige,* worthy of questioning] questions!") (BGE, 1). The conjunction occurs on the body of "woman", Gaia, phantasm of the earth-body, at the point-gap where (her) its truth is revealed (reveiled). The question of truth leads, for Nietzsche as well as for Freud and Lacan, to the womb.

In the opening to the preface—overture to the overture—of *Beyond Good and Evil,* for example. "Supposing truth is a woman?" Here it is a question of seduction, and of the *maladresse* of philosophers, their "improper methods for winning a woman's heart." But successful seduction leads to undressing, to the unveiling of the truth—and here is where the real danger lies. "Perhaps truth is a woman who has reasons for not letting us see her reasons? Perhaps her name is—to speak Greek—*Baubo*?" (*GS,* Preface, 4). Baubo is the demon-goddess of vagina, her simulacrum a figurine impersonating female genitalia. She is veiled as underlying phantasm in Nietzsche, here surfacing as "whatever is kept concealed for good reasons" (*GS,* Preface, 4. Even Freud exercised himself in a mini-essay about her). If truth had a name then, it would be called *Baubo.* If it could be seen, it would be seen "as" the primal opening of woman's body, the sexual, genital opening. Not the Thing but the gap-in-being, which "signifies" castration (Lacan). Or, conversely, the phallus signifying its own absence.

"Woman" also signifies—and is—life itself. Nietzsche has emerged convalescent from his metaphysical illness (the illness of metaphysics), but "with a few more question marks . . . The trust in life is gone: life itself has become a *problem* . . . Even love of life is still possible, only one loves differently. It is the love for a woman that causes doubts in us" (*GS*, Preface, 3). Life is a woman, is a problem, is truth, needs veiling, is undressed with *maladresse* by maladroit philosophers who would dis-clothe their own "origins" (the source of their questioning) in a vaginal abyss, if they were capable of diagnosing their questions "as the symptoms of certain bodies." Their own bodies are asking veiled questions about "woman's" body. "Behind the highest value judgments that have hitherto guided the history of thought, there are concealed misunderstandings of the bodily constitution" (*GS*, Preface, 2).

Nietzsche does not actually claim to know these bodies, this truth, the crack-in-being: "from such abysses . . . one returns *newborn*." In being reborn one has actively forgotten what one knew: "how we learn now to forget well, and to be good at *not* knowing, as artists!" (*GS*, Preface, 4). Re-emerging from the face-off with truth reborn, forgetting, convalescent, yet reminded of what has been forgotten by the blinding vision of the *Baubo*, one no longer knows which way to turn. "The problem of the value of truth came before us—or was it we who came before the problem? Who of us is Oedipus here? Who is the Sphinx?" (*BGE*, 1). Whatever, whoever else he is, Oedipus is one who returned "home" as phallus into the "haven" of the womb from which he had emerged as newborn and departed in ignorance of his origins.[20] "We are unknown to ourselves, we men of knowledge—and with good reason. We have never sought ourselves—how could it happen we should ever *find* ourselves? . . . So we are necessarily strangers to ourselves, we do not comprehend ourselves, we *have* to misunderstand ourselves" (*GM*, Preface).

Something intervenes between Nietzsche and the Truth—a fabula: the European metaphysical-conceptual system, the phantasms of the unknown body, Baubo, the Medusa . . . never a transparent self-deception, always a fabulous agency interceding to mediate oneself to oneself. Something intervened between Oedipus, between Laius, and the best intentions of a father and a son. It was the fabulation of the destruction of the "Oedipal" family, announced as prophecy, as a fate by the oracle at Delphi. The play is the working out of their *reaction* to the message of the god. Never is one *simply* unknown to oneself without an intervening fabulation-phantasm system of the Other meddling, middling, and peddling in duplicity and "self"-deception.

The *Oedipus Rex* represents what is most enigmatic and occluded in European fabulation, a Sophoclean version of the primal trauma which in name has informed the premier psychoanalytic myth, the "Oedipus complex." The play of Sophocles exemplifies, almost too perfectly, not the complex itself, but its construction, its invention, the problem of the reconstruction of the primal scene. It also works as a message-event relay system impelled by an ever-receding, ever-proceeding fabulation complex, a ship of state piloted by a *kubernētēs* ("governor": Laius, Oedipus) who is guided in turn by a message from god, a Fatum.

"What really happened?", always the question, undecidable, to be supplemented with another: given that x (the event) is, in varying accounts, agreed by a historical consensus to have occurred, what are its fabulous generic antecedents? Hayden White has identified and catalogued (in *Metahistory*) the modes, myths, and genres of modern historical imagination and reconstruction—the moods of historians as figured in the rhetoric of their histories. But the question is, what is the mythos that informed the production of the event? What messages arrived from what sources, and how did the actors react? What myths do historical agents themselves believe? That is, what event, what scene do they think they are acting in? What mytho-logoi are they acting out and without knowing it? Nietzsche: "French Revolution—that gruesome farce . . . spectators from all over Europe . . . interpreted it according to their own indignations and enthusiasms for so long, that *the text finally disappeared under the interpretation*" (*BGE*, 38, Nietzsche's emphasis). It may have disappeared as text but as event it reappeared in the "farce" of 1848.[21] The "misunderstanding of the past" (Nietzsche, *ibid.*) is precisely the best rehearsal in preparation for a repetition.

NOTES

1. On the effort to liberate logos from mythos, see Marcel Detienne, *L'invention de la mythologie* (Paris: Gallimard, 1983).

2. G. S. Kirk and J. E. Raven, *The Presocratic Philosohers* (Cambridge: Cambridge University Press, 1957), p. 188.

3. Kant, *Critique of Pure Reason*, trans. Kemp Smith (New York: St Martin's Press, 1929), p. 181.

4. Ibid., p. 183

5. Liddel and Scott, *Greek-English Lexicon.*, S.V. Compare *barbarophōnos*, "speaking a strange or foreign tongue."

6. *Beyond Good and Evil* (=*BGE*), 12. I have followed, with occasional modifications, the translations of Walter Kaufmann. I have adopted the following abbreviations of Nietzsche's texts:

GM = *The Genealogy of Morals*
TI = *Twilight of the Idols*
GS = *The Gay Science*
Z = *Thus Spoke Zarathustra*

7. Compare the supererogatory dialectic between Chomskian "Cartesian" universalists and Sapir-Whorfian relativists. Foucault's "empirico-transcendental doublet," subject to the historical a priori, tips the balance toward relativism, but both epistemological positions are apparently tautological. See *Les mots et les choses* (Paris: Gallimard, 1966), pp. 314–354 et passim. See also Thomas Kuhn, *The Structure of Scientific Revolutions*, 2d ed. (Chicago: University of Chicago Press, 1970).

8. "Narratology" makes this distinction under various sets of opposing terms (e.g. *histoire/récit*).

9. Eco, *A Theory of Semiotics* (Bloomington: University of Indiana, 1976), pp. 7 ff.

10. On the distinction between content and expression forms, see Gilles Deleuze, "Ecrivain non: un nouveau cartographe," *Critique*, no. 343. (1975).

11. Michel Foucault, *Discipline and Punish*, trans. Alan Sheridan (New York: Vintage, 1977).

12. See esp. R. D. Laing and A. Esterson: *Sanity, Madness, and the Family* (New York: Basic Books, 1964); Gilles Deleuze and Felix Guattari, *L'anti-Oedipe* (Paris: Minuit, 1972); Jacques Lacan, "Le mythe personnel du névrosé," *Ornicar?* nos. 17–18 (1979), pp. 289–307.

13. On body- and soul-formation, see Foucault, *Discipline and Punish*, pp. 16–24 et passim; Marcel Mauss, "Les techniques du corps", in *Sociologie et anthropologie* (Paris: PUF, 1949).

14. Eco, *Semiotics*, p. 7.

15. Cf. Pierre Klossowski, *Nietzsche et le cercle vicieux* (Paris: Mercure de France, 1969). Klossowski reactivates Nietzsche returning as himself or "le Baphomet." On the world-fable, see also "Nietzsche, le polythéisme et la parodie," in *Un si funeste désir* (Paris: Gallimard, 1963), pp. 187–228.

16. Jacques Lacan, *Le séminaire de Jacques Lacan XI: Les quatre concepts fondamentaux de la psychanalyse* (Paris: Seuil, 1973), p. 49.

17. See Gilles Deleuze, *Proust et les signes*, 4th ed. (Paris: PUF, 1976); *Différence et répétition* (Paris: PUF, 1968).

18. The preceding paragraph is synthesized from Freud, Lacan, and Alain Juranville's quasi-Heideggerian reading, *Lacan et la philosophie* (Paris: PUF, 1984).

19. See Freud, "The Dynamics of Transference" (1912); "Anaysis Terminable and Interminable" (1937).

20. Sophocles, *Oedipus Rex*, 11. 420 ff., with Simon Goldhill's commentary in Goldhill, *Reading Greek Tragedy* (Cambridge: University Press, 1986), p. 206 f.

21. Marx, *The Eighteenth Brumaire of Louis Bonaparte* (New York: International Publishers, 1963), p. 15.

10

The Mechanized Philosopher

Friedrich Kittler

1

"Our writing instruments contribute to our thoughts."[1] Friedrich Nietzsche, the first mechanized philosopher, was inspired by his brand-new typewriter to make this simple and scandalous statement. The statement, written on the very machine on which it is commenting, has itself never been commented on. Technical progress is sometimes too revolutionary to be recognized. Like Nietzsche's great thought, it arrives on doves' feet.

The typewriter, developed in the second half of the nineteenth century, has changed the practices of writing and literature to such a degree that most contemporaries did not even realize it. Typewriting not only interconnected for the first time the two hitherto separated acts of literary composition and publication,[2] it also did away with a secular monopoly. In classical Germany at least, the honor of seeing their names and manuscripts printed had been a prerogative of males. Women were allowed to inspire as well as to consume these so-called works; the field of writing, however, remained foreclosed. That is why a rather ubiquitous metaphor identified women with naturally or virginally white sheets whereupon a very male slate-pencil would write the glory of its authorship.[3]

This entire metaphysics of handwriting came to a necessary end when, in 1881, the salesmen of Remington and Sons discovered the attraction their hitherto unsellable machine exercised on whole armies of unemployed women. As irony would have it, the male secretaries of the century, having already invested much too much pride in their painfully acquired handwriting, were for a period of eight years from the time of its invention to overlook Remington's innovation.[4] Blinded by the continuous and coherent flow of their ink, that material guarantor of bourgeois in-dividuality, they missed a historical change or chance. Young women, by contrast, who were neither educated nor individualized by higher institutions of learning, at once displayed a tremendous capacity for "degrading themselves into writing machines."[5] Their useless piano fingers increased in economic value.[6] From 1881 on it is the case that "there are more women working at typing than at anything else."[7] "Their so-called 'emancipation,'" in other words, is due to Remington, Underwood, IBM, and their many successors.[8]

The first pre-industrial steps towards the invention of the typewriter were undertaken for the sake of cripples.[9] In 1823, for instance, an Austrian physician invented a mechanical device that, despite its name "Schreib-Maschine," simply guided the writing hands of blind people. It even assisted them in rereading their texts. Significantly enough, Müller's invention was aimed at literate but blind fathers who wanted to re-educate with letters and truths their morally blind sons.[10] Thus such inventions demonstrated that not only authority and authorship but also handwriting and rereading were the laws of classical discourse.

Before writing could be industrialized, our culture had to change its very laws, Physiology, that hard science, replaced a psychological idea of man that had guaranteed that through handwriting and rereading he would find his soul. In the middle of the century, former handicaps—like blindness, deafness, and so on—became starting points for technical reconstructions. Every medium, according to McLuhan, extends and amplifies physiological functions.[11] Thus, from 1840 on, typewriters were built for blind people and in two cases (Foucauld and Pierre) even by blind people.[12] Physicians and engineers lost all interest in possible rereadings. None of the early typewriters constructed before the Underwood in 1897 allowed immediate visual control of its output. Yet this meant a challenge and no longer a handicap. Blind machines compelled people, whether blind or not, to acquire a new historical skill. In 1904 a physiologist's test-person typed into his test-diary: "To-day, I found myself not infrequently striking letters before I was conscious of seeing them. They seem to have perfected themselves just below the level of consciousness."[13]

Typing, in other words, is automatic writing, and its psychology, the unconscious. Just being readable and acceptable no longer defines discourse. From 1881 on, the glory of typing coincides with the enigmatic and meaningless letter itself. And this transvaluation of values was necessarily the job of a mechanized philosopher.

2

Nietzsche suffered from extreme shortsightedness (minus fourteen diopters). His range of vision made the reading of books or scores a difficult and painful task. Even writing posed a problem; otherwise Nietzsche would not have correlated the "telegram style" introduced in *The Wanderer and his Shadow* (this Shadow being obviously blind) with the author's bad eyes.[15] That is why he looked around for a typewriter as early as 1879[16] and as early as 1882 bought one with the help of Paul Rée despite its high price. The model he chose was designed not by one who, like Nietzsche's father, was a Saxon parson, but rather by a Danish parson. Like so many contemporary inventors, Hans Magnus Malling Hansen[17] in Kopenhagen had developed a so-called writing-sphere for the express purpose of assisting his deaf and dumb pupils.[18]

In Genoa, Nietzsche spent two months trying out and repairing, using and describing his favorite toy until the heavy rains of the Riviera spring made it indeed "unusable." A letter, a litter, as Joyce said; wet ribbons left nothing more than meaningless signs on wet paper.[19] The dream of combining literary composition with publication had again melted away into blindness or random noise, that background essential to all modern media.

And yet, it was a love affair. The fact that a German newspaper article on Nietzsche had not "forgotten" his typing-sphere[20] filled him with joy and pride. So precisely did he realize discursive events. As far as I can see—and it *is* difficult to write the literary history of typewriting—no contemporary philosopher would have both accepted and even celebrated his own mechanization. Only popular authors like Mark Twain in America[21] and Paul Lindau in Germany antedated Nietzsche. Their reason, however, was literary mass production and not blindness, their reaction not a metamorphosis like Nietzsche's. "At last," Nietzsche types, "when my eyes prevent me from *learning*—and this will happen soon!—I still can forge rhymes."[22] Instead of a philosophical scholar bound to readings and rereadings, there appears a poet Nietzsche and an automatic writing whose only topic is typewriting itself:

The typing-sphere is something like me: made of iron
Yet easily distorted especially while traveling.
One has to have sufficient tact and patience
And delicate little fingers in order to use us.

In these rhymes three components of textuality coincide: instrument and topic of writing, instrument and agent of writing. An author, however, does not appear, precisely because he remains the poem's addressed reader. Identifying himself with the receptive delicacy of his machine, Nietzsche reverses the phallogocentrism of classical slate pencils. Not authorship but effeminization is his fate.

And indeed, the writer's sex changes with Malling Hansen as well as with Remington, in Europe as well as in America. As a typing poet, Nietzsche is but another female secretary working in a Kopenhagen printer's office.[24] And it is only following the demise of his Malling Hansen typing sphere that he changes again into a man and philosopher. "This machine," he writes to Overbeck, "is delicate like a young dog and causes much trouble—only some entertainment. Now, my friends have to invent a reading machine, too. Otherwise I will deteriorate and miss my necessary mental nutrition. More exactly, I must contact a young man intelligent enough to *work* with me. To this end, I would even contract a two years' marriage."[25]

Love affairs with typewriters put an end to love itself. The mechanization and desexualization of writing clearly undermine the difference between a young man and a wife. As long as women were excluded from textual production, poets like Goethe could dictate to other men like Eckermann, his secretary, or to a certain Geist, that the Eternal Feminine is all men's ideal.[26] A century later, when Valéry retraces the drama between Faust and Gretchen, a female secretary appears at the exact place of love.[27] And when Gottfried Benn dismisses all his concubines, he does so in order to marry a secretary who could type two hundred syllables per minute.[28] Nietzsche's fantasy of a two-year marriage is fulfilled and modern literature established.

3

What took place in 1882 was neither marriage nor literature but philosophy. After his typing-sphere had fallen apart, Nietzsche's sister and mouthpiece had a favor to ask of Malvida von Meysenbug. The old emancipated lady was invited to look out for an "eminent young man able to help Nietzsche's philosophic business by means of excerpting and copying."[29] Instead of Malvida, however, Paul Rée did the research, and instead of an eminent young man, he presented a rather notorious young lady. The friend who already had procured Nietzsche's typing-sphere also procured its human substitute: Lou von Salomé.

Hundreds of scholars have analyzed the most famous *ménage à trois* of literary history. No one, however, has realized that its humble purpose was not erotic at all, but rather guided by the technology of writing. The only exception is Nietzsche himself, who writes to his sister:

> So, your wish is fulfilled. My esteemed friend [Malvida] or rather Dr. Paul Rée has indeed found somebody able to help me. Yet, it is neither an 'enthusiastic young man' nor a young man at all, but a young lady!! Truly I would prefer serious young men or even men of my own age . . . , but the case is exceptional. Fraulein von Meysenbug and Dr. Rée bombarded me with letters and conjurations till I came to Rome where they had found a young lady—born, as they pretended, for my philosophy.[30]

These are lines of terrible historical precision. The question whether or not Friedrich Nietzsche went to bed with Fräulein Salomé may divert psychologists. The question why young ladies of the time could replace Nietzsche's rotten typewriter and even his notoriously rare students has some priority. An answer, once again, comes from his sister and mouthpiece. The monograph on *Friedrich Nietzsche and the Women of His Time* recalls that professors of the University of Zürich had developed a weakness for female students, at least ever since "emancipation" no longer meant war, but rather an "amiable" readiness to work as "teaching assistants and librarians."[31] Consequently, young ladies from Russia or Germany, a country where text-production and higher education still remained a male monopoly until 1908, had every reason to choose the Department of Philosophy or some other department of the University of Zürich. Ex-professors of the University of Basel had every reason to choose them as their teaching assistants and librarians. The deck was stacked long before an enflamed philosopher and his Russian love climbed Monte Sacro.

Nietzsche's philosophy implements the historical desexualization of writing and teaching. In the absence of any colleague or even student sufficiently inspired to fulfill Nietzsche's deepest wish, the foundation of a Zarathustra chair,[32] Nietzsche does away with certain limitations of philosophical discourse. He chooses new students from among emancipated women. Lou von Salomé is only one of the many Zürich students to seek Nietzsche out. The forgotten names of Resa Schirnhofer, Meta von Salis, and, above all, Helene Druskowitz must be added. Strangely enough, what Nietzsche called the future of Germany's system of higher education starts in the peaceful and anchoritic Engadin. Strangely enough, female students traveled to Sils-Maria to visit a "man" who "in their eyes must have been the worst misogynist of all."[33] But such is life. Just as the secular absence of woman from philosophical discourse had idealized her under such names as Nature or Mother, so the inclusion of many different women would also affect that discourse itself. Nietzsche redefines what Hegel had called love as war and hate between the two sexes.[34] His sarcastic comments on women who write instead of mothering are equaled only by the comments on men which his female pupils and "friends" (Helene Druskowitz in particular) will publish.[35] Thus, philosophical discourse loses its unity and truth. Two writers, male versus female, engage in a discursive escalation, thereby proving the new definition of heterosexuality.

Honeymoons between Nietzsche and Lou von Salomé would have been fine and forgotten. Their ever-escalating fight started Nietzsche's fame. Women (and Jews)[36] were the first to discover an almost silenced ex-professor. Whether motivated by hate or not, most of Nietzsche's private female students engaged in writing careers. And this, at the time, was a discursive event in itself. Even though Zarathustra-chairs remained a dream for some decades to come, Nietzsche had done what he could. To quote just one example: to Resa Schirnhofer, in search of a philosophical dissertation topic, he strongly recommended she read *Dawn* and *Gay Science*, calling these fragments goldmines full of excellent topics as well as introductions to his *Zarathustra*.

Nietzsche—I wrote it once and Laurence Rickels has proved it—was no founder of discursivities. May that dubious glory remain to Marx and Freud.[39] What he did was to destroy secular rules and to test, in endless experiments, new fields and technologies of discourse. Like everyone else at the time, Nietzsche had been trained, both in high school and in the university, in handwriting and academic homosexuality. "The influence of women"[40] and of typewriting were absolutely surprising. And yet, in both cases, he realized each as a discursive innovation right from the start. Writing women and writing machines sustain Nietzsche's discourse.

4

"Our writing instruments contribute to our thoughts." This typed thought contains in *nuce* Nietzsche's *Genealogy of Morals*, chapter two. Nietzsche, instead of continuing his failed experiments with the typing-sphere, transcribes it into a theory. Writing is defined no longer as a natural extension of man whose handwriting would simply externalize voice and memory. On the contrary, media are preceded only by blindness in every sense. The animal called man comes out of random noise and forgetfulness. The institution of memory, therefore, is an act of sheer and external violence. Man, instead of learning his in-dividuality through the continuous flow of handwriting, is the blind victim of machines that inscribe and divide his body in a most real way, a mnemotechnical device whose name the readers of Stoker's *Dracula*[41] or of Kafka's *Penal Colony*[42] can easily supply. Both texts describe typewriters of the time before Underwood, that is, without visual control. Their inscriptions have to be read by the very flesh. Nietzsche, in identifying himself with his typing-sphere, spoke of a common "delicacy."

Under these conditions, the genealogy of morals is at once the genealogy of gods. "In order to deny the existence of a suffering that could remain hidden and undiscovered—without witness—mankind was almost compelled to invent gods: that is, beings able to see through darkness and interested in painful spectacles."[43]

It is Nietzsche's ultimate and indeed final experiment to occupy the place of such a demon. If God is dead, gods are easily invented. "The poor man," as Malvida von Meysenbug calls him, "almost blind, unable to read, unable to write (except on a machine),"[44] identifies himself with Dionysos. *The Genealogy of Morals* is put into verse and a painful spectacle, the *Laments of Ariadne*, can begin.[45] The voice of versified Ariadne arises in absolute darkness or blindness. She speaks of and to a "hidden" god who is torturing her body mnemotechnically. Dionysos has no word, no style, except those very torments. That is why his victim can decode only on her body the signs of a desire that is precisely the desire of the Other. After one hundred and fifteen lines of laments, however, she has succeeded. Ariadne now realizes her desire for the desire of Dionysos.

> Come back!
> *With* all your tortures!
> All my tears
> run to you,
> the last flame of my heart
> burns for you.
> O come back,
> my unknown god! my *pain*! my final happiness!

This last cry is no fiction. It almost quotes one of those recently invented female writers. A poem written by Lou von Salomé and set to music by Friedrich Nietzsche includes the line "If there is no more happiness you can give me, well, there is still one more pain to give!" The poet Nietzsche, for once, is nothing but a woman's secretary. That is why their relation has to be inverted again. After the final cry of Ariadne or Salomé, the hitherto hidden and silent god makes his entry.

> Be wise, Ariadne! . . .
> You've got little ears, you've got my ears:
> let me put a wise word into them!—
> Don't we have to hate each other before we shall love?
> *I am your labyrinth* . . .

Dionysos, occupying the aural labyrinth of his victim, is a dictator in both senses of the word. He dictates to a slave or secretary to take his dictation. The new rule of heterosexuality is literally fulfilled when one sex inscribes painful words into the other's ear. Philosophy changes its very pragmatics. Instead of academic, exclusively male discourse within and about an Alma Mater, the two sexes speak to each other about their impossible relation. That is why Nietzsche, having invented a "philosopher" named Dionysos, calls his existence a historical "novelty."[46] Unlike Socrates with his Greek nobles, unlike Hegel with his German functionaries, Dionysos discusses philosophy with a woman. *The Laments of Ariadne* are just one of many "famous dialogues," as Nietzsche put it, "between Ariadne and her philosophical lover on the island of Naxos."[47]

The island of Naxos is no fiction, but rather the future of Germany's higher education system. After the double loss of his Malling Hansen and his Salomé, the almost blind Nietzsche looks out for possible secretaries. The only way to write *Beyond Good and Evil* is to dictate the book. To this end, a certain Mrs. Röder-Wiederhold makes her entry onto the island of Naxos. Forgotten and ephemeral, she is nonetheless a prototype. In many cases, modern text-production takes place on the material base (as Marx would call it) of heterosexual couples who write together instead of sleeping together. Tolstoi and his typing daughter,[48] Henry James and Miss Bosanquet's Remington,[49] Valéry's Faust and his Mademoiselle Lust, Benn and his second wife, Edith Wharton and diverse men, Hofmannsthal and a daughter he had earlier wisely sent to a typing school,[50] Kafka and Felice Bauer,[51] the warlord Hitler and the stenographers he preferred to his whole general staff,[52] all these strange couples are preceded by Nietzsche and his secretary, that human substitute for a rotten typing-sphere.

Mrs. Röder-Wiederhold, it must be said, poses a problem. Unfortunately enough, certain European demons have inscribed onto her the morals of Christianity and Democracy. Confronted with a despotic dictator in both senses, she cannot but suffer. Her own writing hands must transcribe what is beyond Good and Evil, beyond Christianity and Democracy. So it happens that *The Laments of Ariadne* literally come true. Any history concerned with technologies of writing must take into account the fact that *Beyond Good and Evil* was not an easy book to produce. Nietzsche knew it and said so. Mrs. Röder-Wiederhold "wept" much more than he would have "liked."[52]

Muβ *man sich nicht erst hassen, wenn man sich lieben soll?*

NOTES

1. Nietzsche, typed letter to Peter Gast, end of February 1882, in F.N. *Briefwechsel*, ed. Elisabeth Förster-Nietzsche and Peter Gast (Berlin-Leipzig 1902–09), IV: 97.

2. Cf. Marshall McLuhan, *Understanding Media: The extensions of man* (London: 1964) p. 260.

3. Cf. for instance Friedrich Schlegel, *Über die Philosophie: an Dorothea*, Kritische Friedrich-Schlegel-Ausgabe, ed. Ernst Behler (Paderborn: 1958 ff.), 8:42. The metaphor is analyzed in my essay "Writing into the Wind, Bettina." *Glyph*, 7 (1980), 45–48.

4. For amusing historical facts see Bruce Bliven, Jr., *The Wonderful Writing Machine* (New York: 1954), pp. 59–79. The end of handwriting is described in Eduard Weckerle, *Mensch und Maschine* (Jena: 1925), p. 32.

5. Jenny Schwabe, *Kontoristin. Forderungen, Leistungen, Aussichten in diesem Berufe* (Leipzig: 1902), p. 6f.

6. In 1895, two German economists made this point very clear: "Es wird überraschen, hier einen praktischen Nutzen der zur wahren Landplage gewordenen Ausbildung junger Mädchen im Klavierspiel zu finden: die hierbei gewonnene Fingerfertigkeit ist für die Handhabung der Schreibmaschine sehr wertvoll." (Quoted in Ute Frevert, "Vom Klavier zur Schreibmaschine: weiblicher Arbeitsmarkt und Rollenzuweisungen am Beispiel der weiblichen Angestellten in der Weimarer Republik;" In Annette Kulm and Gerhard Schneider (eds.), *Frauen in der Geschichte*, v. I (Düsseldorf: 1982), p. 88.

7. Bliven, p. 3.

8. George Tilghman Richards, *The History and Development of Typewriters*, (1964), p. 1

9. For a historical survey, see Werner von Eye, *Kurzgefaßte Geschichte der Schreibmaschine und des Maschinenschreibens* (Berlin: 1958).

10. Cf. C. L. Müller, *Neu erfundene Schreib-Maschine, mittelst welcher Jedermann ohne Licht in jeder Sprache und Schriftmanier sicher zu schreiben, Aufsätze und Rechnungen zu verfertigen vermag, auch Blinde besser als mit allen bisher bekannten Schreibtafeln nicht nur leichter schreiben, sondern auch das von ihnen Geschriebene besser lesen können* (Wien: 1823), pp. 5f., 11, 16.

11. Cf. McLuhan, p. 64f.

12. Cf. von Eye, p. 16.

13. Edgar J. Swift, "The Acquisition of Skill in Type-Writing. A contribution to the psychology of learning," *The Psychological Bulletin*, 1 (1904), 302.

14. Cf. Gottfried Benn, "Roman des Phänotyp," in his *Gesammelte Werke*, ed. Dieter Wellershoff (Wiesbaden: 1959–61), II, 176. Sherlock Holmes, in the first typewriter-story ever written, wonders if, for the shortsighted heroine, it is not "a little trying to do so much typewriting." Here the great detective commits one of his rare errors. (Arthur Conan Doyle, "A Case of Identity," in *The Complete Sherlock Holmes*, ed. Christopher Morley, [New York: 1930], p. 192.)

15. Nietzsche, letter to Peter Gast, 11/5/1879. *Briefe*, IV, 28. The impact of telegraphy on literature was first described by Robert Lincoln O'Brien, "Machinery and English Style," *Atlantic Monthly*, 94 (1904), 464–472. Nietzsche's phrase, "Unser Schreibzeug arbeitet mit an unseren Gedanken," underscores the fact that typing requires brevity.

16. Cf. Nietzsche, letter to Elisabeth Förster, 8/14/1879, quoted in Kurt Paul Janz, *Friedrich Nietzsche: Biographie* (Munich: 1978–79) 2:27.

17. Hansen—and not "Hansun", as Nietzsche's biographer spells the name. Janz is twice mistaken when he denies to Malling Hansen the Nietzschean title of "Erfinder." Remington (who simply bought Sholes's patent in 1873) cannot have "preceded by ten years" a machine constructed in 1865. Cf. Janz, 2:81, 95

18. Cf. Otto Burghagen, *Die Schreibmaschine: Illustrierte Beschreibung aller gangbaren Schreibmaschinen nebst gründlicher Anleitung zum Arbeiten auf sämtlichen Systemen* (Hamburg: 1898), pp. 10, 119f.

19. Cf. Nietzsche, letter to E. Förster, 3/23/1882, *Briefe*, v. 5 pt. 2, p. 484: "Das verfluchte *Schreiben!* Aber die Maschine ist seit meiner letzten Karte *unbrauchbar;* das Wetter ist nämlich trüb und wolkig, also feucht: da

ist jedesmal der Farbenstreifen auch *feucht* und *klebrig*, so daβ jeder Buchstabe hängen bleibt, und die Schrift *gar nicht* zu sehn ist. Ueberhaupt!!"

20. Cf. Nietzsche, typed letter to Overbeck, March 1882, F.N., *Briefwechsel mit Franz Overbeck*, ed. Richard Oehler and Carl Albrecht Bernoulli (Leipzig: 1916), p. 169. So far, it has been impossible to dig out that "Bericht des Berliner Tageblattes."

21. Mark Twain's rather complex story is told by Bliven, pp, 58–63. Cf. also Burghagen, p.22: "Wir nennen nur Mark Twain, Bret Hart, Farjeon, Fritjof Nansen, Paul Lindau, Gerhard Amyntor und viele andere als die ersten Schriftsteller, welche ihre Werke direkt auf der Schreibmaschine zu Papier bringen." In such catalogues, Nietzsche is usually forgotten.

22. Nietzsche, letter to mother and sister, 4/1/1882, *Briefe*, v. 5 pt. 2, p. 485.

23. Nietzsche, *Werke. Kritische Gesamtausgabe*, ed. Giorgio Colli and Mazzino Montinari (Berlin: 1967ff.), 9:673. Other typed rhymes were sent in a letter to Peter Gast, 2/17/1882, *Briefe*, 4:96.

24. Cf. v. Eye, p. 78. The first female typewriter was probably Lillian Sholes, the inventor's daughter, in 1872. Cf. Richard Nelson Current, *The Typewriter and the Men Who Made it* (Urbana: 1954), p. 54. (Thanks to Heidi Beck of Stanford.)

25. Typed letter, March 1882. *Briefwechsel mit Franz Overbeck*, p. 169f.

26. Cf. for instance Friedrich Wilhelm Riemer, *Mitteilungen über Goethe*, ed. Arthur Pollmer (Leipzig: 1921), p. 313f. "Merkwürdige Reflexion Goethes über sich selbst: daβ er das *Ideelle* unter einer weiblichen Form oder unter der Form des Weibes konzipiert. Was ein Mann sei, das wisse er ja nicht" (11/24/1809).

27. Cf. Paul Valéry, *Mon Faust: Ébauches*, in *Oeuvres*, ed. Jean Hytier (Paris: 1960), 2:292.

28. Cf. his letter to Ellinor Büller-Kinkowström, 1/10/1937, in G.B., *Den Traum alleine tragen: neue Texte, Briefe, Dokumente*, ed. Paul Raabe and Max Niedermayer, (Munich: 1969), pp. 184–186.

29. Elisabeth Förster's note in F.N., *Briefe*, v. 5 pt. 2, p. 488.

30. Letter to E. Förster, end of April 1882, *Briefe*, v. 5 pt. 2, p. 488. Even if this letter—as Karl Schlechta affirmed (F.N., *Werke*, ed. K.S. [Munich: 1954–56], 3:1371)—were one of his sister's falsifications, it is invented in accordance with every documented wish. Cf. for instance Nietzsche's typed letter to Paul Rée, 3/21/1882, in F.N., Paul Rée, and Lou von Salomé, *Die Dokumente ihrer Begegnung*, ed. Ernst Pfeiffer (Frankfurt: 1970), p. 100.

31. Elisabeth Förster-Nietzsche, *Friedrich Nietzsche und die Frauen seiner Zeit*, (Munich: 1935), p. 136.

32. Cf. Nietzsche, *Werke. Kritische Gesamtausgabe*, v. 6 pt. 3, p. 296.

33. E. Förster-Nietzsche, p. 138.

34. Cf. Nietzsche, *Werke. Kritische Gesamtausgabe*, v. 6 pt. 3, p. 304.

35. Cf. Nietzsche, letter to his mother, 10/22/1884, in F.N., *Briefwechsel. Kritische Gesamtausgabe*, ed. Giorgio Colli and Mazzino Montinari (Berlin: 1975ff.), v. 2 pt. 5, p. 435. Helene Druskowitz's hatred of men is most furiously expressed in her last book, *Pessimistische Kardinalsätze: ein Vademekum für die freiesten Geister*, von Erna (Dr. Helene von Druskowitz) (Wittenberg: ca. 1900).

36. The structural identity between women and Jews in Nietzsche is shown by Jacques Derrida, "La question du style," in *Nietzsche aujourd'hui?* (Paris: 1973), 1:235–287.

37. Cf. Nietzsche, letter to Resa Schirnhofer, April 1884, quoted in Förster-Nietzsche, p. 202.

38. Cf. Friedrich Kittler, "Wie man abschafft, wovon man spricht: Der Autor von *Ecce homo*," in *Literaturmagazin* 12 (Reinbek: 1980), p. 153f., and Laurence Rickels, "Friedrich Nichte" (in this volume).

39. Cf. Michel Foucault, "Qu'est-ce qu'un auteur?" *Bulletin de la Société Française de Philosophie*, 63 (1969).

40. Cf. Nietzsche, *Werke und Briefe. Historisch-kritische Ausgabe*, ed. Karl Schlechta and Hans Joachim Mette (Leipzig: 1933–42), 5:245.

41. Cf. my essay "Draculas Vermächtnis," in: *ZETA 02. Mit Lacan*, ed. Dieter Hombach (Berlin: 1982), pp. 116–125.

42. The homologies between Nietzsche's *Genealogy* and this Kafka-story are shown by Patrick Bridgwater, *Kafka and Nietzsche* (Bonn: 1974), pp. 104–111.

43. Nietzsche, *Werke. Kritische Gesamtausgabe*, v. 6 pt. 2, p. 320.

44. Letter to Olga Monod-Herzen, 4/26/1882, in Friedrich Nietzsche, Paul Rée, Lou von Salomé, p. 420: "Der arme Mensch, er ist wirklich ein Heiliger . . . und arbeitet immerfort, obgleich er beinah blind ist, weder lesen noch schreiben (bloß mit einer Maschine) kann."

45. The "dithyramb" is to be found in F.N., *Werke. Kritische Gesamtausgabe*, v. 6 pt. 3, pp. 396–399. Its direct relation to the *Genealogy of Morals* was discovered by Karl Reinhardt, "Nietzsches Klage der Ariadne," in K.R., *Von Werken und Formen: Essays* (Bad Godesberg: 1948), p. 477.

46. *Werke. Kritische Gesamtausgabe,* v. 6 pt. 2, p. 248.

47. *Werke. Kritische Gesamtausgabe,* v. 6 pt. 3, p. 117f.

48. Cf. Bliven, p. 79.

49. Cf. Theodora Bosanquet, *Henry James at Work* (London: 1924), and McLuhan, p. 260.

50. Cf. Hugo von Hofmannsthal and Ottonie Gräfin Degenfeld, *Briefwechsel* (Frankfurt: 1974), p. 385 (6/11/1919). Thanks to Antje Weiner-Petersen of Stanford.

51. On this "impossible rapport sexuael" see Friedrich Kittler, *Aufschreibesysteme 1800/1900* (Munich: Fink Verlag, 1985).

52. Cf. Percy Ernst Schramm (ed.), *Kriegstagebuch des Oberkommandos der Wehrmacht (Wehrmachtführungsstab)* (Herrsching: 1982), 1:139E.

53. Nietzsche, letter 7/23/1885, quoted in Janz, II, 393. A final quotation, applicable both to Ariadne and to Mrs. Röder-Wiederhold, may be recalled. Zarathustra said that "he who writes in blood and sentences, does not want to be read, but to be learned by rote" (*Werke. Kritische Gesamtausgabe,* v. 6 pt. 1, p. 44).

11

History and Mimesis

Philippe Lacoue-Labarthe

Under this title, "History and Mimesis," I am proposing to outline a reading of the second of Nietzsche's *Untimely Meditations*.

I will not attempt this reading here with the sole intention of giving my own interpretation, indeed a new interpretation of this text. Besides, the second *Untimely Meditation* has been read and re-read so often that it is difficult to see today what "new interpretation" could be given—and still more difficult what "personal" interpretation. Nor is it my intention to investigate as an historian of philosophy Nietzschean thought on history. Nietzsche does not himself concern me here. Instead I wish to take this *Untimely Meditation* as one of the major documents in which the German tradition has perhaps laid down its most fundamental thought, that is to say, its thought on history. Other documents could be consulted: besides Hegel, of course, Schiller's aesthetic and "poetological" essays. For example. Or Hölderlin's *Remarks* on Sophocles; or *The Eighteenth Brumaire of Louis Napoleon Bonaparte*; or even Wagner's *Ring*. And there are many others. If I choose to speak of Nietzsche, it is for the single reason that he appears to me to have said with the utmost precision—and in political terms that, to a large extent, fashion European (and world) history in our century, our history therefore—what, in the eyes of the Germans, has been always at stake in the problematic of history. Behind this interpretive essay, then, it will always be necessary to presuppose a question of more

This lecture was first presented on March 3, 1983 at the University of Strasbourg as part of a research project organized by the center for Interdisciplinary Studies and Research in Theology on the topic "Of History."

general aspect, that for the sake of convenience I will distribute along two registers:

1. Why is German philosophy, since the very first of Kant's successors, essentially the philosophy of history?
2. Why is history, in such philosophy, essentiality itself?

Whatever may be, today, the dominant position of "historicism" under its multiple forms or, in terms of its mere opposite, the neoclassical (and more or less weak) controversy to which it gives way, nothing assures us that history has itself been interrogated, still less understood, in its essence. A first gesture in this direction is to address oneself to philosophy itself. Not to find there an answer (any answer would only reinforce our present somnambulism), but to discover there the difficulty of a question.

* * * * *

The question of history, in Nietzsche, is at first the question of historical culture, *historische Bildung*: culture and historical formations, historical education. As so often in Nietzsche—as so often, it is necessary to say, in philosophy—the fundamental preoccupation is pedagogical or, more exactly, "agogical." The second *Untimely Meditation* is in the same vein as the Basel lectures on *The Future of Our Educational Institutions*; it is in a certain way indissociable from that other *Untimely Meditation* to which it is nearly contemporary: *Schopenhauer as Educator*; one must even reread it, more broadly, in terms of the entire enterprise of cultural "propaganda" that, under the name of Wagner, forms the horizon of Nietzsche's first philosophical work, beginning with the work on the Greeks and tragedy.

This second *Untimely Meditation* is entitled: *On the Uses and Disadvantages of History for Life.*[1] It is placed under the authority of a statement from Goethe: "In any case, I hate everything that merely instructs me without augmenting or directly invigorating my activity." History—historical culture—is consequently judged from the point of view of life, that is to say, from the point of view of activity. It is moreover this point of view that determines the primary sense of the "untimely." It is a question of intensity or, and I will return to this, of energy: it is a question of knowing if history—historical culture (here understood as the domination of history over culture and education, as domination from the point of view of history, historicism)—it is a question therefore of knowing if history thus understood increases or decreases vital potential. Life is first thought as *dynamis,* that is, as power. Power, understood as will to power, is already at this time, although the philosopheme may not yet be literally constituted, the key word of the Nietzschean interpretation of being: *it is*—it subsists, exists, endures and imposes itself—it is what *has* power. *It is* what *lives,* that is to say, according to an etymology that Nietzsche borrows from the Pre-Socratics,[2] what breathes. And this goes for every being. But especially for three among them that in Nietzsche's eyes enjoy an absolute privilege: man (in the sense of the individual), people (which one must keep from confusing with nation, in the modern sense) and culture (*Kultur*).

A man, a people, a culture are, in the same way, alive. A living thing is of course alive only if it is not dying or is not threatened by death. The criterion for judging the life of a living thing is essentially that of health. If *to be* means to *live,* to think that which is, that is to say, to philosophize, means to estimate or measure the degree of vitality, the chances that that which is has to live. To discern, therefore, the health of the malady. To philosophize is a critical task, but this critical task arises from medical practice. In notes that are nearly contemporary to the second *Untimely Meditation,* Nietzsche defines the philosopher as "a cultural physician." To philosophize therefore amounts to tracking down the signs of a possible malady or to relieving the symptoms of a real malady. To interpret and to diagnose; that is to say, to return to causes. To set up an etiology. And from there, to attempt a cure, that is, to propose a remedy. (Once having diagnosed the malady as neurosis, Freud will oppose himself to this "plan" in *Civilization and Its Discontents.* It is an old affair of mimetic rivalry.)

It is within this medical, ontologico-medical, optics that the question of history is considered: is history—historical culture (but again understood as "historical sense," the consciousness of belonging to a history and of defining oneself as an essentially historical being)—is history, then, in this sense, useful to life or not? Is it not on the contrary the symptom of a malady, the properly modern malady, that is to say, the malady of what we could call in an emblematic fashion, somewhat as Nietzsche does, the Hegelian epoch?

In principle, we know the answer: if we refer to the living thing par excellence, to the animal—or even, in man, to what was his animal age, to infancy (a double image of the lost paradise, in which man signifies irremediable loss and mourning), then we see that in the first place life derives from the possibility of forgetting. Man is a sick animal because he is sick of memory: he bends under the weight of the past, he is overcome by an incessant *es war* that "reminds him what his existence fundamentally is—an imperfect tense that can never become a perfect one" (1, p. 61). A being, in other words, that endlessly suffers finitude. As such, he is promised to death ("the desired forgetting," the "let me forget" of tragic wisdom, but as end of the present and of existence), a death that always only confirms this Hegelian truth: "Being is only an uninterrupted has-been." If man wants to live, then, it is absolutely necessary that he know how to forget. Forgetting is in no way a loss. Forgetting is necessary to the economy of living; it is the very condition of activity and action that, otherwise, would be paralyzed by the consciousness of repetition. Later, Nietzsche will speak of forgetting or of active "forgetting." Man must know how to extricate himself, not simply from becoming and temporality (and thus to gain instants of eternity, divine, that is, properly in-human moments—a very strong theme up to *Zarathustra* and beyond), but also from the domination of memory. A sign of this is the happiness, the joy, that such a separation, that is, such an ecstasy, brings: the happiness, the joy, of being for a moment, as Nietzsche says, "truly being," that is, in effect, of reaching eternity.

If memory is therefore what essentially threatens the living in man, if memory is the malady of man and his health depends on his capacity to combat memory, historical sense and historical education, the culture of memory—the "rumination of the past" and "sleeplessness"—are the worst fears that can overcome man. This is why Nietzsche can say, and this is his first postulate:

> There is a degree of sleeplessness, of rumination, of the historical sense, which is harmful and ultimately fatal to the living thing, whether this living thing be a man or a people or a culture. (1, p. 62)

Nietzsche, of course, is never naive enough to oppose to this, purely and simply, the absence of all historical sense. Memory is constitutive of that singular living thing that is man. It is even what defines him: man is an animal endowed with memory, that is to say, with language. But when neither memory nor the historical sense can be suppressed (this would be the very negation of man), we see the symptom of a profoundly sick state in which both are cultivated for themselves and, above all, unopposed (even appreciated and encouraged). Historical being defines man; it does not constitute his essence, which is life. In other words, historicity defines the humanity of man, according to what distinguishes him from among all living things. But insofar as he is first of all a living thing, it is relatively inessential to him. Nonetheless, one must understand—and indeed this is what Nietzsche understands—that the essence of history is in no way anything historical. Put another way, if you will, memory rests upon the bottomless fund of forgetting.

Hence Nietzsche's diagnosis: everything in this matter is a question of dosage. Or, since the critique is a medical one (and the medicine critical), of limitation and delimitation. It is not a matter of denying the historical sense, but of containing it, damming it up, bringing it within its just limits. That is to say, of making sure that it does not exceed the point where "it could become overwhelming and harmful": to life, to power, to the will and (creative) energetic desires, to force and fecundity. To health. This is what Nietzsche calls the law of the horizon:

> This is a universal law: a living thing can be healthy, strong and fruitful only when bounded by a horizon. (1, p. 63)

And this leads to the statement of its fundamental principle:

> Peace of mind, the good conscience, the joyful deed, confidence in the future—all of them depend, in the case of the individual as of a people, on the existence of a line dividing the bright and discernible from the unilluminable and dark; on one's being just as able to forget at the right time as to remember at the right time: on the possession of a powerful instinct for sensing when it is necessary to see historically and when unhistorically. This, precisely, is the principle the reader is invited to meditate upon: the unhistorical and the historical are necessary in equal measure for the health of an individual, of a people, and of a culture. (1 p. 63)

It goes without saying that to limit the historical sense is to prevent it from moving towards the lack of historical sense, which is no more negative than forgetting. The lack of historical sense is on the contrary the very condition of acting and doing, at least when acting and doing have a real greatness. Every true act is unhistorical, as every great event—that is, every great *historical* event, every event that "makes history"—presupposes, for its very emergence, a nonhistorical foundation or "climate." The unhistorical is life as the origin of history, since "history belongs to the living" (2, p. 67). To limit historical sense means, then, to reserve its place—the highest—for life and to preserve the very origin, that is to say, the possibility of history. It is therefore to reverse the relation that seeks to install historical culture between life and history, since historical culture is precisely responsible for the decay of history itself. Such a logic consequently requires that life no longer be in the service of history (for this is the malady, and this is death), but that history be put in the service of life as well as in the service of the very thing that makes it possible. It is really a question of preserving history as that which is, in itself, power and potency, creative force. Hence Nietzsche's thesis, which is stated in the following manner:

> History become pure [the scientific claim is one of Nietzsche's favorite targets: I cannot consider it here], sovereign science would be for mankind a sort of conclusion of life and a settling of accounts with it. The study of history is something salutary and fruitful for the future only as the attendant of a mighty new current of life, of an evolving culture for example, that is to say only when it is dominated and directed by a higher force and does not itself dominate and direct. (1, p. 67)

Such is in fact the reason for which delimitation is a matter of dosage. According to a very old logic, and originally linked to the problematic of *mimēsis*, history is thought as drug, as *pharmakon*. Absorbed in small quantity, it does not present any danger: it is even necessary to the survival of the organism. It can cure. But if one abuses it, it destroys and kills. It is a poison. One must therefore use history moderately. And if it becomes overwhelming, if it drugs an entire people for example, then it becomes necessary to oppose it with antidotes. This is practically the conclusion of the second *Untimely Meditation*:

> But it is sick, this unchained life, and needs to be cured. It is sick with many illnesses and not only with the memory of its chains—what chiefly concerns us here is that it is suffering from the *malady of history*. Excess of history has attacked life's plastic powers, it no longer knows how to employ the past as a nourishing food. The evil is dreadful, and yet! if youth did not possess nature's clairvoyant gift no one would know it is an evil or that a paradise of health has been lost. This same youth, however, also divines with the curative instinct of this same nature how this paradise is to be regained: it knows the medicine and balsam against the malady of history, against excess of history: but what is this medicine called?

> Now, one must not be surprised to find that it is called by the names of poisons: the antidote to the historical is called—*the unhistorical and suprahistorical.* (10, p. 120)

All of this is well known, after all, so I will not insist on it. I have nevertheless had to recall it because it is in some way a question there of the official version of this original Nietzschean problematic of history. It is the properly philosophical version. It inscribes Nietzsche within the metaphysical tradition. It refers his interpretation of history itself and his antihistorical strategy—his hatred, not of history itself, but of historicism, that sort of cancer of modernity—to his most obvious interpretation of being. And from there, it enables an understanding of the celebrated distinction, to which the second *Untimely Meditation* is generally reduced among the three forms of history (monumental, antiquarian, and critical) and the very complex relations that Nietzsche establishes among these three forms, whose unity constitutes historicity itself. I will return to this.

Such an interpretation is neither false nor insufficient. It even has its necessity. But because it goes directly to what is essential—by philosophical criteria—because it tends to neglect and underestimate what is apparently, in Nietzsche, of the order of the nonphilosophical (and in fact the *Untimely Meditations* are primarily polemical texts, that is to say, political texts), it does not stop to decipher those statements that it already considers as merely empirical, or at the very least as subordinated to ontological or supposedly ontological statements. This is obviously the case for the political statements—those very ones that Heidegger, during the thirties, will never want to take directly into account. Or to examine them a bit more closely, those that are shown to be governed by a much more twisted logic than that wherein malady and health are opposed within the horizon of the determination of being as life and power. A more twisted logic means a logic fundamentally capable of carrying away and displacing, even of making secondary or subordinate, the so-called "ontological determination."

(I do not wish to indict the Heideggerian interpretation of Nietzsche. I am simply suggesting that Heidegger, who saw very clearly in "Nietzscheanism," after the episode of '33, the principal enemy, could nevertheless not take into account Nietzsche's political statements [I refer to everything on the "conservative revolution" side of Nietzsche] because they were ultimately too close to his own political positions. Even in terms of a certain mistrust vis-a-vis Germany. Heidegger is on the contrary the first to have sensed that Nietzschean discourse—Nietzschean predication—does not rest on anything constituted or received, as it were, from the "past," from "history," from "people," etc. On anything empirical. And therefore to have sensed that politics, in Nietzsche, give way to another ontology, or presuppose a displacement of ontology.)

What does this discourse consist of? What is the political purpose of the second *Untimely Meditation*? It consists of two propositions:

1. Germany does not exist.
2. Germany does not exist because it has no proper being.

This is therefore an observation, a judgment of existence (or, in this case, of nonexistence) and, supporting it, a judgment, a "theorem," a proposition that one must call ontological: to exist (to be) is to have a proper-being (an "identity"). Because of this, you can already see that another type of ontology, or at least of ontological conceptuality, is introduced than that with which we were at first concerned: life (to be is to live, to breathe) comes to be supplanted by the proper or propriety.

First of all, with regard to the observation: Nietzsche is far from being the first to make it. Moreover, in order to refer to this nonexistence, he uses the word that, since Schiller and Hölderlin, if not before, has designated the fundamental sentiment of the Germans: *Not*, distress, interior misery. Such distress, in Nietzsche's eyes, depends above all on the absence of "spiritual unity." "Germany does not exist" does not merely mean that Germany awaits its political unity. In itself a political unity is nothing. Rather, "Germany does not exist" means that the condition of political unity does not exist, that there is no German identity, that what Nietzsche calls "the unity of the German spirit and of German life" is missing. Lacking such unity, the Germans are uncertain of their being: they are never sure of their collective interiority, their personality is weak. Not only are they affected by the modern evil par excellence, by historical evil, which is depropriation ("We moderns have nothing whatever of our own," we are only "walking encyclopedias," we are filled "with the ages, customs, arts, philosophies, religions, discoveries of others"), but in them evil is redoubled by the fact that they have never been anyone, they have never made up a people even though they have everything, perhaps, to become one. The Germans are an absolute non-people. And such is the distress.

The decisive thing here is less in the attribution of causes (moreover, we will see in a moment that the cause is unique) than in the manner in which Nietzsche thematizes and describes this German evil, that is, in the strictest sense of the word, this alienation. He speaks of the scission between outside and inside, the contradiction between form and content, the "strange contrast" between an inward being to which nothing outward corresponds and an outward being to which nothing inward corresponds. Beneath the ethical pathos, it is really an aesthetic thematic that comes to light, and we recognize in the categories that Nietzsche manipulates the traditional lexicon of the theory or philosophy of art: the work of art, the great work of art, has been always thought as that in which the relationship between foundation and form is absolutely necessary, in such a way that a perfect adequation rules between the "inside" and the "outside." Moreover, it is also what defines the noble animal, the organic as such, the living being par excellence. But *work* and *organic* are the same word, and the question of knowing which, art or life, is the model for the other still stands. But which of the following dominate in Nietzsche's thought: an onto-zoology or an onto-mimetology?

In the beginning, at least, the philosophical constraint is double, and sufficiently powerful to oblige Nietzsche to speak in the same breath of the culture of a people in terms of a work of art and of the people itself as a "living unity":

> The culture of a people . . . was once, and I think with a certain justice, defined as unity of artistic style in all the expressions of the life of a people; this definition should not be misunderstood in the sense of implying an antithesis between barbarism and *fine* style; what is meant is that a people to whom one attributes a culture has to be in all reality [*Wirklichkeit*] a single living unity and not fall wretchedly apart into inner and outer, content and form. (4, pp. 79–80)

A people, as well as a man or a culture, a civilization (*Kultur*), does not exist, does not have its own unity, only lives insofar as it is thinkable as a work of art. It is in reality onto-mimetology that prevails and, at least in the "first Nietzsche," that has always already prevailed over onto-zoology. Being, for Nietzsche, is first of all *being worked*. If being, life, is thought as power, as *dynamis*, it is because being is already thought, according to a certain echo of the Greek interpretation of Being, as production, as *poiēsis* (which is moreover also constitutive of *physis*), and because production, in its turn, is thought as setting to work, as *energeia*. Being is energy. But this energy is itself understood in a modern way, under the horizon of the subjective determination of Being. This energy is that of a subject in the sense of subjectivity: it is the proper capability of an artist, whether the latter is human or not. (At any rate, the human artist, when he is truly great, that is to say, when he is truly an artist, is genius. His energy, and on this point Nietzsche is perfectly faithful to the Kantian reinterpretation of *mimēsis*,[3] is natural energy itself.) The artist's capability is defined by his capability to work, in a finished manner, to lead the thing worked or set to work to its term or its end, to its *telos*. Energy is also *entelechy*, completed formation. The only thing that exists as such is what is thus clearly finished in its form. Existence is reality, *Wirklichkeit*: set to work (*Werk*) wholly and completely.

The model of artistic practice, for Nietzsche, is provided by sculpture. This is perhaps, secretly, an echo of Hegel. Not only because they both refer to Greek art (as the paragon of "great art"), but because for the one as for the other, it is of the essence of art that its highest manifestation occurs in the erection of a figure, of a *Gestalt*. Artistic capability—power in the ontological sense—resides essentially in what Nietzsche calls, sometimes in a Kantian or post-Kantian (romantic) mode, the "formative force" (*bildende Kraft*), sometimes, in a mode that is more his own, the "plastic force" (*plastische Kraft*) or the "figurative force" (*gestaltende Kraft*).[4] I would prefer to translate it, in "Latin," by "fictioning force," thinking of the way in which philosophy, that is to say, the construction of "theoretical fictions," should be done according to Nietzsche "with a hammer"—which we must understand, as Heidegger has taught us, in reference to the art of the sculptor. The plastic essence of art is Apollonian insofar as it is formulated as chaos, confusion, and lack.

It is therefore not an accident if, beginning with the first pages of the text, health (that is to say, being-itself or the state of non-alienation, existence as real existence) is related to plastic capability. Life is thought on the model of art, and not inversely:

> To determine this degree and therewith the boundary at which the past has to be forgotten if it is not to become the gravedigger of the present, one would have to know exactly how great the *plastic power* of a man, a people, a culture is: I mean by plastic power the capacity to develop out of oneself in one's own way, to transform and incorporate into oneself what is past and foreign,to heal wounds, to replace what has been

> lost, to recreate broken moulds. There are people who possess so little of this power that they can perish from a single experience . . . on the other hand, there are those who are so little affected by the worst and most dreadful disasters . . . that they are able to feel tolerably well and be in possession of a kind of clear conscience even in the midst of them or at any rate very soon afterwards. (1, p. 62)

But we at once see what happens in real existence: it is not enough to be oneself, one must yet form oneself. The plastic force is the faculty of "growing by oneself" and of completing oneself by oneself. For a subject, whatever it may be, its formation—the only way it is itself—is an auto-formation. And such is in general what is missing in the Moderns, in the men of historical culture, and, more cruelly yet, in the Germans. Germany does not exist because the Germans are not a people, are not, as it were, an auto-organic work.

What does this mean?

Quite simply, that the Germans live *by imitation*. They have a formation and a culture, a *Bildung*, but the latter comes from the outside, it does not correspond to any inward necessity. This is moreover why it is wholly historical and why the Germans are, amongst all the peoples of Europe, more the "historians" than any others.

The description that Nietzsche gives, as you know, is one of pitiless severity: the Germans have never been a proper culture, but a mere knowledge—by itself alienating—of what culture is. Consequently, they have always lived according to conventions: when the conventions they follow originate from a certain solidity (this is the case with those that come to them from the French), the vicariousness of their life still has a certain steadiness. When on the contrary it gets into their head to discard the iron collar of the said conventions (to be "themselves," no longer to imitate or let their behavior be dictated), they are subjugated to even worse conventions because, right away, lacking a true internal principle, they seek their models more or less everywhere. The result is not only that the Germans are not themselves, but that they offer a distressing spectacle. Imitation is an aesthetic category; it belongs originally to the aesthetics of theatre. A distressing spectacle means bad comedy, masquerade, carnivalesque grimaces, monkey tricks. Germany is a pitiable theatre upon whose stage pitiable representations are played. In this sense it resembles imperial Rome: everything there is a role, one poses as a "universal type," one raises cosmopolitanism to the dignity of an institution. But in reality this existence is only for epigones, late-comers, and is further accentuated by the massification that affects all peoples of the industrial age. It is a mass imitation.

All of this amounts to saying that German nonexistence lies in German *passivity.* Conforming to an entire tradition that goes back at least to Plato, Nietzsche at first thinks imitation, *mimēsis,* as passivity. For imitation is not at first that of the actor (subjective genitive), but that of what the actor, imitating, offers to be imitated. Imitation is spontaneously understood as the spectator's identification, that passive mode by which one comes to oneself by submitting to the model of the other, so that being-itself, Plato essentially says, is constituted in the same way that a figure is impressed upon a malleable material when it is struck by a *typos* or "typed."[5] Imitation, in this sense—and Girard, as Freud before him, will retain something of this—is the general regime of the social, of the "bad" social, from the primary in-formation of the child by adult discourse and the narratives (the myths) that we tell him, to the rivalry that necessarily opposes, and not only at the time of the social apprenticeship, the imitator and the imitated, and that threatens to end social cohesion. This is why, if the theatrical metaphor—under all its forms—organizes in a rigorous or constraining fashion the entire description that Nietzsche gives of German nonexistence, it is because under the roles, the masks, the puppets, the derisive marionettes, etc., he does not think of the art of the comedian (which against Plato and within the perspective of the reversal of Platonism, he on the contrary places very highly, in the same way that he does the theatre in general), but he thinks of what Diderot, after many others, called the theatre or comedy of the world. That is to say, a theatre wherein the spectacle is in reality in the playhouse. This is what makes Nietzsche say that the Germans are the "spectators" of a gigantic "universal exposition." And this is above all what, for him, explains the incessant exclusion, by the "real" Germany (that is to say, the "philistines of culture"), of all those that carry or embody its spiritual or creative possibilities. He thinks of Wagner, of course, but in the Basel lectures he also evokes, (already) with more conviction, Lessing, Winckelmann and Schiller—and in any case, as we know, the list is very long.

Germany, finally, "does not exist" because of its lack of art, or the refusal to recognize its art: the great music of Germany, from the Lutheran chorale to Wagner, of which *The Birth of Tragedy* speaks. This means that as long as German art does not exist or German art is not recognized by the Germans themselves, there cannot be a German people; the German people will remain unable to form themselves and to erect themselves as a living work of art: "art flees away if you immediately conceal your deeds under the awning of history" (5, p. 83). Historical culture, imitation, prevents Germany from all access to itself, that is to say, to its proper being. Imitation is depropriation.

But art is itself, since the Greeks, since Plato and the Aristotelian determination of *technē*, imitation, *mimēsis*. Nietzsche obviously does not ignore this. Or more exactly, he does not escape, he does not succeed in avoiding the power of this determination any more than anyone else. But, in his eyes, the imitation at work in art—which one must understand literally—is in no way a passive imitation. Moreover, it is on this point, very precisely, that Nietzsche opposes himself to Plato and, whatever he says or believes, follows Aristotle. (The critique of Aristotle that *The Birth of Tragedy* contains is a critique of the neoclassical interpretation of Aristotle; it does not in any way touch Aristotle himself.) Properly artistic *mimēsis*, that is to say, productive or producing *mimēsis*, is on the contrary the highest degree of activity. It is, moreover, what is properly virile in human activity in general since, as you know, in conformity with one of the oldest and most obscure constraints that exists in philosophy, Nietzsche distributes the virile and the feminine according to the distinction between the active and the passive.

The struggle against imitation and historical culture consists, then, essentially, in a conversion of *mimēsis*—as does in general the struggle carried on by the aesthetic against receptivity, the point of view of the amateur and of the spectator, of consumption, in short, of taste. To convert *mimēsis* is to *virilize* it. This is done so that it can cease to take the form of submission in order to become truly creative. And if what is involved in the passive imitation is a bad relation to history, it is this relation itself that one must convert and transform into a creative relation. And indeed history—history "well understood," says Nietzsche—is "the eternally manly" (5, p. 87).

In a way closely analogous to what occurs in the Diderot of the *Paradox of the Comedian*, this virile conversion of *mimēsis* is the conversion of *pathos* into *ēthos*. It is a properly heroic conversion, or more exactly, one that is subordinated to the great agonistic model of heroic imitation, such that it dominates all or nearly all of ancient pedagogy, despite the collapse—desired by Plato—of the archaic aristocratic *paideia*. This is why nonhistorical imitation is placed under the invocation of Plutarch and his *Exemplary Lives*:

> If . . . you acquire a living knowledge of the history of great men, you will learn from it a supreme commandment: to be-

come mature and to flee from that paralyzing upbringing of the present age which sees its advantage in preventing your growth so as to rule and exploit you to the full while you are still immature. And if you want biographies, do not desire those which bear the legend "Herr So-and-So and his age," but those upon whose title-page there would stand "a fighter against his age." Satiate your soul with Plutarch and when you believe in his heroes dare at the same time to believe in yourself. With a hundred such men—raised in this unmodern way, that is to say become mature and accustomed to the heroic—the whole noisy sham-culture of our age could now be silenced forever. (6, 94–95)

Three traits, principally, characterize this second *mimēsis* (it goes without saying that I am schematizing a great deal).

First of all, as we have just seen, its function, paradoxically—but mimetic logic is always paradoxical; this is even what defines it or undefines it—is to assure auto-formation or auto-organization itself. The paradox is of the following form: the more I believe in heroes, the more I believe in myself. That is to say: the more I imitate, actively, deliberately, constructively (in the manner of that imitation which is fundamentally that of the authentic actor, who does not at any moment submit to his model, but instead consciously elaborates upon it—in all coldness, as Diderot says)—the more I imitate, then, the more it is myself, by myself, that I construct. Authentic *mimēsis* is the interiorization of the model, that is to say, a reconstruction. By this, and only by this, can we explain how mimesis is a means of identification: it is, and this is why it has no proper being, the appropriation of a model. The most extreme depropriation provides the only chance for authentic appropriation.

The model—and this is the second trait—the hero, is Greek. This is another mark of the "untimely" (yet again so German): I am, says Nietzsche playfully, "a disciple of antiquity." These are the Greeks at the moment of their "greatest power," the Greeks who, for the first and only time, are themselves and by themselves formed (worked) without recourse to any model whatsoever. These are the Greeks of a purely unhistorical effraction (and moreover, at the same time, suprahistorical, as is indicated in their two most powerful creations: art and religion—"aesthetic religion," as Hegel would have it). These are therefore the Greeks of a breach or rupture in historical continuity, who, as such, created history:

> If history in general were nothing more than "the world-system of passion and error," mankind would have to read it

> as Goethe advised his readers to read *Werther*: as if it called to them "be a man and do not follow after me!" Fortunately, however, it also preserves the memory of the great fighters *against history,* that is to say against the blind power of the actual, and puts itself in the pillory by exalting precisely these men as the real historical natures who bothered little with the "thus it is" so as to follow "thus it shall be" with a more cheerful pride. (8, p. 106)

The Greeks, in other words, do not belong to history: they are not historical beings. And it is in this alone that they are worth being imitated. But there is here—and this is the third trait—another paradox: what relation to the Greeks is in fact thinkable, if it is not a historical relation? It is, we are told, a matter of pharmaco-logic. We know how it functions: it is all the same to history, as Nietzsche says, how one "resolves the problem of history." A bit of history, a reasonable dose, is the most effective antidote. And yet it is not: in a parallel way, in another stratum or according to another guiding thread of the same text, the paradox is assumed in its most extreme paradoxical aspect: it involves, in the imitation of the Greeks, a nonhistorical relation to the being, itself nonhistorical, of the Greeks. That is to say, at bottom it involves an entirely other conception of history and historicity.

A relatively simple way of understanding what is at play here for Nietzsche is to resituate his effort in the horizon wherein by itself, discreetly but with insistence, it is situated after *The Birth of Tragedy*: that is to say, within the horizon of agonistic rivalry, in view of the appropriation of "means of identification," with neoclassical imitation, the imitation of the French (the second *Untimely Meditation,* as all of Nietzsche's early writings, is written under the influence of the deception following 1870: even the war against France changed nothing of the state and dispositions of Germany); and beyond the rivalry with neoclassical imitation, the rivalry of the Renaissance, that is to say, the rivalry with the proper Latin and catholic style of renascent imitation. At stake is obviously the possibility that the land of Reform produce its renaissance, or rather an unprecedented *birth.*

For everything, in fact, is a problem of birth, that is to say, of origin. As always in Nietzsche. Let us not forget that it is at bottom the sole subject of his first book. One must substitute the imitation of what is original in the Greeks—their creative and auto-creative power, their capacity for effectuation, their formative force—for the Latin type of imitation which, after Rome, is historical—and which is historical in the sense that it is modeled upon the *results* of Greek culture, upon its works. One must substitute the imitation of *poiēsis* itself, of power, for the imitation of *poiēmata*. One must, like them, be born by oneself, be auto-engendered and auto-constituted—one must work oneself. Imitation is here thought upon the Kantian model of inspired exemplarity (*Nachfolge*, as opposed to *Nachahmung*, servile imitation), such as Kant tries to define it in the third *Critique*.[6] What Nietzsche expects the Germans to do is succeed to the heritage of the Greek *genius*.

This presupposes two things.

On the one hand, as we can well imagine, that Greeks other than those of Latinity be exhumed and brought to light. This is why, in the direct line of Schlegel's romanticism, of Hölderlin, and of Hegel, Nietzsche opposes two Greeces: not simply, as we always say, the Dionysiac Greece and the Apollonian Greece (Dionysiac and Apollonian, in their organic unity, comprise only one Greece, the tragic Greece); but this tragic or, as Nietzsche says, "classical" Greece is opposed to the "declining" Greece, that following Euripides and Socrates, which is political, sophistical, philosophical—at bottom, already historical—and no longer produces anything, but lives upon the greatness of the original auto-production.

But as on the other hand this tragic Greece, whatever its greatness has been, is partly to blame for the appearance of the declining Greece, and then of the Latin interpretation of the latter (one must presuppose, as Hölderlin had already done, an accident or a catastrophe in Greek history; that is to say, in Nietzsche's lexicon, a sudden decline in tension, an unexpected weakness, a lessening of creative power), to imitate the Greeks ought to mean: to do better than they. The imitation that is involved in the "monumental" conception of history—and I will soon speak of nothing else: the monumental is exemplary, it is what is worthy of being imitated (2, p. 70)—should aim, says Nietzsche, at "overcoming models" (2, p. 68). We recognize here, in its matrical form, that agonistic imperative which, after Winckelmann and (at least) up to Heidegger, restricts all of German tradition and regulates its—irregulable—relation to the Greeks. Ultimately—and in a certain way it will have nearly always been so; Nietzsche is neither the first nor the last to suffer it in its extreme form—it prescribes imitating the Greeks without imitating them or, more exactly, imitating the Greeks only up to the point where they have ceased being inimitable and have become responsible for the *imitatio* of the Ancients. As I have believed it possible to show in relation to Hölderlin, this is a perfect *double-bind* structure.[7] It will have delivered Germany, at least up to the Third Reich, to a destiny that one must call psychotic—a destiny, moreover, from which Hölderlin and Nietzsche, each in their own way, were unable to escape.

But beforehand there is always the hope of a solution. That is to say, the hope of a possible cure or of a possible preventive treatment. The strategy, in Nietzsche—a strategy that answers moreover to a logic curiously enough like that which governs, on another register, Marx's first texts—is founded upon this: only the disinherited, that is to say, those for whom the burden of the past is so great that they are no longer anything, those who have absolutely nothing proper to them, are able to find, in this extreme alienation and depropriation, the force of being born, the force of finding the grandeur of a beginning: "The greatness that once existed was in any event once *possible* and may thus be possible again" (2, p. 69). But one must realize this, and such a realization constitutes a rupture: an effraction outside of history.

The man of monumental history, the "active and powerful" man, the one who "fights a great fight" for no other reward than "glory," that is to say, exemplarity, confidently believes that "the great moments in the struggle of the human individual constitute a chain, that this chain unites mankind across the millenia" (2, p. 68). The agonistic enchainment produces an historical continuity, "a solidarity and continuity of the greatness of all ages" (2, p. 69). But the repetition must not be deduced from the continuity. And we know moreover that it is in order to avert this danger that Nietzsche for the first time mentions, and rejects, the (empirical) hypothesis of the eternal return:

> At bottom, indeed, that which was once possible could present itself as a possibility for a second time only if the Pythagoreans were right in believing that when the constellation of the heavenly bodies is repeated the same things, down to the smallest event, must also be repeated on earth: so that whenever the stars stand in a certain relation to one another a Stoic again joins with an Epicurean to murder Caesar, and when they stand in another relation Columbus will again discover America. Only if, when the fifth act of the earth's drama ended, the whole play every time began again from the beginning, if it was certain that the same complex of motives, the same *deus ex machina,* the same catastrophe were repeated at different intervals, could the man of power venture to desire monumental history in full icon-like *veracity,* that is to say with every individual peculiarity depicted in precise detail: but that

> will no doubt happen only when the astronomers have again become astrologers. (2, pp. 69–70)

In other words: the danger that monumental history conceals, when it does not imply rupture, is that "of becoming somewhat distorted, beautified and coming close to free poetic invention [*Erdichtung*]." "There have been ages, indeed," says Nietzsche, "which were quite incapable of distinguishing between a monumentalized past and a mythical fiction, because precisely the same stimuli can be derived from the one world as from the other" (2, p. 70). This is why monumental history has need, at its end (and in order to correct it), of antiquarian history—pious history that conserves and venerates the past, thus preventing it from being reduced to the mere emergence of great moments—and above all of critical history, history that judges and summons the past before its tribunal in order to measure it according to the criterion of the service it renders to life. One must have force, Nietzsche says again, in order to live, "to break up and dissolve a part of the past" (3, p. 75).

This necessity of rupture, of a violent effraction like that of birth, is obviously never tantamount to a rejection of the Greek model. Rupture is always thought, fundamentally, as rupture with the present—and with what of a past, and of a past hardly worth being imitated, burdens the present. Nevertheless, the rupture, the will to rupture—which is pure creative will: will of the forthcoming (l'à-venir)—is such that it falls back upon the apprehension of the model. Very precisely, it renders the model enigmatic. Or more precisely still, it restores the model to the enigma of the rupture that it itself produced.

It is to such a rupture, and therefore to the invention of what is forthcoming that the oracular motif refers (the allusion is always, of course, to the Delphic oracle, to the Apollonian oracle): "when the past speaks it always speaks as an oracle: only if you are an architect of the future and know the present will you understand it" (6, p. 94). And he adds almost immediately: "form within yourself an image to which the future shall correspond, and forget the superstition that you are epigones." As an oracle, as an enigma, the past only bears and offers this single indication: the future is to be constructed. It is the enigma of the pure indication of the future. This is why when, in the final pages of his text, Nietzsche exhorts "young Germany" to work, or rather to work toward the birth of Germany, he cannot avoid recalling the delphic precept and the interpretation that Heraclitus gives of the oracular enigma:

> And how can we attain that goal? you will ask. At the beginning of a journey towards that goal, the god of Delphi cries to you his oracle: "Know yourself." It is a hard saying: for that god "conceals nothing and says nothing, but only indicates," as Heraclitus has said. (10, p. 122)

The past is therefore only a model insofar as it is the pure indication of a possibility: of a "great possibility." It allows only the imitation of an occurrence, but not of anything that has already occurred. Historical *mimēsis,* such as Nietzsche conceives it, does not consist of repeating the Greeks but of recovering the analogue of that which was their possibility: a disposition, a force, a power—the capability of extricating oneself from the present, of breaking with the past, of living and committing oneself under the constraint of what has not yet happened. This *mimēsis* does not admit any constituted model; it constructs its models. It is a creative *mimēsis*. It is a "poietic": it is great art itself.

We see that the relation to the Greeks is in reality of the order of the sublime, and not of the beautiful. The sublime, says Nietzsche, is "the incomprehensible event" (5, p. 83). The Greeks are such an incomprehensible event, and it is this that defines their very exemplarity. An event that is no less incomprehensible should therefore correspond to the sublime example. And such is the meaning of the rupture or effraction to which Nietzsche appeals. It is a Schillerian lesson: Germany can exist only if it is raised to the height of the sublime. That is to say, in another definition of the sublime, if it cannot in any way be measured. The sublime is the incommensurable. The *mimēsis* of which Nietzsche thinks is an imitation of the incommensurable.

It is moreover in this sense that history—the writing of history—raises itself to great art. The disposition required of the historian is explicitly related to the disposition of the sublime artist: "it is analogous to that aesthetic phenomenon of detachment from personal interest with which a painter sees in a stormy landscape with thunder and lightning, or a rolling sea [these are the Kantian *topoi* of the sublime], only the picture of them within him" (6, p. 91). But such a meditation is equivalent as well, adds Nietzsche, to a "complete absorption in the things." And he continues:

> It is a superstition, however, that the picture these things evoke in a man possessing such a disposition is a true reproduction of the empirical nature of the things themselves. Or is

> it supposed that at this moment the things as it were engrave, counterfeit, photograph themselves by their own action on a purely passive medium? [As is usual at the time, photography is the paradigm of passive *mimēsis*].
>
> This would be mythology, and bad mythology at that: and it is forgotten, moreover, that that moment is precisely the strongest and most spontaneous moment of creation in the depths of the artist, a moment of composition of the highest sort, the outcome of which may be an artistically true painting but cannot be an historically true one. (6, p. 91)

Not accidentally, moreover, Nietzsche assimilates this sort of sublime objectivity of representation to the "mysterious work of the playwright," that is to say, of the good mimetician, of the active and creative mimetician: of the one who constructs the real and does not reproduce it, who "creates new images according to given types" (not to facts), who welcomes—in the wording of Grillparzer—"events impenetrable to him," and whose "powerful poetic faculty" is charged with evoking, for this very reason, "that which is the highest and the rarest"—pure greatness as such.

IV

One of the rare passages, in *Being and Time*, where Heidegger refers directly to Nietzsche is the passage from paragraph 76—Birault has devoted a long commentary to it in his book on *Heidegger et l'experience de la pensée*—where, seeking to establish the ontologic-existential origin of history (of historical science, historiology) in terms of the historiality (*Geschichtlichkeit*) of *Dasein*, Heidegger explicitly evokes the second *Untimely Meditation*. He writes:

> The possibility that historiology in general can either be "useful" for one's life or "a disadvantage" to it is grounded on the fact that one's life is historical in the roots of its Being, and that therefore, as factically existing, one has in each case made one's decision for authentic [*eigentlich*] or inauthentic historicality. Nietzsche recognized what was essential to "the uses and disadvantages of history for life" in the second of his *Untimely Meditations* (1874), and said it unequivocally and penetratingly. He distinguished three kinds of historiology—the monumental, the antiquarian, and the critical—without explicitly pointing out the necessity of this triad or the ground of its unity. *The threefold character of historiology is adumbrated in the historicality of Dasein.* At the same time, this historicality enables

> us to understand to what extent these three possibilities must be united factically and concretely in any historiology which is authentic. Nietzsche's division is not accidental. The beginning of his *Meditation* allows us to suppose that he understood more than he has made known to us.[8]

I cannot here enter into the "thing itself." This would require that the bases of the existential analytic of temporality and the historiality of *Dasein* be perfectly understood. I will content myself therefore with a very brief schematization, meant simply to indicate what is at play there.

At first, Heidegger's purpose does not present any difficulty: it is simply a question of showing how the three *ecstasies* of temporality—whose "essence," says Heidegger, "is the temporalization of the very unity of these different ecstasies"—correspond to the three historical instances offered by Nietzsche. That temporality is ecstatic means that time does *not stand still,* or that temporality is "the original 'beside oneself.' " As temporal, then, *Dasein* ek-sists, that is to say, it is always a movement that breaks away from the present and transcends being-present towards its being. Or, if you prefer, the movement by which it relates to its present only insofar as, projected towards its future, it is referred to its past, in such a way that the present itself—the authentic *instant*—is pure division, the distension between past and future; and *Dasein,* because time does not exist as being, is the abyss of presence in the present.

What is remarkable here is that Heidegger adopts in his turn, under the motif of ecstasy and in a register of an entirely different profundity, the Nietzschean sublime. The monumental, for example, the past in its grandeur, because temporality is originally temporalized in terms of the future, is borne by this future and found in reality to be always "before us." The past is a pure possibility. Similarly, in antiquarian history, what takes place is the appropriation of what has been by virtue of the constitution of a world that can be said to be "mine": of a fatherland or of a "home" (*Zuhause*). But this world is not any region in the world, it is in no way given or consistent—it is moreover "the place" of "dis-placement" itself, of the *Unheimliche* or of the *Un-Zuhause,* by which Heidegger, in a Hölderlinian mode, will later qualify the Greek *deinon,* the terrifying or monstrous, that is to say, the sublime. It is moreover why, says Heidegger, "in an existential or ontological way the not-being-in-itself should be understood as the most original phenomenon." With regard to critical history, it opens the present as critique of the present, that is to say, as the possibility of escaping from the actuality of today and of being painfully separated from its declining public-being. It possesses the possibility of an effraction. And it is finally the sublime, that is to say, trans-cendence or, as Heidegger would then claim, meta-physics as such, that constitutes the very unity of the three instances and, consequently, the very unity of authentic history.

Of course, Heidegger does not breathe a word about the problematic of imitation. Though some paragraphs before, the relation to the past is defined according to the possibility, for *Dasein,* of "choosing its heroes" (§74)—and what is a hero, if not a model or an example?—in other words, in a general way, the entire Heideggerian enterprise is in its political significance one and the same with the project of a "repetition" of the Greek beginning, a repetition that is all the more violent and sublime as it addresses itself, in this beginning, to what remained concealed in it, to what did not properly occur but remained "in reserve" and, as such, passed over the present and fell before it. It is, strictly speaking, the Nietzschean scheme of historicity. That is to say, that which, under the name of the sublime, calls for a *mimēsis* without models and a (re-) establishment, ultimately impossible, of history.

I will not pronounce upon what the Heideggerian dissimulation dissimulates of the mimetic problematic. I simply state that it happens at least once, to Nietzsche as well as to Heidegger, when their thought on historicity is implicated in a determinate politics, that of Bismarck or that of Hitler. The same thought, however, in terms of its sublimity, should have prevented such a compromise before it occurred. However, it did not, and I ask myself whether, as long as we do not seriously comprehend what, in historical reality, has authorized this kind of compromise, we will not remain entirely unprovided for before a world bequeathed to us by a tradition in which these compromises were not inevitable.

Translated by Eduardo Cadava

NOTES

1. *On the Uses and Disadvantages of History for Life,* in *Untimely Meditations,* trans. R. J. Hollingdale (Cambridge: Cambridge University Press, 1983). All subsequent references to this text are to this edition and will be inserted parenthetically within the essay by section number and page. When necessary, this translation has been modified slightly.

2. *Philosophy in the Tragic Age of the Greeks,* trans. Marianne Cowan (Chicago: Henry Regnery, 1962), §XI.

3. *The Critique of Judgement*, trans. James C. Meredith (Oxford: Oxford University Press, 1969), §46.

4. In another semantic register, formation and culture (*Bildung*) communicate with statuary (*Bild*, "image," also signifies "statue").

5. See "Typographie" in *Mimesis des articulations* (Paris: Aubier-Flammarion, 1975), pp. 165–270.

6. *The Critique of Judgement*, §47 (cf. §32). Kant has difficulty defining this form of *mimēsis*: "The possibility of this [the transmission of a model] is difficult to explain. The artist's ideas arouse like ideas on the part of his pupil, presuming nature to have visited him with a like proportion of the mental powers. For this reason the models of fine art are the only means of handing down this art to posterity." This amounts to explaining *mimēsis* through *mimēsis*.

7. On this point, see "Hölderlin et les Grecs," in *Poétique* 40 (1979), 465–74.

8. *Being and Time*, trans. John Macquarrie and Edward Robinson (New York: Harper and Row, 1962), p. 448. The translation has been modified slightly.

12

Namely, Eckermann

Avital Ronell

Er könne nichts für mich thun, und der
Vater im Himmel würde schon für mich sorgen.
Damit leuchtete er mir die Treppe hinunter.
Bitte lache.
("He could do nothing for me, and our
heavenly Father would surely look after me.
With these words, he lit the way down *the stairs*
for me.
Please laugh.")[1]

1. Going Down

There has always been, in the immunopathological activities of certain texts, a place for hygienic writing. Each thinking text, to the extent that it develops strategies of protection against outside interference or parasitism, is run by an immunopathological drive. Perhaps every text can be shown to be fantasmatically producing antibodies against the autoimmune community it has established within itself (a within that is constantly leaking, running an excription machine,[2] exposed precisely to a contaminating "outside"). The immunological drive is as truly lodged in the Heideggerian corpus, which is always cracking down on impurities, as it is housed by the symptomatologist, Friedrich Nietzsche. Still, Heidegger and Nietzsche did not hire the same company to cordon off spaces of impurity, though both share a certain predilection for cleanliness, ever repelling sites of toxic invasion. This is why Nietzsche is constantly throwing up, and Heidegger inhales the pure air of forest paths.

Self-cleaning texts are made everywhere available. For instance, they are thematized in the works of Franz Kafka by implacable figures of cleaning women who are associated with tremendous hermeneutic insight. These agents of hygiene dwell in radical proximity to the residue for which they are responsible. They are the steadily invading contaminators against which the text tries to protect itself. Consider the three angels of dust: the woman, on the edge of writing, who sweeps aside Gregor Samsa's corpse; the cleaning woman who signs the suicidal rush of Georg Bendemann at the tail end of "The Judgment"; the *Castle*'s landlady straightening out those who are the leftovers from another regime of being. The cleaning lady, who in Kafka poses a threat to narrative purity, also always runs the risk of being fired. When she's on her way out, she tends to wear a quill in her hat.

Whether it is a matter of the house of being or the prison house of language, people get paid for keeping it clean.

The cleanup job is something for which Nietzsche-criticism, like the commentary surrounding many great figures, has made itself responsible. It is an economical way of domesticating a figure, particularly one who, like Nietzsche or even Goethe, also trails behind him a dirty story or the film of history. When submitted to the sanitation department of some institutions, these figures come out clean, like laundered money and safe text. They are made digestible by the huge garbage disposal systems which universities sometimes are. I personally have nothing against this. It just so happens that I, like Eckermann, work the night shift, when everyone has gone but an odor still lingers. It's not that God is dead, says Nietzsche, but his corpse has not been disposed of. Hence the odor. Don't get me wrong—show me no pity. I am neither fascinated nor particularly disgusted by the job. It rather depends on whom you work for. The cleanup crew tends to retain traces of filth; it is never itself clean. There's always a stain that hasn't been removed.

In any case, the cleanup crew tends to show up when the boss is gone or on the way out. We know everything about them, and empty their litterature. We don't resent them but form a couple with them. Not in any ideal or sentimental way, of course. Still, we create the bosses, and even their secretaries. They depend on us. We have thought and lived the Nietzschean saying, "I am ugly created the beautiful." Suprised? Philosophy is never where you expect to find it: since at least Hegel, it's been working the night shift, however.

No writer has been more alert to pollution systems circulating in texts than Nietzsche. As catalytic converter—how many times does he gasp for clean air!—Nietzsche is the place where the sanitation department cooperates with a hermeneutics of obsessional neurosis. He knows how to smell a rat in the most uptown areas of thought. And Nietzsche hangs out in these doubles spaces, drawing an *Übermensch* out of a leftover. As Heidegger has noted, the *Übermensch* can be thought of as a bridge, a transhuman, linking up over an abyss.

When Nietzsche names Goethe in the context of the transhuman, he stumbles and stammers, landing on "Eckermann"—Goethe's leftover. The syncopated gulp separating what is indissociable, namely, the Goethe-Eckermann couple, opens a space for what Freud has called a "dreckology." Eckermann is the immunocompetent guarantee of the Goethean corpus. Debased, forgotten, late on arrival, he corresponds to the essentially modern character of what Heidegger epochalizes as "we latecomers." As master slave, Eckermann, this link and leftover, offers exemplary access to one among the impressive number of *couples* that compelled Nietzsche's attention. Nietzsche's rapport with the couple—the alterity that is double or nothing—is indeed so striking as to render Nietzsche the thinker par excellence of the couple: Lou and Paul, Dionysus and Apollo, Ariadne and Dionysus, Dionysus and the Antichrist, Wagner and Nietzsche, and what he becomes when he is: I am my mother and my father, *Ich bin der und der,* and so forth. When it comes to the couple Goethe-Eckermann, Nietzsche switches on the transvaluating machine, going for the one over the other (the one *as* the other), reinstalling the gigantic but hidden cleaning apparatus of what we call Goethe.

2. . . . and Out

I suppose, if it is not too late, I could speak to you about depression—about depressions and openings, that is; about the way down and about *dejection* (I shall ask you to consider dejection in its medical sense as well, where it means an evacuation of the bowels, or the matter evacuated—excrement). The topological displacements which depress the Nietzschean text—a text so peculiarly riddled with holes, cuts and enigmatic openings—have been treated under various guises, and often in terms of what has been taken to be a *feminine* element. The opening, a certain figuration of outwardness, has been regarded as a deep, unfathomable inside, for instance a Medusian hole (*trou*) in Bernard Pautrat's reading of *Zarathustra* or, in Gilles Deleuze, as the depths and caverns, the "pits" to which woman is assigned or of which she is a sign.[3] In his *Twilight,* Nietzsche himself—assuming it is still possible to say "Nietzsche himself"—links such interpretations of woman's depth to the hopelessness of ever getting to the bottom of things. Perhaps, indeed, some gynecologist of morals would go down too far, would risk losing himself in the obscure atopy or groundlessness of his pursuit (*"Man hält das Weib für tief—warum? weil man nie bei ihm auf den Grund kommt"*).

But let us withdraw the speculum of vaginocentric readings and remain close to another source of Nietzschean depression, for there are other apertures and openings in Nietzsche—and we should not too soon forget the nasal and anal cavities of the *Genealogy* which are indeed contracted or held closed (*zugehalten*), for we have had to stop inhaling degenerate life; thus, we pinch our noses to ward off the stench of our revolting productions (*Erzeugungen*) such as spittle, urine and dung (II, §7) and at the same time we have stopped relieving ourselves (*entladen*). Except for the artist, perhaps, who is in a sense the form of his own relief, or, in Nietzsche's words "under certain circumstances the dung and manure from which [the artwork] grows." We shall return to these circumstances. For now let us note simply that the words Nietzsche uses to designate "decency" such as *anständig* and *aufrichtig*, point up to a posture of uprightness which Freud has explained precisely as a posture of maximum distance from the smells produced from our lower regions—in other words, the beginning of all morality.

Yet, even beyond his special nostrils and the ears that he commands to open, there are still other holes in Nietzsche; perhaps they have let too much blood and perhaps they are the silent wounds of too great a catastrophe. This at least is what Blanchot suggests when he compares Nietzsche to Goethe in a section entitled "André Gide et Goethe" in *Faux Pas*. Goethe, he writes, has been unfaithful to shipwreck; he has proven himself guilty in the face of darkness: he knew catastrophe but elected to circumvent it. In short, Goethe willed everything *including* his rescue. Nietzsche, on the other hand, threw himself into catastrophe with the certitude "qu'en se perdant il accomplissait son destin" ("in losing himself thereby he fulfilled his destiny").[4] And though it may seem that in this respect Goethe owes one to Nietzsche, Blanchot reminds us of Nietzsche's love and admiration for Goethe, for his Apollonian force and his Dionysian dreams.

It may well be that Blanchot has named for us the law of Goethe's singularity, namely, that he has been rescued from the catastrophe which he, like Nietzsche, knew. And Nietzsche himself rescues Goethe from countless catastrophes, for example, in his poem entitled "An Goethe" which begins:

Das Unvergängliche
Ist nur dein Gleichnis!

If Goethe could resist catastrophe and avoid being overturned (*katastrephein*), it is not because he didn't foresee it or read the chart of his descent. He foresaw it and he even dictated it, in a sense, by telling the story of his life to himself, namely, to Eckermann.[5] Eckermann was the anonymous vessel who let his body be invaded by Goethe, and Eckermann knew that he was the rescue vessel for a hero (*Held*) whom he could not allow to sink, as he says in the preface to the Third Book of the *Conversations*.

No rescue mission was formed to save Nietzsche, nor did he necessarily will it. Yet one of the fissures or cracks, one of the openings that he names in the *Genealogy* occurs, as you know, when Nietzsche, giving definition to his ascetic priest, calls out in his text "mehr Schmerz! mehr Schmerz!" When he dissolves this section, he does so by asserting Goethe's position with regard to the ascetic ideal: "*Goethe*, in case you hadn't known as much, was no ascetic priest," writes Nietzsche. "He—knew more." Goethe—knew more. What more did Goethe know when he rent a hole into a passage naming the desire for more—dash—pain?

Goethe is out of the question; Nietzsche brings him into the picture to illustrate its outside, to place him, paradoxically, as its external reference: he is incorporated into the text of ressentiment to be expulsed, propelled outside the body of this concern; and as such, he is also the life-line that brings Nietzsche to the other side of ressentiment. And we shall see how Goethe affirms the position of master precisely because he *knows* how to maintain pain in the element of its exteriority.

Thus, he is brought in—flown in, we could say—to be expelled, dropped, excused from the conference of ascetic priests; he saves Nietzsche, if only momentarily, and thereby gains infinite credit for his name.[6] And if Nietzsche's credit line, if *Goethe*, comes to be the horizon against which we measure ressentiment, it is not a horizon whose limits are fixed within the boundaries of the German-speaking text: when Baudelaire offers some free advice to a young poet, he admonishes him to remain free of debt, upholding Goethe as the figure par excellence who can be *imagined only* in the role of creditor (*créancier*), never in debt or at fault.

But I was suggesting another typology of the fault and it may be that Goethe has always been used to cover a debt or fault—a fissure—that he has been held up as a fetish or substitute for some thing that has been cut off, missing, disintegrated; and often he has been used to cover or substitute for Germany itself—if we can still say "Germany itself."

But what about the position that Goethe occupies in Nietzsche's reading and elsewhere? We think we know that Nietzsche will never merge Goethe with the category of the *Unvermögen* which so often identifies the man, and certainly the woman, of ressentiment. This word means impotent as well as impecunious. I need not recall the position that impotence assumes in Nietzsche's corpus, nor Goethe's own delicate maneuvers around *unvermögend.* Nietzsche perhaps is most attentive to the way Goethe seems to keep a *Dis-tanz* from such a predicament. Thus, when Nietzsche names Goethe, he necessarily addresses the question of a declining age and the fiction of the writer as a stylized human being. In a note, he writes that:

> *Goethe* is exemplary: the impetuous naturalism which gradually becomes severe dignity. As a stylized human being he reached a higher level than any other German ever did. No one is so bigoted as to reproach him therefor and even to censure his becoming old. One should read Eckermann and ask oneself whether any human being in Germany ever got so far in noble form.

If Friedrich Schlegel had censured Goethe for becoming old, Nietzsche employs another strategy, one that shows Goethe, if not becoming old, passing into noble form. But to apprehend the form of that nobility and the stylization of the human being, one must look away from Goethe; in fact, "one should read Eckermann." And from the *Gay Science* we know what type of aesthetic surgery is required to attain such a high level of stylization: it is a "great and rare art." "Here a large mass of second nature has been added; there a piece of original nature has been removed. . . . Here the ugly which could not be removed is hidden; there it has been reinterpreted and made sublime" (p 99). One should read Eckermann. And if one reads Eckermann, one will find that he stylizes or "reinterprets" *Goethe* with a finely cut diamond.

In Nietzsche—and for Goethe—Eckermann is accorded a place, which is not really a *place,* between the writer and himself, at a moment when the signatory *Goethe*—the italicized Goethe—no longer coincided with: Goethe. Thus, Eckermann's first assignment in the summer of 1823 will be to determine which of the papers in Goethe's possession were actually written by the master: Goethe no longer knows, and asks Eckermann to find, identify, perhaps to invent his style. Eckermann will spend the entire summer identifying Goethe in order to return to him his findings at the beginning of the Fall. Goethe is satisfied with the results and yet we shall never know who interpreted when Goethe decided that Eckermann interpreted his style and signature correctly.

By way of introduction—though it is getting rather late for that—we can say that Eckermann created the fiction of the self-composed, Olympian Goethe; in Blanchot's words, he witnessed the poet in his solitude. Of the *Gesamtbild* we may still carry of Goethe, he was credited with having handed down its principal elements. As for his own image, what can be said but that he was a shadow, a phantom, a writing hand attached to Goethe's voice. He wanted to make a name for himself. He was thirty years old in June 1823. It was getting late.

In the end, Eckermann's style would become indistinguishable from Goethe's; scholars would be unable—and still are—to determine whether he copied his notes from Goethe's diary or whether Goethe reconstituted his diary from Eckermann's notes. The history of the *Conversations*, a long one, is a history of incertitude which involves among other things constant questioning of proprietorial rights, joint ownership, the writing couple, the one and the other. Sometimes you will find the book under Goethe's name with the title, *Conversations with Eckermann*; or you might find it listed under "Eckermann" as *Conversations with Goethe*. While some call it Goethe's last work, or his spoken text, others call Eckermann himself Goethe's last work—and not necessarily his best at that. Indeed, it would seem that Goethe had a hand in organizing and producing this fragile part of himself that was to be sacrificed to the fiction of *Goethe*. Goethe arranged his survival as fiction and as life, as the fiction of life (*Dichtung der Wahrheit*) that only the Romantics dared attack and decline. It is hardly fortuitous if Goethe kept Eckermann at his side, forbidding the instinctive wanderer from straying too far up the Rhine. Eckermann was to be shielded from the Romantic illness, but more importantly he was to shield Goethe from this impertinent, rebellious generation or degeneration of writers. Eckermann became in a sense the deflecting object, the *conduit* as Nietzsche would say, that attracted the ressentiment of a whole generation. His lot, of course, will eventually come to resemble the one reserved for widows, those creatures left behind with a body of works and who become the petty functionaries of its future institution. Eckermann, always to a certain extent Goethe's widow, his void, will be severely punished for the profit he made and for the proprietary rights he exercised over Goethe's works. The punishment begins almost immediately. Heine mocked Eckermann as did countless others. And even in the twentieth century, if one deigns to mention Eckermann, this embarrassing leftover, it is mainly to exercise one's venomous spleen. Friedenthal and other Germans have discovered Eckermann to be beady-eyed, his nose is/was too long, at any rate he is servile and he is ugly. *He* is ugly. In addition or rather in subraction: "Er ist ein Halber, aber er hat ein ganzes, rundes Werk geschaffen, das zu Goethes Oeuvre gehört."[7] This type of mutilation to which Eckermann is subject has been, I believe, largely dictated by Goethe, and perhaps it was only a sly and terribly ironic Nietzsche who could overturn these nearly universal judgments, though Nietzsche himself—I say this in passing—would suffer the indignities of a ferocious widow and philosophical executor: Elisabeth—F. N.—Förster-Nietzsche.

Now, Eckermann arrived to take over—to execute Goethe's oeuvre and life; it will be *his* desire and command that Goethe complete *Dichtung und Wahrheit*—complete his autobiography, his life. And Goethe will do the same by doing the opposite for Eckermann, that is, he will not let him complete his life or oeuvre, he will finish Eckermann, for Goethe considers himself a kind of finishing school for the young writer, who until the age of fourteen was wholly illiterate. Goethe will make Eckermann indissociable from himself; he will lend him his name and his style, which Eckermann will then bend into our readings and misreadings of a beautiful Goethe. So many works of scholarship presumably occupied with Goethe will import this somewhat foreign body, this Eckermann, to lend a certain buoyancy to their claims; they will say that "Goethe said . . ." but append Eckermann's name to what Goethe is said to have said. Nietzsche—knew better; he knew about fortifications against pain and about that which is left behind.

Thus wrote Nietzsche:

> Wenn man von Goethes Schriften absieht und namentlich von Goethes Unterhaltungen mit Eckermann, dem besten deutschen Buch, das es gibt: Was bleibt eigentlich von der deutschen Prosaliteratur übrig, das verdiente, wieder und wieder gelesen zu werden? (*Menschliches, Allzumenschliches*)

About whom or what does Nietzsche write when he writes that he is writing about Goethe's writing—the best German book? Goethe, by the way, is no longer italicized. What remains, what deserves the eternal return of the reader is, according to Nietzsche, not entirely

Goethe nor Eckermann, but the name of Goethe's supreme writing: namely, Eckermann. And it is indeed with Goethe's remains—with what remains of Goethe's signature—that Eckermann will write the remainder of his life.

Eckermann warns in this best of German books that if the *Conversations* are not added to one's reading, "one will not be able entirely to have the authentic Goethe" ("den eigentlichen Goethe nicht vollständig haben, wenn er nicht auch diese *Gespräche* hinzufügt").[8] The *Conversations,* then, will give you the authentic Goethe. (Eckermann will have beautiful nightmares, by the way, about having produced a more authentic Goethe than Goethe himself produced in his works.) They are at once an addition or supplement to Goethe's corpus while they also guarantee its totality. Yet, as totality, they in fact revert to the function of a half. The authenticating supplement, the authenticating signature: at one point the couple disagrees on which of them will authenticate, underwrite the other. In any case Eckermann wished his book to be published wearing the same jacket as Goethe's collected works (*Ausgabe letzter Hand*), and to serve in the terms spelled out by his contract as introduction and supplement—as the appendage and the ground. As if Eckermann had to make Goethe presentable to us. If Eckermann is capable of giving away the authentic Goethe it is, according to most receivers of this extraordinary gift, because the gift—the *Conversations*—is itself in the first place Goethe's property.

In the introduction to his work, Eckermann seems largely to concur with this assumption; in fact, he promotes it himself. Yet he also writes at one point, "Übrigens erkenne ich dasjenige, was in diesen Bänden gelungen ist, zu meinem Eigentum zu machen, was ich gewissermaßen als den Schmuck meines Lebens zu betrachten habe."[9] The rights of ownership, it would seem, would not go to Goethe, for the writer recognizes or knows how to make the successful part of this work his own property, what is proper to himself (*Eigentum*): what is successful namely, is Eckermann. This is where a momentary reversal takes place: Eckermann is not the supplement or addition to Goethe and his life, but Goethe, who remains unnamed at this point, is the addition, the decoration or the parergon to Eckermann: the jewel of my life. This is not to say that Goethe relinquishes his position before the beginning of the *Conversations* proper; it is momentarily displaced and in a certain sense reversed. Eckermann will carve a subtle argument into these reversals when, in the introduction, he turns the adornment of his life into a hardstoned diamond. The facet whose emanations Eckermann will capture authorizes him to claim: "dies ist *mein* Goethe."

Eckermann's strategy here is, at bottom, to safeguard Goethe. The pathos of rescue with which Eckermann approached Goethe from the very beginning always should be kept in mind. In the first place, in announcing "this is *my* Goethe," he is immunizing his enterprise against any possible contestation that might be brought to bear upon this text. In asserting a part of Goethe that is wholly his own, namely Eckermann's, he makes this work invulnerable to attack. Of course, if this were a critical work about Goethe's oeuvre—a mere interpretation—Eckermann would have to assume full responsibility for his writing; but here he establishes the status of the text as testimony and, as such, the only criteria for truth must be derived from the purely subjective effect that Goethe produced on Eckermann. At the same time, Eckermann is giving back to Goethe what is his own. For the only truth of Goethe, of this diamond, can be the different perceptions that one receives from it. The diamantine cut of this text guarantees the reception of the testimony while also saving Goethe from a scientific operation. As the object of testimony, Goethe will remain mysterious, elusive, and safe from any attempt to pin him down. In this respect, Eckermann returns *everything* to Goethe. Everything I say, he says in effect, is not equal to the grandeur and multiplicity of the phenomenon, Goethe. However, the same holds for anything anyone else might say or write about Goethe, for anyone else would be perceiving another, singular facet. As an assembly of multiple facets, Goethe will never be, strictly speaking, identifiable with what one can say about him. In fact and as facet, "this is *my* Goethe." Eckermann's project is a delicate one. If this is *his* Goethe we cannot properly have any access to him; and if, then, Goethe is unknowable as a total object of any discourse, then Eckermann is also, at the very beginning, disclaiming any possibility for representing the true Goethe. Yet, in saying "this is my Goethe, this facet of Goethe is the reflection that I perceive" he is claiming to disclose precisely this facet of Goethe which is the only image or manifestation of Goethe to which one can ever hope to accede. Eckermann knows this much: his project is an impossible one; his text and testimony are impossible—and yet they are true. Goethe, Eckermann in effect says, will never be identifiable with what I am about to say. This text is Goethe, but it never attains him. And Goethe is also the signatory of this text, for this is the only way he showed himself to me, Eckermann. But because this is the way Goethe showed himself, I, Eckermann, have to sign myself.

This structure guarantees the text as Eckermann's property, insofar as it is an instance of subjective testimony. In this respect it is unique: nothing else can be substituted for this testimony, it is irreplaceable. As such, we have to assume its truth; however, to assume that it is true, we have to attribute it: to Goethe. As exclusive receiver, Eckermann *is* the owner of the speech. A diamond only shows itself in this way; it is therefore the truth of the diamond. The logic of the argument runs something like this: the subjective effect that Goethe had on me was multiple appearance; therefore I tell the truth (if the object shows itself only as appearance, then that very appearance must be the truth of the object). However, Goethe is the divine source about which only one thing can be said, although none of this is really correct: therefore, everything is only approximation. By thus divinizing his text, Eckermann renders it superior to any criticism or refinement. My text is better than it is, my signature is even more illustrious: it is *my* Goethe. *I* have written the best German book. As signatory of the *Conversations,* Eckermann is the center without a place, face or facet in this text. Goethe, on the other hand, is pure facet that can be neither centered nor touched.

If Eckermann's strategy has been one of safeguarding Goethe, of keeping him in a certain sense untouchable, secret and at an eternal distance, it is because Eckermann is the caretaker of someone who is vanishing, and who has been vanishing for a long time. Unfortunately, I shall not be able to trace this structure of parasitical inclusion along the lines of a cryptonomy here. In other words, I believe it is possible to demonstrate that Goethe by no means provides an original instance of corporeal invasion for Eckermann—and that Eckermann had already found a home for someone else's suffering within him. Some other figure is agonizing in Eckermann; he is a fosterparent to an alien body which has been deposited within him—and all this is thrown up in a sense toward the end of the *Conversations,* when Eckermann teaches Goethe about birds (says he), instructing him that certain of these have been known to swallow their adoptive parents (*Pflegeeltern*). Goethe, the adoptive parent, opens his ears as they enter a precarious discussion about moulting, losing one's plumage—or excreting—in order to sustain *Gesang.* The phantom agitating in Eckermann and who demands that his host continually feed him—this phantom who has long before Goethe taken up residence in his body, will have to be confronted elsewhere, however.

Now, if Eckermann's predatory habits seem finally to correspond to Goethe's desire, it is because Goethe had spontaneously proposed himself as Eckermann's host. In fact, Goethe gives *his* body to Eckermann so that he can constitute it as a body. Eckermann's task, as Goethe defines it, will be to transform the fragments and remains—the bits and pieces of Goethe's writings—some of which date from the 1770's, into the body of Goethe's works. Thus if their relationship may appear at first sight to be grounded in dissymmetry—and it certainly is—this does not preclude the relationship's being always in a certain sense reversible, however. For Goethe preys on Eckermann in order to nourish his body, which, henceforth, will never be entirely his own. In fact, Eckermann underscores this aspect and the secret reversibility of their relationship when he feeds Goethe back his own lines from a work whose completion is, according to its author, due to Eckermann. The subject in question on December 16, 1829 is Homunkulus, that mysterious figure capable of reading the mind and dreams of Faust when he lies unconscious. "Sie empfinden das Verhältnis sehr richtig, sagte Goethe" whereupon Eckermann quotes to him the text referring to the relationship of their relationship:

Am Ende hängen wir doch ab
Von Kreaturen die wir machten.

This is an example of Eckermann making Goethe swallow Goethe in order to digest Eckermann: in the final analysis, in the end, we do indeed depend upon the creatures that we have created. We hang from them, like limbs. If Goethe created Eckermann at the end of his life, it was because this end also depended upon him. In the *Conversations* these lines revert to Eckermann; they are presented as his lines which he picks from Goethe's body, citing from Goethe's masterpiece in order to establish his mastery over their relationship: "Sie empfinden das Verhältnis sehr richtig, sagte Goethe." Thus inciting Goethe to authorize the legitimacy of his claims and the correctness of his interpretation of Goethe, Eckermann likewise affirms the proper functioning of his assimilative or digestive systems.

Eckermann has long been assimilating Goethe's body to his own and his position has always been one of hanging on to the Goethean body, be it in the prehistory of their intimacy, at the time he wrote *On Poetry with a Particular Reference to Goethe,* be it as the *Kompendium* to Goethe's *Farbenlehre,* be it as that member of Goethe's familial branch who as early as June 19, 1823, can assert that Goethe "mich zu den Senigen zählt und mich als solchen will gehalten haben" ("counts me among his own and wants to keep me that way")—or be it in the form of the *Conversations* which was first appended to Goethe's collected works. Eckermann himself hangs on to Goethe's body of which he constitutes an appendage, limb or member (*Glied*) which is however best viewed as a type of prosthetic device that, all Goethe-scholars agree, can be dislocated from the joint legacy. Perhaps we shall have to amend this notion of Eckermann as *Glied* in a moment, as the movement of our narrative carries us to another body.

But to remain within the precinct of this body—of the detachable, attachable parts and reversibility—let me just say that neither was a notion of mutual perforation nor one promoting corporeal exchange ever directly addressed in the recorded exchanges between Goethe and Eckermann. However, in the third volume of his conversations with Goethe, Eckermann inserts an account of a dream he had narrated to Goethe. He had dreamt his dream the night preceding March 12, 1828. "I saw myself namely," Eckermann begins, "in an unknown region among strangers, but I was altogether in a good mood" (this is a dream, needless to say). "At lunch time we consumed our meal" and then, while walking about they saw a coastline spread before them at a distance. " 'There's only one thing to be done,' said the one to the other: we must undress and swim over there.' 'You can say that easily enough,' I (Eckermann) said; 'you happen to be young and beautiful and beyond that, you're good swimmers. I however swim badly and, anyway, I don't have the kind of figure (*ansehliche Gestalt*, "eminent or distinguished figure") that would allow me to appear on shore in front of strangers with any pleasure or ease.' 'You're a fool, said one of the most beautiful. Just get undressed and give me your form (*Gestalt*) and you can have mine in the meantime'. . . . With these words I quickly undressed, leaped into the water and immediately felt, in the other's body (*Körper*) that I was powerful swimmer. I had soon reached the coast and, naked and dripping, I stepped among the people with the most cheerful confidence—I was happy in the feeling of these beautiful limbs (*dieser schönen Glieder*), my behaviour was unforced, and I was immediately at home with the strangers at table." The others eventually reach the shore to join them and the only one missing turns out to be the young man "with my form in whose limbs I felt so well." Finally he approaches the shore "and I was asked if I wouldn't care to see my former self (*mein früheres Ich*). At these words a certain uneasiness (*Unbehagen*) overcame me, because I felt no great joy about myself (*keine große Freude an mir selber*), in part because I feared that my friend would immediately ask me back for his own body. Nonetheless, I turned toward the water and saw my second half swimming not far in our direction and, turning his head sideways, he looked up at me laughing: 'There's no bouyancy (*Schwimmkraft*) in your limbs!' he called to me. 'I've really had to fight the waves and breakers, and it's no wonder that I'm arriving so late and am last of all.' I immediately recognized the face: it was mine, rejuvenated and somewhat fuller and wider, and freshly colored. Now he stepped onto the shore and when, setting himself upright, he took the first steps, I had a general view of his back and his thigh (*Schenkel*, also "hinged leg; limb") and was pleased about the perfection (*Vollkommenheit*) of this form. . . . How is it possible, I thought to myself, that your small body grew up so beautifully!—Did the primal forces of the sea have such a wondrous effect on it or is it because the youthful spirit of the friend permeated or penetrated our members (*die Glieder durchdrungen*)? I quietly wondered why the friend didn't act as if he wanted to exchange his body once more. Actually, I thought, he looks so stately and, at bottom, it could be all the same to him; it is not all the same to me, however, for I am not sure whether I could be pieced back together in that body or whether I would shrink to my former size. —In order to arrive at some certitude about the matter, I took my friend aside and asked him how he felt in my limbs (or "member," *Glied*). 'Just fine!' he said 'I have the same sense of my being and strength (*Kraft*) as before. I don't know what you have against your limbs! As far as I'm concerned, they are perfectly all right, and you see that one only has to make something of oneself. Stay in my body as long as you please, for I am completely content to abide in yours for all eternity (*für alle Zukunft*).' I was very happy about this statement, and insofar as I, too, felt completely as before in all my sensations, thoughts and memories there came to me in the dream the impression of a complete independence of our souls and the possibility of a future existence in another body."

And the possibility of an existence in another body. The other body to whom the contents of this dream have been confided responds with the characteristic ambivalence that he seems to reserve for Eckermann's more delicate revelations. "The muses are particularly favorable to you at night," Goethe comments "for you will surely admit that in your waking hours it would be difficult for you to come up with something so peculiar (*Eigentümliches*, also "proper to yourself") and pretty." "I hardly understand how I arrived at that," Eckermann replies, "for in the past days I have been feeling greatly depressed, which would make the idea of so new a life seem rather remote." Although I cannot propose an analysis of this dream at this time, I shall ask you to retain only this: to make something of oneself means to enter the other body, possibly an institutional body—and we shall examine the consequences of this fantasmatic entry in a moment. For at bottom, there is always a way out.

Eckermann himself, however, gives us a clue to where a primary dream source might be found. He supposes it to have arisen somewhere in the conversations of the previous evening. We might take a brief glimpse at that exchange to see how it might have left its imprint in Eckermann's dream. That conversation—of March 11, 1828—engaged Goethe in a reflection on genius for which, Eckermann notes, Goethe has exchanged the term "productivity." "Every divine illumination in which the extraordinary arises (*das Außerordentliche*) will always be bound up with youth and productivity." What determines productivity will not be a quantitative mass of creations but their *life* and *endurance (Leben und Dauer).* There was a pause after Goethe linked productivity to life: then, Goldsmith, for instance, can be considered a productive poet precisely because the little he produced was capable of sustaining its indwelling life (*ein inwohnendes Leben hat das sich zu erhalten weiss*). This gave rise to a pause (*Es entstand eine Pause*) during which Goethe continued to pace up and down the room. Eckermann interrupts the pause by asking whether genial productivity resides only in the spirit of an important person or whether it might also be lodged in the body (*oder liegt sie auch im Körper?*). "At least," Goethe replied, "the body has a great influence over it.—There was however a time in Germany when one thought of a genius as being small, weak and even hunchbacked; however, I praise the genius who has the appropriate body.—" One can well imagine how this part of the exchange between Eckermann and Goethe might have been translated into the dream had that night by "le petit Docteur Eckermann" (as he was known). The pause itself should give pause, as it introduces a dead moment into the question of life. Genius has something to do with youthfulness—this, by the way, is the same conversation in which Goethe makes his notorious assertion associating genius with repeatable puberty (*wiederholte Pubertät).*

Eckermann, the questioner, the listener, the writer of genius—though that genius may not be proper to him or embodied in his appearance—is now old by comparison to Goethe; he is doubled over Goethe, hunchbacked, writing this down, depressed. He may not know how to sustain life—his own life—he may lack the necessary bouyancy. He was perhaps never young. He was a latecomer (he was even born belatedly as the last son of a second marriage, he was born to elderly parents—Goethe gets him on this, too). And Goethe cannot resist talking to Eckermann about the physical constitution (*körperliche Konstitution*) of a writer who might not be solid or well—one who, on the contrary, would be subject to dejection. The productions of such a writer, he presumes, must frequently come to a standstill (*häufig stocken*); this type of writer is depressed and suffers blockage. Goethe has advice for him: "My advice, therefore, is to force nothing." Eckermann's dream that night in one sense enforced this admonition, but in the other body: "I felt very fortunate in these beautiful limbs," he dreams, "my behavior—I—was not forced." As one of Goethe's beautiful members, I do not force my writing. I am young and healthy. Elsewhere, Eckermann has told us that swimming and writing amount to the same activity. Nietzsche will advance a similar hypothesis, notably when he writes that the decision to start writing is like leaping into cold water.[10]

If Eckermann adjoined himself to the Goethean body, in fact, if he dreams of the possibility of an existence in another body—and he tells Goethe that this *is* his dream—then he forever runs the risk of being removed or excreted from the other body, that is, of being subject to a peculiar form of survival to which the name of Eckermann always returns us—what the German language would designate as *weiter* rather than *überleben*. Eckermann's so-called survival after 1832 can be grasped neither in terms of life or death, strictly speaking, but rather as another delay—his final delay, in fact, for Eckermann was even a latecomer to his own death. When George Elliot writes of her visit with Eckermann in the 40's, she astutely notes that she had seen him before his "*total* death." Perhaps this partial and incalculable death, this delay that supplants survival as such, needs to be called by its name: namely excrement—as that which continues to grow after a body according to biological determination ceases to live. The first meaning that excrement takes is that of any appendage or outgrowth on the body, such as hair, nails, feathers and so on; it is related to the Latin *excrescere*, to grow out, to rise. Goethe himself seems to have intuited immediately Eckermann's place in terms of supplementary growth. His several letters and diary entries from as early as June 10, 1823 refer to Eckermann as something that has "*sich an mir herangebildet*." Nor should the history of Eckermann's own complicated attachment to hair and feathers be left entirely out of the picture: when he first encounters Goethe he must burn his hair to accomodate the style that was agreeable to Goethe; and his last temptation and wish will be to cut a lock of hair from Goethe's corpse. Any consideration of Eckermann's relationship to his not quite so proper name (namely, excrement) would have to take into account as well his pathological preoccupation with feathers, and particularly the fact that after Goethe's death he lived in a cramped room with forty odd birds (including birds of prey) whose droppings would fall on his papers: all this belongs to the issue of excrement.

But the other meaning, more familiar to us, need not be excluded and also has something to do with a type of survival, as an early and largely unpublished poem of Goethe's tells us.

The poem in question not only thematizes scatological survival, but is itself carried along by such a movement. This is *Werther's* void, entitled the "Joys of Young Werther." We have stopped suffering:

Freuden des jungen Werthers

Ein junger Mensch, ich weiss nicht, wie
Starb einst an der Hypochondrie
Und ward denn auch begraben.
Da kam ein schöner Geist herbei,
Der hatte seinen Stuhlgang frei,
Wie's denn so Leute haben.
Der setzt' notdürftig sich aufs Grab
Und legte da sein Häuflein ab,
beschaute freundlich seinen Dreck,
Ging wohl eratmet wieder weg
Und sprach zu sich bedächtlich:
"Der gute Mensch, wie hat er sich verdorben!
Hätt er geschissen so wie ich,
Er wäre nicht gestorben!"

The Joys of Young Werther

A young man, I don't know quite how,
Once died of hypochondria
And was therefore also buried.
Then a beautiful spirit came by.
He had to relieve himself
As one must after all do.
He went to his necessity upon the grave
And deposited there his load,
Observing amicably his dirt
And went thence with a sigh of relief, breathing
And spoke to himself, reflecting:
"The good man, oh, how has he ruined himself!
Had he shat like I did
He would not have died!"

Excrement is that which allows the *Geist*, which strictly speaking belongs neither to the living nor the dead, to survive—or, at least, to sustain its peculiar stirrings. As *Dreck*, this dejection is *not* ugly, hideous or repulsive in any way; on the contrary, the "beautiful" Geist—thus, one aesthetically valorized—looks upon his droppings in a friendly manner, without averting its gaze, to leave relieved, breathing, living on. This is not to say that we are interested solely in constructing an image of *Dreckermann* per se, but rather in showing, among other things, the place that Goethe had made for excrement as something that follows upon a work, in this case, as something following the sorrowful self-elimination thematized in Werther. The choice presented in this poem is precisely one between self-elimination and elimination, of doing oneself in or relieving oneself outwardly.

Perhaps it is not even necessary to dramatize the conditions of Eckermann's "life" after Goethe's biological death to suppose that he belongs at once to the class of the young hypochondriac who no longer lives while he is also the delayed *Erzeugung*, as Nietzsche would say, of Goethe's *Geist*—and thus a sign of his maker's survival. This would be just one of the ways Goethe left Eckermann behind.

Excrement, then, is the name which Goethe leaves to the company of a work—work understood as corpse—as its guardian and as the mark of its death, marking the end of a process but also the beginning of another one, one that begins with the droppings on the grave, if we also consider that this substance has fertilizing properties as well. But what is to be fertilized here is above all that layer of ground covering the buried opus; it is precisely the ground under the legacy, from which the posterity and the legend of the work will spring. And since the question of *Geist* or *genius* has already solicited a certain notion of productivity in relation to the body, we might remember, too, that the production of excrement presupposes the proper and healthy functioning of all sorts of assimilative systems: this process not only holds for the making of a work, but also for the type of *Bil-dung* in which Eckermann and Goethe seem to be engaged. This brings us back to the large question, which is never held at a distance from what Eckermann writes or Goethe says, of the relationship between property or (self-) possession (*Eigentum*) and the extraneous or foreign (*das Fremde*), which pertains to excrement in both senses we have developed: first as something growing out from the body and from which it is most easily detachable, belonging thus to that body and removable from it to become foreign matter, and in the second sense, as the end-station or destiny of what has been taken into the body to be discharged, secreted, or excreted.

It would not be difficult to demonstrate that Goethe swallowed Eckermann whole in order to assure the after-life of the work which for him is already buried. In fact, those critics who designate Eckermann as Goethe's last work would no doubt agree with our excretory interpretation of work. Eckermann must grow out of Goethe's work which he must assimilate after Goethe has assimilated him to his systems. He is to fertilize the work whose condition of survival he is: he will permit Goethe's *Geist* to move freely from the graveyard of his productions. As Goethe's outgrowth or delayed death, as his charge and discharge, Eckermann relieves Goethe of the responsibility towards those works he had more or less completed, though he felt they were not ready to be published as part of his complete works. We can think here of Nietzsche's notion of ennobled irresponsibility which, in this case, permits Goethe's spirit to move on to other projects, such as *Faust II*, to take one example.

If Eckerman's task and "dirty work" is to secure Goethe's posterity, to remain behind with the work, at its graveside, this does not mean, however, that Eckermann will not stir to rebel against his lot. As an outgrowth of Goethe, as his follower and pupil, Eckermann will not always be something upon which Goethe can cast a friendly glance. This becomes especially clear in the case of the *Farbenlehre (Theory of Color)*, a work which initially left Eckermann baffled. Let me interrupt this argument for a moment to remind you that Nietzsche, the sovereign subject of this Symposium, preferred the *Conversations* to *Faust* and to *Dichtung und Wahrheit*. In a note, he wrote with unbaffled certitude that "Goethe, in his Color Theory, was wrong" (1876 or 1877). I am led to suspect that Nietzsche took particular pleasure in reading this section of the *Conversations*, and not only in order to oppose Schopenhauer, who sided with Goethe. Nietzsche, needless to say, takes the part of Eckermann.

Now before asking him to write the compendium, Goethe organizes another property transaction when he directs Eckermann to appropriate the theory (*Lehre*) as his own (*zu eigen machen*), promising that what he passes on to him will begin to live in Eckermann's care. Goethe predicts that "this science will soon be your property (*Eigentum*)." He leaves Eckermann in possession of this work, but something begins to take root which Goethe did not exactly foresee; namely, "an unsuspected difference" arises (*und so gerieten wir in eine unvermutete Differenz*) which, given the gravity of the matter, Eckermann feels obliged to impart.

The question that interests me here is not so much who is right in the course of this development, but rather Eckermann's need to assert precisely the *Differenz* between his own careful (*sorgfältig*), superior insight and Goethe's observations. As we go over some of the elements of this difference, we should not forget that the subject at hand is a *Lehre*, i.e., the stakes here involve not only Goethe's teaching of color but his status as teacher, as master of

Bildung, which Eckermann, however, continually affirms. In this light—in the light of the one submitted to *Bildung*—it is noteworthy that Eckermann's privileged instrument of verification most often is *Kerzenlicht*, a funereal beam that he casts over Goethe's corpus. Indeed, given everything that science meant to Goethe and his passionate crusade against Newton, this is not a matter of indifferent *Differenz*.

The problems first arise when Eckermann takes a look at the *Farenlehre* in order to test whether he would be at all capable of meeting Goethe's "friendly request" (*Aufforderung*, "challenge, demand"). While considering the phenomenon of blue shadowing in an empirical light, however, he comes to realize "with some surprise" that Goethe's argument is "based on error." He describes how he arrived at this conclusion, making his case increasingly solid: "in order to be absolutely sure . . . and now there was no further doubt," and so on. "The color was there, outside of me, independently, and my subject(ivity) had no influence upon it." Goethe had classified this phenomenon as a subjective manifestation, and it is perhaps not exactly fortuitous that Eckermann will seek to diminish subjective power in Goethe's theory at the same time he tries to affirm his own subject. It is equally important that in the act of refuting Goethe, of risking parricidal writing, he can fathom an "outside."

In the days that follow, Eckermann finds the opportunity to confirm the truth of his hypothesis, for example, "in this case, according to Goethe's teachings, the freshest blue tonality was supposed to emerge. It did not however emerge." After several more days of experimentation, Eckermann establishes that "Nature could not confirm" Goethe's argument "as true"; the corresponding paragraphs thus "urgently required revision." Eckermann does not stop at this: "I encountered something similar with colorful double-shadowing" which, after anxious observation, he was compelled to dismiss. However, this time, he does not limit himself to his experiments, but calls upon Shakespeare to bear witness. Although reference to *Romeo and Juliet* may not seem scientifically compelling, Eckermann probably could not have taken a more deadly aim at Goethe. If Shakespeare's couple meets a tragic conclusion, the one inscribed in this book now faces doom as well. For Shakespeare is the only name to which Goethe, in the *Conversations* and elsewhere, ascribes powers of mutilation. Eckermann could have found no higher tribunal to sit in judgment of Goethe: Goethe claims he had been forced to rid himself of Shakespeare—to get him off his body ("vomHals schaffen")—in order to be able to write at all. Eckermann knew this only too well; as early as January 5, 1826, he had scribbled on one of his papers that "Shakespeare alles andere verleidet." There may be no end to Shakespeare, as Goethe's essay on that subject argues, but his would be the name of Goethe's end. Eckermann's strategy of including Shakespeare in a demonstration that, with the exception of this reference, remains purely empirical, belongs to the logic of his crime, to his assertion of an outside, the possibility of independence and the doubt he casts on the "double shadow":

> Das Resultat meiner Beobachtungen ging demnach dahin, daß auch Goethes Lehre von den farbigen Doppelschatten nicht durchaus richtig sei, daß bei diesem Phänomen mehr Objektives einwirke, als von ihm beobachtet worden, und daß das Gesetz der subjektiven Forderung dabei nur als etwas Sekundäres in Betracht komme.

Eckermann is dealing in law, in Goethe's law of subjective claim which he will allow only a secondary position: doubles, shadows, secondariness; this all sounds desperately familiar.

Goethe disregarded too many things; given his fixation on what has once been recognized as law (*am einmal erkannten Gesetzlichen*) and his way of presupposing his law/the law even in such cases where it appears to be concealed, he could very easily be misled (*verführt*, "seduced") into making large syntheses and perceiving a law of which he had grown fond (*ein liebgewonnenes Gesetz*) even in a place where an entirely different law was operative.

Therefore, "when Goethe mentioned his *Farbenlehre* today and asked me what was happening with the Compendium we had discussed, I would have gladly concealed the points developed above, for I was unsure (embarrassed) about how I was supposed to tell him the truth without hurting (*verletzen*, "wounding") him." Eckermann was embarrassed about telling Goethe the truth—a truth which he however freely imparts to his readers. And this truth cannot be told without inflicting a wound on Goethe, one whose proportions Eckermann will disclose only at the end of this entry.

He does tell Goethe, for he had no other choice, he writes, that after careful observation, he finds himself in the position (*Fall*) of having to deviate (*abweichen*) from Goethe. Goethe, it appears, begins to gain in stature in Eckermann's rendering of the scene, for "it is not given to me to develop a subject of great length in oral conversation (*im mündlichen Gespräch*) with any clarity . . . I would do that later, in writing." Later, in writing. "However, I had hardly begun to speak when Goethe's lofty and cheerful nature grew clouded (*verfinsterte*) and I saw only too clearly that he did not appreciate my objections." Eckermann saw too clearly; he saw too clearly in his experiments with light and shadow, and he sees too clearly when Goethe's brilliance is clouded over, darkened. As you see, the experiment is now being carried over to Goethe; and if Goethe appears too obscure in his writing, and Eckermann can so easily give umbrage, it is also because Conversation is at stake. Having asserted his inferiority in oral conversation (*mündlichen Gespräch*), Eckermann will now shift the sense of the mark to announce the possibility of triumph: "it can happen, however, that the mature (*Mündige*) are overprecipitous whereas the immature (*Unmündige*) find it." Goethe flushes and returns with mockery: "As if you had found it! With your conception of colorful light, you belong in the fourteenth century." Goethe makes Eckermann's immaturity a question of age, of the dark ages, injuring him with his charges of obscurity. But "the only thing which is good about you, is that at least you are honest enough to come out with what you are thinking." That would be the only thing good about Eckermann.

The stakes are high, and Goethe does not refrain from naming them. Eckermann's deviation in his veneration for Goethe already has a place in intellectual history: "*Es geht mir mit meiner Farbenlehre gerade wie mit der christlichen Religion*. One believes for a while to have faithful pupils and before one turns around they deviate and form a sect." Eckermann is indeed about to take the form of a sect, to be cut-off from Goethe's body, to be ex-communicated. " 'You are a heretic just like the others, for you are not the first to have deviated from me. I have become estranged from the most excellent people because of disputed points in the *Farbenlehre*'. . . . He named for me a few important names."

Goethe, then, has severed relations with the most excellent people, among whom Eckermann may or may not count himself, precisely for the type of objections that Eckermann raises. The immediate consequence of Eckermann's heresy is indeed a form of excommunication: they had finished eating (for they always eat) and conversation ceased (*das Gespräch stockte*). Yet if conversation was blocked, the *Conversations*, it must be said, has rarely flowed so freely, for this is also among the lengthier "conversations" that Eckermann would record: an instance of interrupted intercourse sustaining Eckermann's desire to write (*conversatio*). Now arrives the moment of sublime triumph, in which the younger becomes the master, at once the elder and the child, in short, the part who is not suffering:

> Goethe stand auf und stellte sich ans Fenster. Ich trat zu ihm und drückte ihm die Hand, denn wie er auch schalt, ich liebte ihn, und dann hatte ich das Gefühl, daß das Recht auf meiner Seite und daß er der leidende Teil sei.

This is the magnanimity of power: if Eckermann concedes to Goethe in this manner it may be due to love, as he suggests, but it is most certainly because he has justice on his side: he is right, and this right surpasses Goethe's threat of vengeance. Goethe has been judged—by Shakespeare and by Eckermann—justice is on this side, but the other part or member (*Teil*) suffers. Thus, "it was not long before we conversed and joked about indifferent matters." The *Differenz* appears to be suspended, the division repaired. Yet when Eckermann leaves, promising Goethe a written version of his objections—he reminds Goethe that if he would not concede to him his right, it was simply a consequence of the awkwardness in "my oral delivery"—Goethe cannot refrain from saying a few things about heretics and heresy as Eckermann was in the doorway. Goethe throws his comments at Eckermann "halb lachend, halb spottend." Half and half: the halves are beginning to multiply again with the non-suffering half upon which Goethe casts half scorn half laughter, half inside, half outside Goethe's house. If Goethe is himself divided, it is because "*Goethe*" is as such divided, as Eckermann proceeds to explain:

> If it should seem problematic that Goethe could not easily tolerate opposition regarding his *Farbenlehre*, whereas with his poetic works he showed himself to be wholly gracious, accepting each well-founded objection with gratitude, then perhaps the riddle (*Rätsel*) can be resolved when we consider that as poet he received the fullest gratification from the outside (*von außen her*), whereas in the case of *Farbenlehre*, this largest and most difficult of all his works, he experienced nothing but blame and disapprobation.

Eckermann is still wandering on the parricidal path. He understands and explains patiently why it was particularly painful for Goethe to meet up with any opposition concerning the *Farbenlehre*. It is a question of the outside, and Eckermann puts himself entirely in line with this outside-of-Goethe which repudiates his most difficult work. And this outside comes at him from all sides, for the better half of his life, forcing Goethe into the stance of a reactive warrior who is not afraid to cut to the quick. Nor is he afraid to amputate. Eckermann, as we noted, runs the risk of being cut off. At the same time, he qualifies Goethe's reactive instinct as natural:

> Ein halbes Leben hindurch tönte ihm der unverständigst Widerspruch von allen Seiten entgegen; und so war es denn wohl natürlich, daβ der sich immer in einer Art von gereizten kriegerischen Zustand und zu leidenschaftlicher Opposition stets gerüstet befinden muβte.

Armed for battle on the field of science, Goethe is the warrior whom Eckermann challenges, if not to a fight quite to the end—though his end is always in sight—then at least to a "natural" duel on Nature. But the difference between the painful duality taking shape here and the mass of other conflictual pairs who have fought over this particular text is that Eckermann does not belong to the legions of slavishly uncomprehending opposition: he stands his ground alone, he is honest, as Goethe has said, and forthright; he does not hide among the ranks of that army raised by Ressentiment. In Nietzsche's terms, *he also knows how to be an enemy.* This is of course precisely what makes him a most dangerous opponent.

Yet Eckermann has just told us that, in the case of the *Farbenlehre,* he has been in effect all along describing and engaged in a riddle (*Rätsel*); and when riddles are at issue, the myth of Oedipus does not always lag that far behind. However, this wanderer, we shall see, will find a devious, if not ingenious solution to the riddle, thereby bypassing the path which he has been hitherto pursuing, the parricidal path upon which he has nonetheless and, it would seem, irrevocably entered. The detour that he takes, the deviation from the killing of the Father, the solution and resolution of the riddle is in fact simple: Goethe, it turns out, is, in this case and connection, not the father but the mother, the *good* mother: "He was, in connection to the *Farbenlehre,* like a good mother." A good mother, that means a mother who has not been violated, not by Eckermann namely, for it was precisely his earlier recognition in this episode of the "unsuspected difference" that stopped and deadened the urge for intercourse. Goethe, the father, will not have been killed and Goethe, the mother, will retain her integrity. As for Eckermann, he will certainly not have to pay for what was almost a crime. He can write against the Father without remorse.

NOTES

1. In H. H. Houben, *J. P. Eckermann: Sein Leben für Goethe* (Leipzig: H. Haessel, 1925–28), 1: 45.

2. Jean Luc Nancy organized a reading around Sylvia Plath in terms of "excription" in his Berkeley seminar on "Philosophy and Literature," Spring, 1988.

3. "Nietzsche Médusé" in this volume, and *Nietzsche et la Philosophie* (Paris: PUF, 1962).

4. Blanchot, *Faux Pas* (Paris: Gallimard, 1943), p. 316.

5. This of course is a translation of the opening lines of *Ecce Homo* which in turn reads as a translation, of sorts of the name "Ecke(r)-mann." I thank Werner Hamacher for pointing out the syntonic qualities linking *Eckermann* to Nietzsche within the concept of another recess or depression, namely as "niche." Another hereditary state of recession or depression of the Nietzsche family, whose types we always risk matching, bears the name, "Nichte," as Laurence Rickels has astutely demonstrated. (See "Friedrich Nichte" in this volume.)

6. For a discussion of name and credit, see Jacques Derrida, "The Otobiography of Nietzsche," tr. A. Ronell (New York: Schocken Books, 1984).

7. Friedenthal, *Goethe* (chapter on Eckermann).

8. *Gespräche mit Goethe*, Introduction.

9. Ibid.

10. I am grateful to Rainer Nägele for having discerned a peculiarly Nietzschean moment in this dream-narration in terms of the second tractatus, 16th section of the *Genealogy*, which addresses the origin of humanity or the becoming-of-humanity of water animals (*Wassertiere*) as they first step onto land: "als es den Wassertieren ergangen sein muss, als sie gezwungen wurden, entweder Landtiere zu werden oder zugrunde zu gehen, so ging es diesen . . . glücklich angepassten Halbtieren—mit einem Male waren alle ihre Instinkte entwertet und 'ausgehängt.' " In the same section Nietzsche traces the becoming of the human soul not as something that grows inside the body but rather *onto* the body; thus "dies ist das, was ich die *Verinnerlichung* des Menschen nenne: damit wächst erst das an den Menschen heran, was man später [seine] 'Seele' nennt." In a way, Nietzsche describes the becoming of the soul almost as Goethe describes Eckermann's growing onto him, Nägele suggests, as the enabling fiction of immortality—a belated supplement to the concept of the specifically human.

Index